Digital Enterprise Transformation

Digital Enterprise Transformation

A Business-Driven Approach to Leveraging Innovative IT

Edited by
Axel Uhl *and* Lars Alexander Gollenia

Routledge
Taylor & Francis Group

LONDON AND NEW YORK

First published 2014 by Gower Publishing

Published 2016 by Routledge
2 Park Square, Milton Park, Abingdon, Oxon OX14 4RN
711 Third Avenue, New York, NY 10017, USA

Routledge is an imprint of the Taylor & Francis Group, an informa business

Gower Applied Business Research
Our programme provides leaders, practitioners, scholars and researchers with thought provoking, cutting edge books that combine conceptual insights, interdisciplinary rigour and practical relevance in key areas of business and management.

Notice:

Product or corporate names may be trademarks or registered trademarks, and are used only for identification and explanation without intent to infringe.

British Library Cataloguing in Publication Data
A catalogue record for this book is available from the British Library

ISBN: 978-1-4724-4854-5 (hbk)

Library of Congress Cataloging-in-Publication Data
Uhl, Axel.
  Digital enterprise transformation : a business-driven approach to leveraging Innovative IT / by Axel Uhl and Lars Alexander Gollenia.
      pages cm
  Includes bibliographical references and index.
  ISBN 978-1-4724-4854-5 (hardback) -- ISBN 978-1-4724-4856-9 (ebook) -- ISBN 978-1-4724-4855-2 (epub) 1. Organizational change. 2. Management--Technological innovations. I. Gollenia, Lars Alexander. II. Title.
  HD58.8.U448 2015
  658.4'038--dc23
                                                                                2014029434

Printed in the United Kingdom
by Henry Ling Limited

Contents

List of Figures

List of Tables

About the Editors

Prof. Dr Axel Uhl, Head of Business Transformation Academy, SAP AG
Prof. Dr Uhl is head of the Business Transformation Academy at SAP. He has been a professor at the University of Applied Sciences and Arts Northwestern Switzerland (FHNW) since 2009. Axel Uhl received his Doctorate in Economics and his Master in Business Information Systems. He started his career at Allianz and worked for DaimlerChrysler IT Services, KPMG, and Novartis. His main areas of research are sustainability and IT, leadership, and business transformation management. Contact: a.uhl@sap.com.

Lars Gollenia, Head of SAP Business Transformation Services, SAP AG
Lars Gollenia is Head of Business Transformation Services (BTS), the global management consultancy organization of SAP. Previously, Lars held various management positions in the management consulting sector. Prior to his current role he was responsible for Business Consulting for EMEA. Lars has a graduate degree in Business Administration from the Friedrich-Schiller University of Jena, Germany, and he studied Strategic and International Management at Harvard University, Boston. Contact: lars.gollenia@sap.com.

Notes on the Contributors

Dr Matthias Born, Management Consultant/Entrepreneur
Dr Born is an entrepreneur and independent management consultant specializing in process management, business transformation, and technology trends, as well as market innovations. As a digital native, he constantly designs, and implements new business concepts applying the latest technology and innovation trends. Prior to this, Matthias worked at the research department of SAP AG for many years and received his PhD in business informatics in 2012. Contact: matthias.born@bp-expert.de.

Amadou Diallo, Chief Executive Officer, DHL Freight
Amadou Diallo is the CEO of DHL Freight. Mr. Diallo has an MBA in International Business and a Master of Science in Information Services and Process Management. He is responsible for the performance and long-term strategic development of Deutsche Post DHL, a member of DHL Global Forwarding, Freight Management Board, and is a member of the Singapore Economic Development Board. Contact: amadou.diallo@dhl.com.

Tomasz Janasz, Research Analyst, SAP AG
Tomasz Janasz is a business administration graduate from the University of Hamburg. In 2008, he joined SAP as a business consultant with a main focus on project management and quality assurance in major transformation initiatives. Since 2010 he has been a research analyst at the SAP Business Transformation Academy where he co-developed the Business Transformation Management Methodology (BTM²) and the Digital Capability Framework. Tomasz is pursuing his PhD at the University of Wuppertal (Germany) conducting his research on innovative concepts for urban mobility. In 2013 he was awarded the Swiss Electric Mobility Award from Touring Club Suisse (TCS). Contact: t.janasz@sap.com.

Ruediger Jung, Business Enterprise Chief Consultant, SAP AG
Ruediger Jung has more than 16 years' SAP experience starting out with global implementations in different industries throughout different regions. After moving to SAP AG from America he joined the Business Transformation Group for Management Consulting. He is currently a Business Enterprise Chief

DIGITAL ENTERPRISE TRANSFORMATION

Consultant leading a specific engagement model called 'Value Partnership' to establish a long-term, sustainable customer relationship for Samsung. In his role as strategic advisor for business transformation he is working together with C-Level Executives on complex business challenges and industry innovations. He is a member of the Business Transformation Academy community after being certified through the Master Certification Program as Global Business Transformation Manager (GBTM) in 2010. Ruediger is SAP certified in Management Accounting (Controlling) and Financial Accounting (Finance). Contact: r.jung@sap.com.

Dr Agnes Koschmider, Postdoctoral Researcher, Karlsruhe Institute of Technology
Dr Koschmider is a post-doctoral researcher at the Institute of Applied Informatics and Formal Description Methods (AIFB) at the Karlsruhe Institute of Technology (KIT). In 2007 Agnes received a Doctoral Degree in Applied Informatics from the University of Karlsruhe. She studied from 1998–2003 and received her Diploma degree in Business Administration from the Goethe University Frankfurt/Main in 2003. In September 2013 she was named a junior fellow of the German Informatics Society (Gesellschaft für Informatik). In 2014 she received the Wolfgang-Heilmann-Preis 2013/1014 for outstanding contributions to modern information technology.

Nils Labusch, Research Assistant and PhD student, University of St. Gallen
Nils Labusch is a research assistant and PhD student at the University of St. Gallen (HSG). After graduate studies and work in Münster and New Jersey he joined Prof. Dr Winter at the Institute of Information Management in 2011. His current research topics are related to the support of business transformations and the related information requirements. Contact: nils.labusch@unisg.ch.

Kim MacGillavry, Head of Customer Experience, DHL Freight
Kim MacGillavry is head of Customer Experience at DHL Freight and member of its management board. During the last 20 years Kim was responsible for product and service innovation as well as brand management in various multinational companies. Designing, developing, and launching a multitude of products and services, he gained a lot of experience in dealing with the complexities of innovation in large enterprises. Kim has a Master in Applied Economics from the University Faculty Saint-Ignatius Antwerp in Belgium. Contact: kim.macgillavry@dhl.com.

Dr Christoph Meier, Business Consultant, SAP AG
Dr Meier works as a Business Consultant at SAP's Management Consultancy, in the EMEA SCM team. There he supports global SAP customers in transforming their supply chains into digital businesses leveraging emerging technologies.

Prior to his role at SAP Christoph was a consultant at FIR Institute for Operations Management heading the 'IT and Operations' practice. He holds a PhD in Industrial Engineering from RWTH Aachen University (Germany) and a Diploma in Industrial Engineering and Management from Ilmenau University of Technology (Germany).

Prof. Dr Michael Rosemann, Director of the Information Systems Program, Queensland University of Technology
Prof. Dr Rosemann is author/editor of seven books, more than 200 refereed papers, Editorial Board member of ten international journals, and co-inventor of two US patents. His research projects received funding from industry partners such as Accenture, Brisbane Airport, Infosys, Rio Tinto, Queensland Government, SAP and Woolworths. Prof. Dr Rosemann is a Visiting Professor at Viktoria Institute, Gothenburg, Sweden. Contact: m.rosemann@qut.edu.au.

Norizan Safrudin, Research Assistant and PhD Student, Queensland University of Technology
Norizan Safrudin is a research associate and PhD candidate within QUT's Information Systems School. Her research focuses on Business Transformation Management and is funded by SAP BTA. In her PhD studies, Niz adopts a metaphor approach to explain how services from various management disciplines are composed and orchestrated in business transformations, similar to that of a jazz music orchestra. Prior to her PhD, Niz's background is in Business Process Management, where her Honours study on how novices design business processes won a best paper award at a BPM conference in the USA. Niz is also an enthusiastic sessional academic who has delivered lectures and tutorials in Corporate Systems and Business Process Modeling for both under- and post-graduate students at QUT, and also internationally. Contact: norizan.safrudin@qut.edu.au.

Dr Theresa Schmiedel, Assistant Professor, University of Liechtenstein
Dr Schmiedel is Assistant Professor at the Hilti Chair of Business Process Management at the University of Liechtenstein. She holds a PhD in business economics from the University of Liechtenstein and a Diploma in economics from the University of Hohenheim, Stuttgart, Germany, which she conducted partially at York University, Toronto, Canada. Her research focuses on social phenomena in IS research, particularly on the interconnection of culture and BPM. Her work has been published in journals, including *Information and Management* and *Business Process Management Journal*, as well as in academic books and conference proceedings. She is an invited speaker in the field of business process management.Contact: theresa.schmiedel@uni.li.

Prof. Dr Jan vom Brocke, Professor and Director of the Institute of Information Systems, University of Liechtenstein

Prof. Dr vom Brocke is Professor of Information Systems, the Hilti Chair of Business Process Management, and Director of the Institute of Information Systems, University of Liechtenstein where he has been Vice-President since 2012. Jan has over 15 years' experience in IT and BPM projects and he has published more than 200 papers in renowned outlets, including MIS Quarterly (MISQ), that have also been cited in major popular magazines such as the Financial Times Germany. He has authored and edited 20 books, including *Business Process Management – Driving Innovation in a Digital World*, the *Business Process Management Handbook*, and *Green BPM – Towards the Sustainable Enterprise*. Jan is an invited speaker and trusted advisor on BPM, serving many organizations around the world. Contact: jan.vom.brocke@uni.li.

Prof. Dr Winter, Professor and Director of the Institute of Information Management, University of St. Gallen

Prof. Dr Winter is a full-time professor of Business and Information Systems Engineering at the University of St. Gallen (HSG) and Director of the Institute of Information Management. In addition to research in situational method engineering, he is responsible for projects and publications (over 150 journal articles and books) in areas such as enterprise architecture and transformation management. Contact: robert.winter@unisg.ch.

Foreword

AXEL UHL AND LARS GOLLENIA

Everything is changing. Most importantly, the global population has almost doubled since the 1950s and is expected to break the 9 billion barrier in 2040 (United Nations, 2013). At the same time, the extent of extreme poverty has been reduced considerably in recent years: It fell from 43.1 percent in 1990 to less than half that level (20.6 percent) in 2010 (PovcalNet, 2014).

Employment options are a necessity for income and prosperity, but just to maintain the employment rate at a constant level would require the number of jobs worldwide to increase by 600 million within the next 15 years (World Bank, 2013).

Another global trend is the increasing level of urbanization. In 1990, there were just 1.5 billion people in cities (World Bank, 2013a): By 2011, this rose to some 3.6 billion people, which equated to around 50 percent of the world's population, and according to a study by the United Nations the number will increase to about 6.3 billion in 2050 (United Nations, 2011). Even now, many megacities are already approaching their capacity limits, making it necessary to develop new supply, employment, and mobility concepts.

The increasing globalism of markets is another megatrend that cannot be ignored. Most goods and a growing number of services are 'made in the world' and are no longer produced in just one country (OECD, 2013).

The increasingly globally networked world, however, also presents new risks.

Indeed, the five greatest risks faced by mankind are; 1) an increasing inequality of income distribution between the rich North and the poor South, 2) increasing debt levels in countries and communities, 3) the increase in greenhouse gases, 4) a scarcity of drinking water, and 5) rising numbers of elderly people in several important industrial nations.

We will only be able to meet these challenges through advances in technology. After all, technical advances have always ensured the survival of Homo sapiens.

Today, the Internet plays a dominant role: Global Internet traffic has increased more than fourfold in the past five years, and will increase threefold over the next five years (Cisco, 2013). Ninety percent of this data volume is accounted for by videos, which are distributed via Internet portals such as YouTube and Snapchat (Cisco, 2013) so it is hardly surprising that globally stored data might reach 40,000 exabytes respectively 40 trillion gigabytes in 2020 (compared to 130 exabytes in 2005) (IDC iView, 2012).

Mobile communication is also growing rapidly – by the end of 2014, there will be more mobile devices on the planet than there are people (Cisco, 2014). People in the United States spend an average of five hours and 46 minutes each day using their online and mobile devices (eMarketer, 2014).

Social networks also play a major role: Facebook has more than a billion members and other social networks are also expanding tremendously (Meeker and Wu, 2013).

We do not generally tend to embrace change, preferring instead to maintain what we have and how we live but change is an integral part of life – whether we want it or not. Change represents both an opportunity and a risk, and our attitudes to change greatly influence the way in which we deal with changes and how successful they are in improving our lives.

The same applies to companies. They, too, are subjected to changes that require them to adapt accordingly. Not all companies achieve this with the same level of success. For example, more than 40 percent of the Fortune 500 companies in the year 2000 were no longer on the list by 2010 (Solis, 2013).

Supply and demand change in all markets. For example, the number of letters that were sent via the US Postal Service fell from 250 million in 2006 to just 50 million in 2012. The reason for this? E-mails.

Since 2000, the advertising revenue of newspapers in the US has dropped by over $40 billion (Chisholm et al., 2013). This has been caused by an increasing shift in advertising business towards the Internet.

Age and social structures in companies are also set to change. By 2015, generation Y (those born in 1980 or later) will constitute around 75 percent of the world's labor force and thus have a considerable influence on corporate culture and expectations, and this younger generation frequently has quite different values from their predecessors. For example, only 11 percent of them define one of their goals as being to earn a great deal of money (Solis, 2013).

The new generation of highly qualified workers will come from Asia – Asian students currently account for the largest proportion (53 percent) of youths and young adults studying abroad, most of whom come from China, India, and Korea (OECD, 2013b).

How Can Companies Best Prepare Themselves to Ensure That They Remain Competitive in the Future?

The customer will, however, remain the focus of attention – and there is still plenty to do here. According to one study, US companies lose some $83 billion in turnover each year due to their poor service and poor customer experience (Genesys, 2009). Only 37 percent of US companies achieved a rating of 'Excellent' or 'Good' in Forrester's 2012 Customer Experience Index. If you consider that 12 positive experiences are needed to compensate for one unresolved negative experience, it is easy to imagine just how important customer experience is (Help Scout, 2011). Furthermore, it is six to seven times more expensive to acquire a new customer than it is to retain an existing one (Reichheld, 2003).

But where will companies find their customers? On the Internet, mobile devices, and social networks. Here, too, the Asia Pacific market is the leader (comScore, 2012).

Social networks provide a unique opportunity to acquire new customers and to retain them in the long term. Millenials – people who were born around the turn of the millennium – follow brands on social networks with particular frequency (Solis, 2013). This age group also believes the reported experiences of other consumers on the Internet more than company advertising messages (OECD, 2013a). According to a study conducted by Brian Solis (2013), 70 percent of the consumers surveyed said that their purchase was influenced by the online recommendation of a friend or relative.

Innovative companies have long since taken advantage of such developments. Apple revolutionized the hardware, software, music, and retail markets, and Google did the same with the markets for research, navigation, and travel planning. Amazon is stirring up the markets for books, music, and retail, while at the same time revolutionizing the logistics industry. Skype modified the telecom service range, and Facebook is reforming the banking industry through community banking and community insurance.

High time to prepare for the future! Or do you consider it too difficult to adapt so quickly to the digital age because of your company's history and associated 'burden', such as systems, structures, and employees? And do you feel that the digital world should wait for you? Well, digital companies will probably not treat you so politely and considerately.

Innovation means progress and is a 'must' for every company. Not every company, however, can boast a world-class innovator and leader like Apple's Steve Jobs. Can innovation be created or managed? Numerous articles, books, and magazines give tips on how to make companies more innovative. Apparently, all you have to do is to look at what the Googles and Facebooks of the world would do, but such recipes are usually of little help – what works for company A will not necessarily work for company B.

Innovation is more than just having a good idea or being creative; innovation can sometimes be very simple, and sometimes breathtaking. It can be integrated easily or it can revolutionize a company. It is easier said than done, and it sometimes means overhauling an entire strategy. So how are you supposed to catch this mythical beast that has so many different faces?

A healthy dose of openness, curiosity, and expertise cannot hurt. Learning about the technologies and use cases in various industries is an effective and efficient way to drive business model innovation. Coca-Cola recently announced that it will sell its products in 'capsules' in the future, in a similar way to Nespresso. This will change their entire business model. Coca-Cola will save itself the expensive deposit bottles and transport costs and instead sell or rent both the capsules and the drinks vending machines. A similar scenario has developed for the pasta manufacturer Barilla, who wants to allow its customers to print out its pasta themselves using 3D printers.

But our generation has a common problem. In a world of social networks, mobile applications, cloud and big data management, which offer us more opportunities than ever before, we sometimes lack the basic skills to make them happen. We can obtain all the new technologies and ideas to reinvent our businesses, but we have trouble with the basic skills needed to transform the organization behind them.

This book is therefore dedicated to the combination of transformational capabilities and new digital skills to be developed.

The Digital Capability Framework presented here is based on the business transformation management method that has been applied successfully for a number of years.

The Digital Capability Framework is a strategic management tool that is similar to a balanced scorecard, however, the framework goes far beyond that. It enables organizations to obtain clarity about what maturity level an organization has in terms of the six defined Digital Capabilities, what maturity level they wish to attain, and how they intend to achieve this. The digital use cases also help to develop a clear picture of the processes to be optimized and the technologies that should be used. A customized plan to transform the organization into a digital company can be defined as a result.

We would like to take this opportunity to express our sincere gratitude to all the authors who invested a considerable amount of effort to develop this book. In particular, we want to thank the following organizations and institutions: SAP AG, the University of Applied Sciences and Arts Northwestern Switzerland, the University of St Gallen (Switzerland), Queensland University of Technology (Australia), the University of Liechtenstein (Principality of Liechtenstein), the Karlsruhe Institute of Technology (Germany), Samsung SDS (South Korea), Finanz Informatik (Germany), IBM, and Hilti AG (Principality of Liechtenstein). Not only did they contribute to this publication but they have also given us such loyal and lasting support for so many years.

Special thanks go to the project team, who coordinated the entire development, review and publication process: Tomasz Janasz, Dr Matthias Born, Dr Sue Nielsen, and Andrea Daria Anner.

References

Chisholm, J., Kilman, L., Milosevic, M. and Henriksson, T. (2013) World Press Trends Report 2013, WAN-IFRA – World Association of Newspapers and News Publishers, 2013.

Cisco (2013) Cisco Visual Networking Index: Forecast and Methodology, 2012–2017, http://www.cisco.com/c/en/us/solutions/collateral/service-provider/ip-ngn-ip-next-generation-network/white_paper_c11–481360.pdf, last accessed 6 June 2014.

Cisco (2014) Cisco Visual Networking Index: Global Mobile Data Traffic Forecast Update, 2013–2018, http://www.cisco.com/c/en/us/solutions/collateral/service-provider/visual-networking-index-vni/white_paper_c11–520862.pdf, last accessed 6 June 2014.

comScore (2012) 2013 Europe Digital Future in Focus, http://etc.-digital.org/digital-trends/mobile-devices/mobile-smartphones/regional-overview/europe/, last accessed 9 June 2014.

eMarketer (2014) Mobile Continues to Steal Share of US Adults' Daily Time Spent with Media, http://www.emarketer.com/Article/Mobile-Continues-Steal-Share-of-US-Adults-Daily-Time-Spent-with-Media/1010782, last accessed 6 June 2014.

Genesys (2009) Genesys Report – The Cost of Poor Customer Service, Genesys Telecommunications Laboratories, Inc., http://www.marketingdeservicios.com/wp-content/uploads/Genesys_Global_Survey09_screen.pdf, last accessed 9 June 2014.

Help Scout (2011) What Bad Customer Service is Costing You, https://www.helpscout.net/blog/what-bad-customer-service-is-costing-you/, last accessed 6 June 2014.

IDC iView (2012) The Digital Universe in 2020: Big Data, Bigger Digital Shadows, and Biggest Growth in the Far East, December 2012, http://www.emc.com/leadership/digital-universe/2012iview/executive-summary-a-universe-of.htm, last accessed 9 June 2014.

Meeker, M. and Wu, L. (2013) Internet Trends: D11 Conference, KBCD Online Report, http://www.kpcb.com/file/kpcb-internet-trends-2013, last accessed 6 June 2014.

OECD (2013) Interconnected Economies: Benefiting from Global Value Chains: Synthesis Report, http://www.oecd.org/sti/ind/interconnected-economies-GVCs-synthesis.pdf, last accessed 6 June 2014.

OECD (2013a) Electronic and Mobile Commerce, OECD Digital Economy Papers, No. 228, OECD Publishing, http://dx.doi.org/10.1787/5k437p2gxw6g-en, last accessed 6 June 2014.

OECD (2013b) Education at a Glance 2013: Highlights, OECD iLibrary, http://www.oecd-ilibrary.org/education/highlights-from-education-at-a-glance_2076264x, last accessed 10 June 2014.

PovcalNet (2014) The on-line tool for poverty measurement developed by the Development Research Group of the World Bank. Poverty and Equity Data. Hg. v. The World Bank Group, http://povertydata.worldbank.org/poverty/home/, last accessed 9 June 2014.

Reichheld, F. (2003) *Loyalty Rules: How Today's Leaders Build Lasting Relationships*, Boston, MA: Harvard Business Press Books.

Solis, B. (2013) *What's the Future of Business: Changing the Way Businesses Create Experiences*, Hoboken, NJ: John Wiley and Sons Inc.

United Nations (2013) World Population Prospects: The 2012 Revision Key Findings and Advance Tables, New York, http://esa.un.org/wpp/Documentation/pdf/WPP2012_%20KEY%20FINDINGS.pdf, last accessed 6 March 2014.

United Nations (2011) World Urbanization Prospects: The 2011 Revision World – Highlight, Population Prospects: The 2012 Revision Key Findings and Advance Tables, New York, http://esa.un.org/unup/pdf/WUP2011_Highlights.pdf, last accessed 6 June 2014.

World Bank (2013) Moving jobs center stage: Main Messages, World Development Report, http://siteresources.worldbank.org/EXTNWDR2013/Resources/8258024–1320950747192/8260293–1322665883147/Main_Messages_English.pdf, last accessed 6 June 2014.

World Bank (2013a) Global Monitoring Report 2013: Rural-Urban Dynamics and the Millennium Development Goals, Europe and Central Asia. http://siteresources.worldbank.org/INTPROSPECTS/Resources/334934-1327948020811/8401693-1355753354515/8980448-1366123749799/GMR_2013_Full_Report.pdf, last accessed 14 July 2014.

The Importance of Technological Trends and How to Exploit Them for Business Excellence

AXEL UHL, MATTHIAS BORN,
AGNES KOSCHMIDER AND TOMASZ JANASZ

1.1 Introduction

Social media, mobile technology, cloud computing or big data – the evolution of these technological trends and the ubiquitous and reliable connectivity to online services change the way successful companies operate. In the digital world, consumers, employees and other business partners alike are more technologically demanding than ever before. In addition, the digital trends provide an enormous source of information about consumer behavior, requirements and needs; something which was not available in the past. Companies can offer completely new services, engage interactively with customers and provide an entirely different working environment. More than ever, digital technology plays a critical role in corporate strategy.

Today, even small startup companies can grow from zero to new market leader at tremendous speed and be a new competitor in tomorrow's market within a few months. The traditional communication and sales channels, radio and TV, needed 38 and 13 years, respectively, in order to reach 50 million consumers (Chui et al., 2012), however, the Internet only needs four years and the iPod just three years to reach the same number of people (Webb and Romano, 2010). New records were set by social media platforms. Facebook reached 50 million people within a year from its launch in 2004 and Twitter after just nine months (Chui et al., 2012). By the end of 2013, WhatsApp – a cross-platform mobile messaging app founded in 2009 – counted 400 million active users per month after only four years (Koum, 2013). These examples show how quickly companies can attract a high number of customers in the digital era. Some important facts are (Manyika et al., 2013):

* The use of mobile Internet technology is already widespread, with more than 1.1 billion people currently using smartphones and tablets.
* By 2015, wireless Web use is expected to exceed wired use.
* More than nine billion devices around the world are currently connected to the Internet, including computers and smartphones.
* By 2025 most IT and Web applications and services could be cloud delivered or enabled, and most businesses could be using cloud facilities and services for their computing resources.

These facts have implications for marketing:

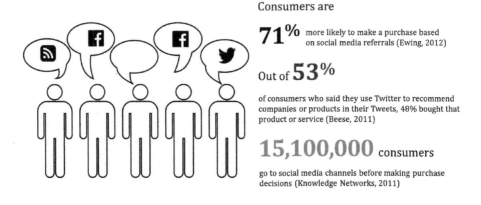

Consumers are

71% more likely to make a purchase based on social media referrals (Ewing, 2012)

Out of **53**%

of consumers who said they use Twitter to recommend companies or products in their Tweets, 48% bought that product or service (Beese, 2011)

15,100,000 consumers

go to social media channels before making purchase decisions (Knowledge Networks, 2011)

Figure 1.1   Implications of social media for (online) marketing

The digital revolution has begun, and companies are being fostered to transform their businesses, to catch up with – or be ahead of – technological trends, such as social media, cloud computing, mobile connectivity or big data. Considering the current pace of market penetration, we can observe a huge difference in today's market from a decade ago. For instance, retailers shifted from traditional value chains to social and collaborative activities such as social merchandizing (customer feedback is used in order to promote products online) or collaborative consumption (customers share their experiences of products). Although digital trends open up new ways of doing business, companies claim that the adoption of these trends is complex and slow.

The key to business excellence is to properly exploit technological trends, which means that the risks of investing into these new technologies must also be identified. Companies which have the right instruments to monitor these trends and make the right strategic adjustments can become so-called Digital Enterprises, which are likely to survive, exceed their competitors and make a profit.

This book provides guidance for the journey towards becoming a Digital Enterprise. It shows the potential of exploiting technological trends and provides instruments to support the digital transformation. The first chapter focuses on the importance of digital technology, highlights the most promising recent technological trends and summarizes the key characteristics of a Digital Enterprise.

Challenges in Digital Transformation:
1. Identify potential application areas for new technological trends.
2. Transform technological innovation into financial profits.
3. Sustain or develop business excellence by considering the latest technologies.
4. Provide guidance for efficient adaptation of new technological trends.

1.2 Importance of Technology

In the last century the digital world changed fundamentally. New technological developments and socio-political trends emerged continuously. Recently, big data, social media, cloud computing and mobility are proclaimed as technologies that will change future business models (Manyika et al., 2013). Companies like Google, YouTube, Facebook or Twitter, enable new ways of communicating and strongly influence our social, business, and political life. In 2011, the Middle East revolution was strongly supported by social media initiatives, facilitating the individual need for freedom of expression and terms like 'Facebook Revolution' and 'Twitter Revolution' were coined. These developments and trends can be described as democratization. The same happens in business environments where customers, employees and other stakeholders gain more influence on business and IT. The interests of all groups must be respected and taken into account more carefully than ever before. In short, the technological and socio-political trends influence the way successful companies operate. In this section we introduce some of the major technological developments in recent years and discuss their potential influence on various industries.

1.2.1 MOBILITY

Mobile connectivity summarizes the trends around mobile devices, such as smartphones or tablets, and communication technologies such as mobile internet or near field communication (NFC). These technologies provide new communication channels with customers, employees, and other stakeholders. Mobile connectivity allows new ways of working together: worldwide, at any place, at any time.

A great example of possible application areas was introduced by Tesco in 2011: The company launched the world's first virtual grocery store in subways in Seoul, South Korea. This virtual wall, which includes a range of different daily items from milk and apples to pet food and stationery, allows commuters to do their shopping on their way to work in the morning. They just need to scan their groceries and their items will be delivered that same evening. This allows commuters to use their waiting times to do the shopping and avoid wasting time in the evening.

The results of the initiative are impressive in terms of numbers: online sales between November 2010 and January 2011 increased by 130 percent, with the number of registered members rising by 76 percent (Tesco, 2011).

Considering such developments, we can envision totally different grocery shops in the future. For example, future shops may focus on presenting only available products, using virtual representations. Customers place the products into their virtual mobile shopping basket and get them delivered within a few hours. As a benefit, customers would not need to carry heavy items anymore. In addition, the stocks will be stored in centralized, remote warehouses, which will be automated to a large degree. The company profits from lower rents as they can store their entire portfolio centrally and avoid having to rent huge stockrooms for each individual grocery store. Furthermore, the staff can be reduced and might change from traditional checkout clerks to a service-oriented staff, which will help customers with their shopping decisions.

The mobile device also allows shops to present real-time offers to their customers, establish new forms of loyalty programs, or use the mobile device as an electronic payment service. With small add-on devices mobile phones or tablets can be upgraded to electronic cash systems and easily accept credit cards.

In order to reduce delivery times in electronic commerce different concepts are emerging. An interesting approach was introduced by mytaxi,[1] which managed to revolutionize the taxi market in less than ten months. For the first time, the customer could order a taxi directly via an innovative taxi-app, which makes dispatch centers obsolete. Taxi drivers only pay small trip fees without having to pay any monthly fixed costs to dispatch centers. Recently, the app-based service has started using its fleet of drivers to offer one-hour courier deliveries in Germany: Taxi drivers, who would usually spend their time waiting for customers, now have the opportunity to use their free time to deliver parcels.

Another example is the mobile strategy of the financial service company Tokio Marine Insurance. They developed a platform to offer location-based products to their travelling customers. As soon as the mobile app on the customer's mobile device detects that the owner has reached a location where special insurance offers could be provided (for example, ski slopes, airports, golf courses) the client automatically receives a suitable insurance offer. A first promotion of the new app resulted in a 300 percent sales increase; mainly customers in their 30s and 40s who decided to procure insurance on the same day – or in the evening of the day before – as the risky activity.

We still have not leveraged the full potential of mobile apps. Concepts like mobile wallets, virtual reality or mobile commerce are in the early stages of development and customer acceptance. There will be great business opportunities for all industrial branches in the future.

Potentials for Organizations:

1. Direct connection and communication to stakeholders (including customers and employees).
2. Additional information about customer behavior.
3. Customer-oriented offers.
4. Mobile payment and ordering systems.

1.2.2 CLOUD COMPUTING

Cloud computing describes the approach of delivering, sharing and charging different types of computing concepts such as infrastructure, platform, software, or even business processes, over a computer-based network. The central cloud-based system relies on sharing resources to achieve coherence and economies

---

1 http://www.mytaxi.com.

of scale. An advantage is that the effectiveness of shared resources can be maximized. Cloud resources are not only shared by multiple users but are also dynamically reallocated according to demand.

The new model of renting software applications (services) in the cloud not only decreases initial costs but also increases competitive advantage, which is the result of a faster deployment of the application.

A study conducted by Rackspace Hosting with support from Manchester Business School in 2012 (Nicholson et al., 2012) revealed that:

* 88 percent of cloud users point to cost savings,
* 56 percent have been able to increase profits through using cloud services,
* 49 percent have been able to grow their business through use of the cloud,
* 60 percent say that cloud computing has reduced the need for their IT team to maintain infrastructure, giving them more time to focus on strategy and innovation.

An interesting example of cloud services is the use of finance and control systems in combination with a wide range of services. Suppliers of tax consulting and auditing services might provide finance systems via the cloud, meaning that the client enters bookings directly into the tax consultant's or auditor's own system. This simplifies the tax consulting or auditing processes and saves the client the expense of installing relevant software. A further example is associated with the use of Business Intelligence (BI) software and tools: If a company does not have a permanent need for BI it can obtain the necessary service on demand from a cloud, use it, and terminate it afterwards. This can save a lot of costs because no maintenance and CPU runtime is needed. The BI services are only running when required.

Along with the benefits, there are also drawbacks. Data security is a frequently mentioned risk in the context of cloud services. As the data is no longer physically stored in and controlled by the company's own data center, misuse and loss of data have to be considered when evaluating the service. Outsourcing data to a cloud is also a matter of trust, and it certainly comes with a certain political dimension, where political stability and data protection regulations are relevant.

Potentials for Organizations:

1. Increased user mobility by a ubiquitous approval of information on any device.
2. Flexibility and cost savings by eliminating the need for heavy local installations of end-user applications and high-powered client computers.
3. Boost of your business by the shift from fixed to variable costs.

1.2.3 SOCIAL MEDIA

'Social Media is a group of Internet-based applications that build on the ideological and technological foundations of Web 2.0, and that allow the creation and exchange of user generated content' (Kaplan and Haenlein, 2010). Users create, share, circulate or make use of online information with the intent of educating one another about products, brands, services, issues and solutions (Blackshaw and Nazzaro, 2006).

Today, almost all products, services and businesses are visible on social networks like Facebook, LinkedIn or Twitter. Basically, we can distinguish between two types of content. On the one hand, content is actively managed and disseminated by the company itself. On the other hand, consumers, journalists, business partners, or any other stakeholders publish their own kind of information about the product, service or company. Consequently, this leads to a new level of transparency: Users discuss openly their job experiences or salaries, topics which were not public in the past. As a result, companies need to react to these developments in order to be attractive employers.

Throughout the world consumers join forces with the help of social networks, gaining immense power to either strengthen or destroy a company's brand and image. This situation pushes certain companies to pro-actively manage their image, like Lufthansa or Deutsche Bahn. Both companies analyze social media streams (like Twitter) in order to study how customers react in cases of transport delays. This allows them to derive proper response actions. The aim is to avoid negative comments and improve the communication with customers.

The social media movements force companies to rethink traditional business models and involve stakeholders in the production and sales cycle more deeply. For instance, the customer relationship for retailers is now dominated by social merchandizing[2] and collaborative consumption.[3] Furthermore, traditional

---

2 *Social merchandising* efforts focus on driving momentum and engagement for specific product rather than driving conversation about the brand in general.

3 *Collaborative consumption* is a class of economic arrangements in which participants share access to products or services, rather than having individual ownership.

value chains are subject to change. Producers might cut out the middleman and sell directly to their end-consumers. A good example is journalists or authors who do not rely on publishers anymore. Today they are able to sell their own electronic version of their publication on Amazon or other platforms, and use social media platforms, like Facebook, to advertize it.

Social media also provides companies with the opportunity to involve consumers early in the lifecycle. Companies have started to use social media interactively for innovation processes, involving the customers more in the development of new products and services. As an example of such 'co-creation' the insurance company Direct Line set up an 'Ideas lab' to engage existing and potential customers in the development of a new app. During a four-week campaign using a new iPhone app they asked Facebook users to pick features and choose the layout in order to determine the best features and functionality: Several hundred users participated. The result was a new 'On the Road' app, including a route planner and a 'Help for accidents and claims' tool. Besides evaluating design or product alternatives, social networks are also used for trend research. In the fashion business, so-called 'trend scouts' use social media platforms in order to spot new fashion trends. The most promising are taken up, produced, and offered as new and stylish fashions in shops. The finance sector in particular uses social networks in an attempt to regain lost confidence. Transparent and easy-to-understand financial service products are presented and explained on social platforms. At the same time consumers can provide ratings and add their own comments, which sometimes unveil risks that the company had not thought of.

Potentials for Organizations:

1.   Faster information sharing by direct and proactive communication with various stakeholders.
2.   Early brand and consumer feedback.
3.   Cost saving with the reduction of product lifecycles.
4.   Transparency of organization processes.

1.2.4 CROWDSOURCING

The term crowdsourcing was coined in 2005 and is a combination of the words 'crowd' and 'outsourcing'. The idea of crowdsourcing is to outsource certain business activities to a crowd of people. Crowdsourcing offers companies new ways of doing business, efficiency and accuracy. The outsourced solutions are likely to be superior to traditional ones.

Organizations can use crowdsourcing to advertise themselves in foreign countries by letting a crowd of people translate text or digitize paperwork – a task that previously seemed to be very laborious. For instance, the free language-learning website Duolingo[4] uses the crowd in order to automatically translate websites. The service is designed in such a way that users simultaneously help to translate websites and other documents while progressing through their lessons. Duolingo does not charge its customers for learning a new language. Instead, their business model is to sell their translation service to customers who want to have their content translated.

Companies have already started to outsource other business activities such as product marketing. As a result, product information, previously provided by the product marketing division, is created or updated by customers themselves. Customers might add pictures, videos or text to share their own sentiments while using the product. Such information increases confidence and may convince future buyers. In the same way, crowdsourcing could be used to create instruction manuals using blogs or videos which are geared to the needs of certain types of customers. In general, content provided by other customers is perceived as more likely to be a helpful and honest testimonial rather than a pure sales message. Some further ideas of crowdsourcing are:

- crowd testing of prototypes and newly developed products; people voluntarily attract other people to analyze prototypes,
- collaborative product development (for example, in the automobile industry, retail),
- suggestions about product features.

The great advantage of crowdsourcing is that it delivers innovations which arise from a crowd of people that work voluntarily and effectively at (usually) no cost.

Potentials for Organizations:

1. Increase the volume of sales by higher customer involvement in your processes.
2. Competitive advantage with unique product descriptions.
3. Increase of online visibility with access by a lot of people.
4. It fuels business innovations.

---

4   See http://www.duolingo.com, last accessed 14 July 2014.

1.2.5 INTERNET OF THINGS

The Internet of Things represents the paradigm that all devices and 'things' can be connected with each other and communicate autonomously (Atzori et al., 2010). It refers to the use of sensors, actuators, and data communication technology built into physical objects that enable those objects to be tracked, coordinated or controlled across a data network or the Internet (Manyika et al., 2013).

The basic idea is that the variety of things and objects in our daily lives are enhanced with modern wireless telecommunications, such as Radio-Frequency IDentification (RFID) tags, sensors, actuators, or NFC chips. Based on a unique addressing scheme the individual devices are connected to each other and cooperate with their neighbors to reach common goals (Atzori et al., 2010). Everything can be said to be 'smart' in the Internet of Things world and the possible impacts on our private and professional lives are huge. We are on the way to smart homes, smart cities, smart energy nets and so forth.

Thinking more about the business side, logistic and manufacturing processes can be greatly supported with these technologies. Some fashion labels are already experimenting with the RFID technology: Every single product is tagged with a unique chip and can be easily identified throughout the shipping process and in stores. Another case for application is the sale of fresh food where the Internet of Things provides new market opportunities. Sensors can provide information on where the food comes from and how fresh it is. It can literally track food from growth to shelf-life in a grocery store. Libelium, a company that designs and manufactures hardware technology, has deployed their wireless sensor systems to monitor food from production and harvesting to consumption and bio-waste outputs.

The Internet of Things paradigm potentially has a huge impact on the entire environment – the first 'smart cities' are emerging. The term refers to broadband communications infrastructure, a flexible, service-oriented computing infrastructure based on open industry standard and innovative services to meet the needs of governments and their employees, citizens and businesses. In the following, we list some possible future ideas that have been already tested (Vermesan and Friess, 2013):

- Smart parking – Every parking slot in a city is connected to a central infrastructure. Cars are automatically directed to the free parking spaces.

- Smart waste management – Every trash bin has a chip and sends a signal if it needs to be cleared. Thus, garbage collection can be optimized.
- Intelligent transportation system – A future system shows us the cheapest and quickest way from our current location to the final destination; no matter if it uses shared cars, shared bikes, subway, train, a ride with another person or any other means of conveyance.
- Smart environment – Such a system informs all people within a certain area about the danger of a certain event, like high air pollution, bushfires, hail storms, etc.
- Smart energy – Household devices are connected to an energy system and certain devices, such as washing machines, are triggered once the energy price is below a certain threshold.

Potentials for Organizations:

1. Ease of micro-productivity, i.e. an economy of shared and connected things.
2. Improvement of logistic and manufacturing processes with digital identity.
3. Interaction of computing systems will deliver new business value.

1.2.6 INDUSTRY 4.0

Industry 4.0 yields an autonomous organization of production units and is closely related to the Internet of Things movement. Such smart factories increase the flexibility of available value-creating networks by the application of cyber-physical production systems (Acatech, 2013). In such smart factories the product lifecycle is digitized and data from different resources is aligned with processes, which allow ad-hoc reactions to changes in the production. Machines can adapt their behavior to the changes, reconfigure and re-optimize themselves. Factories have to be moved from old, centralized control systems to a distributed cyber-physical system aiming to increase the production of smaller batch sizes.

The automotive industry greatly benefits from the Industry 4.0 paradigm. Customers can change their order requests (for example, the color of the car) more easily, even once the production process has been initialized. The modularization of all components of the production processes reduces changeover time. In cases where any unexpected irregularities in the production processes occur, then improvements are started autonomously. New services can be fulfilled even while production is running. This allows companies to offer product variations for acceptable prices.

Potentials for Organizations:

1. Ad-hoc reaction to customer changes (paintwork, delivery address, etc.) and changes in the supply chain (absent deliverers can be replaced readily).
2. Optimization of the tasks of staff members (rescheduling of machines).
3. Uncover irregularities in the production processes and automatically correct them.

1.2.7 BIG DATA

The quantity of available electronic data is growing exponentially. Data and information overload will change our lives. Big data sharing and analysis take place whenever we are browsing the Internet, using a mobile device or social media. Even when we are shopping, banking or using our car, data is collected and analyzed. Every second, around 3.7 million emails are sent worldwide. According to IBM 90 percentof worldwide data today has been generated in the last two years alone (IBM, 2013).

Big data denotes the growing challenge of organizations dealing with extremely large and fast-growing information pools and data sources (Gantz and Reinsel, 2011). When combined with artificial intelligence, big data can lead to completely new applications. A possible application area is the offering of limousine services in major cities. As a result of growing transportation demand, limousine services are an attractive business model. So far this business model has been limited by the availability of qualified dispatchers for the control centers. These coordinators decide which driver is to be sent on which assignment, based on clearly defined decision parameters. They take into account information like the limousines' locations (provided by the Global Positioning System, GPS), the collection and drop-off points, traffic bottlenecks, and other pending assignments. Thanks to big data analysis technology, all of this information can now be evaluated in real time and the assignments are managed automatically.

Another business case for big data is a 360° view on customers. Customers purchase a coffee while shopping, and pay with their credit card. The payment transaction including data about the location of the customer is transmitted and coupons for the nearest retail location are sent in real-time to the customer's mobile phone. When customers buy products, sensors – included in the products – measure customer's sentiments and feedback from the transmission (for example, the location of customers) is used to improve products.

Big data also opens up the possibility of efficiently analyzing outages and incidents. When an outage or an incident is reported, then real-time information (for example, location, weather conditions, traffic situation) and social media (real-time information from social media chatter) are also linked with the report in order to find details otherwise unknown to the provider.

Further possible applications can be found in the banking sector when trading currencies or securities, or in the health sector in optimizing patient care.

Potentials for Organizations:

1. Obtain real-time access into customer behavior.
2. Monitor a massive volume of data in order to detect inconsistencies.
3. Forecast opportunities and events of interest.
4. Analyze real-time data in order to improve decision-making quality.

1.2.8 3D PRINTING AND 3D SCANNERS

Another technological development is called 3D printing, which has the potential to revolutionize entire industries. In the past 3D printers have been particularly used in industrial prototyping and reduced costs and production time. Nowadays the use of 3D printing to manufacture end-consumer parts is also occurring. Whether or not 3D printers will ever be feasible for domestic use, the potential future application is immense. For example, 3D printers could be used to create all sorts of spare parts for all manner of products. Nowadays, it is too costly to store most spare parts separately as part of a store's inventory. Thus, in the future, we will be able to repair many more products rather than throwing them away because of a small broken part. Faulty goods will be able to be taken to a local facility that will retrieve the appropriate 3D model for the spare part online and simply print it out. Furthermore, 3D printing allows manufacturers to produce once more in industrial countries. In the past a lot of manufacturing was outsourced to emerging economies in order to save on costs. With 3D printing it actually does not matter where the printer is located. In fact, it is cheaper to print the products in the country where they are required and save unnecessary logistical and transportation costs.

The prices for 3D printing have dropped tremendously in the past few years; designers and private individuals have started to design their own 3D models online. For example, Shapeways, iMaterialize and Sculpteo allow anybody to upload their 3D digital models to have their designs 3D printed and marketed online.

Nowadays, objects like jewellery or spare parts can be printed at home, however, 3D printing is not limited to small objects. Actually, the vision is that entire houses can be printed in the future. There will also be big changes in the health industry where researchers have already printed individual organs. Even the food industry is experimenting with 3D printing and predicts that everyone will be able print his or her own meal in the future.

The innovation of 3D printing is not just limited to the printers themselves. The entire system, including 3D scanning or modelling, faces great improvements. The technology is, likewise, a threat for existing manufacturers as it provides enormous opportunities for future business models.

Potentials for Organizations:

1. Democratization of manufacturing capabilities by removing high startup costs.
2. Reduction of inventory costs.
3. Flexibility and rapid reaction to customer demand.

1.2.9 SUMMARY

All these technological trends open up new types of business models and customer relationships. Scenarios for three industries are shown in Table 1.1.

Table 1.1 Overview of technology trends

	Mobility	Cloud Computing	Social Media	Crowd-sourcing	Internet of Things	Big Data
Health-care	Medical professionals can access health records during patient exams	Patient data is stored in the cloud and not in each single hospital	Doctors chat with patients online (patient care)	Outsourcing of medical transcription; the community reports on experiences	Real-time patient home care	Personalized services based on the access of data points about patients
Retail	Virtual communication with potential customers	Anyplace access to the product location and digital catalogue	Outsourced activities of product marketing	Collaborative product descriptions	Products tagged with RFID	Real-time delivery management
Banking and Finance	End-to-end mobile banking	Client data is stored in the cloud instead of having databases for each location	Onetime balance monitoring	Cardholders vote about credit card features	Real-time balance monitoring	Targeting appropriate customers in marketing campaigns

1.3 The Transformation to a Digital Enterprise

Current and future technologies allow companies to create competitive advantages. Their success depends on early movement and a clear strategy of how the company can profit most from these technologies. Companies must be able to transform themselves digitally. Digital transformation uses the latest technology in response to socio-behavioral changes, to establish a culture of agility, innovation, empowerment, and engagement.

This is not simply about implementing the latest technology. Instead, it is more about adapting corporate culture in order to benefit from the opportunities provided by the latest technology (Solis, 2013). The latest research studies show that digital transformation radically improves corporate and financial performance (Bonnet et al., 2012).

Just consider Apple's iPad as one example, introduced to the market in 2010. Restaurants capture orders and payments electronically, doctors offer virtual magazines in their waiting rooms instead of traditional paper-based magazines, sales forces use it to present products or services to customers in a more enjoyable and flexible way; the transformation possibilities are endless. However, companies which had established long-term IT strategies before 2010 did not consider the opportunities of such devices. Consequently, those departments, which still stick to the initial plan, are not able to react appropriately to the new market requirements.

Digital Transformation – *is a specialized type of business transformation where IT plays a dominant role. In the digital age, new business opportunities arise and enterprises transform their strategy, structure, culture and processes using the potential and power of digital media and the Internet.*

Companies that are unwilling or unable to adapt to the digital world will fall under what is known as *Digital Darwinism* (Schwartz, 1999). Only 71 companies out of the original Fortune 500 list from 1955 still exist today (Collins, 2008). Companies like Scott Paper, Zenith, Rubbermaid, Chrysler, Teledyne, Warner Lambert, or Bethlehem Steel were among the most celebrated companies in history. Today, they have disappeared from the list and other businesses like Intel, Microsoft, Apple, Dell, and Google grew from zero to market leaders using entirely new technologies (Collins, 2008). The recent economic crisis confirmed yet again that there is no business too big to fail. At the same time, there are many small startup businesses, which proved to be successful, with exceptional growth rates. According to a study by MIT research

(Westerman, 2012), 78 percent of respondents said that achieving digital transformation will become critical to their organizations within the next two years, however, 63 percent said that the pace of technology change in their organization is too slow (Fitzgerald et al., 2013).

Companies which have the right instruments to monitor technological and socio-political trends and make the right strategic adjustments are more likely to survive in the future. In short, companies that transform themselves digitally are able to stay competitive in a rapidly-changing market. We refer to such companies as Digital Enterprises.

Digital Enterprise: The term designates a company – irrespective of its history or its industry – whose IT plays a dominant role in the corporate strategy, i.e. where IT is used in internal and external operations to create a competitive advantage.

Even if a company can rapidly sense and respond to new technologies, it must also create business value from the technology investment. Digital Enterprises know how to make money by leveraging digital technologies and they can use them in a way that is beneficial for all parties involved in their business chain. The transformation to a Digital Enterprise depends on a variety of criteria and plenty of organizations have failed to transform: But what distinguishes a successful digital transformer from its competitor?

An example of a failed digital transformation is Kodak, a company known as an innovator since 1888 and whose laboratories produced many innovations and techniques. Although Kodak owned most of the patents for digital-photography technology and invented the first digital camera in 1975, the company has struggled since and is currently trying to recover. Kodak's business in the 20th century was to sell films, and they feared that digital products could reshape the market. Instead of marketing the new technology, the company aggressively kept promoting their traditional, lucrative, film business. By the time they realized that they were in a 'memories business' rather than a 'film business' they had been overtaken by their competitors and are still having a hard time recovering (Dan, 2013). Kodak was not able to come up with new, innovative concepts that convinced their customers. They did not understand how to transform digitally and commercialize their innovations.

In contrast, the Benetton Group successfully transformed to become a digital player. They implemented a holistic mobile strategy with Apple's iPad as a major device (Apple, 2013). The sales division uses the iPad to visualize the fashion catalogue, replacing the hardcopy catalogue that was costly to produce and difficult to change. The new IT solution enables last minute updates of the collection. Thus, changes can be realized faster and with significant time savings. The marketing division uses the iPad to allow people to share comments and to preview details of the collection through iPads installed in the stores. Consequently, the company provides confidence by making the production transparent. Benetton also uses the iPad as a communication channel between employees. The employees can access the collection, all Benetton stores, mail, calendars or contacts anytime and at any place. A geographically distributed workforce is fully supported. Digital Enterprises have the right toolset for the transformation and proactively react to new technologies instead of just considering transformation when revenues decline (for example, due to a competitor's advantages).

A Digital Enterprise excels in *innovation* and figures out how to derive a real financial benefit out of it. It also has an excellent *transformation* ability.

Digital Enterprises even develop entirely new business models based on new technology, like social media: Friendsurance, in co-operation with Facebook, developed cheap insurance products relating to liability, legal protection, and smartphones. In the event of damage, minor claims are settled within the network itself ('shared risk'); the insurer is liable only for larger claims. The insurance premium is determined depending on the actual damage incurred. This model is based on the sharing of risk between the customer group and the insurer. As a result, a noticeable drop in insurance fraud, a positive risk selection, as well as lower marketing and administration costs could be reported.

Companies that are successful in the long term have the ability to rapidly identify the changing environment and can quickly respond to new situations. Google, for instance, either acquires new application providers[5] or the company builds its expertise from the ground up. Google's IT product portfolio is diversified and the most important point is that their products are seamlessly integrated. Consequently, Digital Enterprises align new technologies seamlessly with the existing IT infrastructure. Another example is the global recruitment company Hays, which decided in 2008 to replace its entire IT landscape with the goal of establishing a flexible, scalable and adaptable IT platform. They took a step back and completely rethought their IT landscape. Their software selection was based on open standards and they also considered cloud-based

---

5   For example, Google bought the free GPS navigation app Waze and plans to offer a comparison site for car insurance.

solutions. The initial part of this IT transformation was completed in 2010 and the company established its basis for a stable and yet flexible infrastructure. The open standards-based architecture allowed them, for instance, to connect to the LinkedIn platform and provides them with new business opportunities. In addition, they use the Google Search Appliance and Oracle business intelligence tools, which provide additional value from the growing mass of data.

A Digital Enterprise excellently exploits the potential of new technologies and, as a consequence, the business.

Nowadays enterprises with a traditional supply chain, such as in the automotive industry, still tend to focus only on the next link to which they ship their products. BMW announced its new electric car, the BMW i3, in July 2013. The really interesting announcement with respect to digital transformation was the multi-channel sales model, including an online sales platform. For the first time, a car manufacturer sells its cars directly to its customers via an online shop. In the past, customers could configure their cars online but the sales occurred at the dealership.

This leads us to another characteristic of Digital Enterprises, namely the closer connection to customers. Social media and other technologies alike enable entirely different forms of communication between and with customers. Amazon is another example, as the company allows its customers to write individual product reviews and make virtual recommendations to other customers that share the same preferences. However, examples in the food service industry show us potential problems if we do not monitor our customer segments carefully. Recently many premium restaurants offered Groupon deals: Groupon runs a deal-of-the-day website that features discounted vouchers usable at local venues. The general concept is that a company has to give a minimum of 50 percent reduction and Groupon earns 25 percent of the remaining price. The restaurants participated with the goal of acquiring more customers. One goal was to provide cross-selling premium offers to the customers, which were not included in the initial deal. However, in fact, the deals often attracted bargain hunters who were not willing to invest any extra money, for instance for additional premium wine. As another result, the typical types of customer in the premium restaurants changed from higher earners to middle class customers who could normally not afford to buy an expensive meal. This has had a negative impact on the regular premium customers, who want to differentiate themselves and do not want to be part of the 'standard' middle class. Consequently, they visited other premium restaurants. Eventually, these premium restaurants managed to attract new customers, however, these were not really spending a lot of money. At the same time, the restaurants were losing their valuable existing customers. Careful customer segmentation beforehand and a focus on the premium customers could have avoided this loss of image.

A Digital Enterprise is capable of focusing on the most valuable customers by using modern technologies.

Digital Enterprises consider the technology impact on the entire organization. As such, they have a solid corporate culture, including visionary and communicative leaders (and thinkers) who are capable of bringing a vision onto the market, and productive workers, who are excellent in translating the vision into a product. A great example is Google, a company that understands how to manage diverse types of knowledge workers. Google aims to provide more than just a nice working environment; it offers many at-work leisure facilities as employees should enjoy their day in the office. In the past, Google also gave employees free reign over 20 percent of their working week, where they could work totally freely on their own ideas – this resulted in some of Google's biggest innovations including AdSense and Gmail.

The automotive manufacturer Volkswagen AG is another example, which offers an idea platform where every employee can make proposals, in addition to a creative working environment. The ideas can range from enhancing the working environment, improving operational processes, to new products. In 2011, Volkswagen collected around 60,000 proposals from its employees, which resulted in cost savings of approximately 100 million Euro.

A Digital Enterprise has knowledge workers who do not believe they are paid to 'work 9 to 5' and that smart businesses will 'strip away everything that gets in their knowledge workers' way' (Drucker, 1959).

The integration of new technologies requires interplay between IT, business processes and data. The manufacturer Rossignol aligned its business processes and data with social media and successfully created a business value from this investment. Initially, Rossignol offered a mobile app measuring the skiing performance of a single person. With the app the company creates a social profile of its customer and is also capable of suggesting the appropriate equipment based on the performance level of the customer. When people communicate their location then the closest stores are indicated. The company can react to customer needs on time. In return customers give feedback on the service and on products, which shortens the product life-cycle.

Modern process and IT infrastructures also support the analysis and capturing of relevant information: It is important to derive the right conclusions from the available data. Let us consider the case where a food company positions a new product on the market. After a few successful months, the revenue for this product decreases tremendously: As the management is only looking at the number of products sold, they conclude that the quality of the product is not good enough so they decide to take it off the market. However, competitors selling similar products were having a hard time as well. Therefore, if the management had monitored the market more closely, and taken the general decreasing demands for a certain period into account, this might have led to a different decision. Digital Enterprises avoid making wrong assumptions and decisions based on limited data. Rather, they have a clear strategy about which numbers have to be measured and are of importance in the entire ecosystem.

A Digital Enterprise aligns its processes, data and IT with the digital technology.

In summary, Digital Enterprises appropriately exploit new technological trends and can quickly adapt their business to them. Beside business and IT issues, IT governance has to cope with the needs and requirements of stakeholders, such as customers and employees, in order to establish competitive advantages through information technology. Often this results in a restructuring of the product and service portfolio and a continuous adjustment to customer needs. Then, the appropriate usage of the technologies can revolutionize the business.

Digital Enterprises recognize how to respond to technological trends and are able to:

- Provide rapid and innovative responses to environmental changes;
- Understand customers' and employees' needs and have digitally-enabled relationships with them;
- React faster to customer needs;
- Offer 24/7 availability;
- Reduce product life-cycles;
- Increase customer confidence;
- Provide transparency;
- Recognize the potential usage of technological trends.

1.4 Structure of the Book

Digital Enterprises continuously assess the maturity of their skills and competencies and aim at improving them. This book presents a sound and empirically validated framework that supports companies to successfully exploit digital technological trends. The Digital Capability Framework provides an instrument which allows companies to take the necessary steps towards a successful digital transformation.

The Framework was developed by the Business Transformation Academy in cooperation with leading-edge institutions of information technology: the University of Applied Sciences and Arts (Northwestern Switzerland), the University of St. Gallen (Switzerland), Queensland University of Technology (Australia), the University of Liechtenstein (Principality of Liechtenstein), and the Karlsruhe Institute of Technology (Germany). The Digital Capability Framework encompasses four parts:

- **Digital Capabilities** – the key skills and capabilities a company requires to transform itself into a sustainable and successful business by considering digital technology as the enabling component.
- **Digital Capability Maturity Models** – structured assessment to evaluate the digital maturity of an organization.
- **Digital Use Cases** – ways of showing how to enhance the Digital Capabilities within a specific industry.
- **Digital Transformation Roadmap** – we presents the six steps of how to proceed to a Digital Enterprise transformation.

The book is intended for a wide audience: reflective managers, consultants, C-level executives, academics and also non-profit organizations – it is useful for everyone who is involved in (digital) transformation in general.

Objectives of this book:

1. Learn about the benefits of new technology and how Digital Enterprises make business with these technologies.
2. Discover new business opportunities which are based on digital technology.

This handbook is organized in the following chapters:

Chapter 1: The Importance of Technological Trends and How to Exploit Them for Business Excellence highlights the importance of technology, which is the key to the success and support of companies to become Digital Enterprises. In addition, we show the typical characteristics of such a Digital Enterprise.

Chapter 2: Digital Capability Framework: A Toolset to Become a Digital Enterprise provides a general overview of the framework and presents a roadmap for how to become a Digital Enterprise.

Chapter 3: Innovation Capability analyses the emerging opportunities when leveraging the enterprise's innovation management. This chapter also illustrates how innovation is managed in a leading and global enterprise.

Chapter 4: Transformation Capability elaborates how to succeed in a digital transformation. This chapter uses IBM as an example of a company that avoided failure.

Chapter 5: IT Excellence analyses the understanding of the possible usage, benefits and risks of IT systems with respect to business excellence. This chapter discusses the IT Excellence of the German IT banking provider Finanz Informatik.

Chapter 6: Customer Centricity discusses all aspects of the customer in order to implement a customer-centric value chain. The findings are illustrated based on the Walt Disney case.

Chapter 7: Effective Knowledge Worker assesses to what extent organizations can improve the working environment and how this impacts on business excellence. This chapter summarizes how Google manages to lead knowledge workers.

Chapter 8: Operational Excellence discusses which opportunities the digital age offers for organizations to realize a new level of operational excellence. The findings are illustrated based on the global company Hilti.

Chapter 9: Digital Supply Chain Management introduces a set of different Digital Use Cases related to Supply Chain Management. The chapter explains the characteristics of the individual cases and describes how to analyze and assess the Digital Use Cases in order to derive a strategic efforts-benefits portfolio and to build up a Digital Transformation Roadmap.

Chapter 10: Digital Transformation at DHL Freight concludes the book and explains how the board of DHL Freight has developed a strategy that establishes aspirations and guidelines for transforming the company by deploying the Digital Capability Framework.

References

Acatech – National Academy of Science and Engineering (2013) Securing the future of German manufacturing industry. Recommendations for implementing the strategic initiative Industrie 4.0: http://www.acatech. de/fileadmin/user_upload/Baumstruktur_nach_Website/Acatech/root/de/ Material_fuer_Sonderseiten/Industrie_4.0/Final_report__Industrie_4.0_ accessible.pdf, last accessed: 27 December 2013.

Apple (2013) The Benetton Group. iPad in Business. http://www.apple.com/ipad/business/profiles/benetton/, last accessed: 27 December 2013.

Atzori, L., Iera, A., and Morabito, G. (2010) The Internet of Things: A survey. *Journal of Computer Networks*, 54(15), pp. 2787–2805.

Beese, J. (2012) Social Networks Influence 74% of Consumers' Buying Decisions. Published on SproutSocial. Retrieved from http://sproutsocial.com/insights/social-networks-influence-buying-decisions/, last accessed: 27 December 2013.

Blackshaw, P., and Nazzaro, M. (2006) *Consumer-Generated Media (CGM) 101: Word-of-mouth in the age of the web-fortified consumer*. New York: Nielsen BuzzMetrics.

Bonnet, D., Ferraris, P., Westerman, G., and McAfee, A. (2012) Talking 'bout a revolution. *Digital Transformation Review*, 2(1). http://www.capgemini.com/resources/digital-transformation-review--edition-2, last accessed 6 July 2014.

Chui, M., Manyika, J., Bughin, J., Dobbs, R., Roxburgh, C., Sarrazin, H., Sands, G., et al. (2012) The social economy: Unlocking value and productivity through social technologies. http://www.mckinsey.com/insights/high_tech_telecoms_internet/the_social_economy, last accessed 6 July 2014.

Collins, J. (2008) The Secret of Enduring Greatness. Fortune. http://www.jimcollins.com/article_topics/articles/secret-of-enduring-greatness.html, last accessed 27 December 2013.

Dan, A. (2013) The Death Of Scale: Is Kodak's Failure An Omen Of Things To Come For Corporate America? http://www.forbes.com/sites/avidan/2013/08/20/the-death-of-scale-is-kodaks-failure-an-omen-of-things-to-come-for-corporate-america/, last accessed 27 December 2013.

Drucker, P.L. (1958) *Landmarks of Tomorrow*. New York: Harper and Bros.

Ewing, M. (2012) 71% More Likely to Purchase Based on Social Media Referrals. Published on Hubspot. Retrieved from http://blog.hubspot.com/blog/tabid/6307/bid/30239/71-More-Likely-to-Purchase-Based-on-Social-Media-Referrals-Infographic.aspx, last accessed 27 December 2013.

Fitzgerald, M., Kruschwitz, N., Bonnet, D., and Welch, M. (2013) Embracing Digital Technology. A New Strategic Imperative. http://www.es.capgemini-consulting.com/resource-file-access/resource/pdf/embracing_digital_technology_a_new_strategic_imperative.pdf, last accessed 14 July 2014.

Gantz J., and Reinsel, D. (2011) Extracting Value from Chaos. IDC IVIEW. http://idcdocserv.com/1142, last accessed 27 December 2013.

IBM (2013) Big Data at the Speed of Business. http://www-01.ibm.com/software/data/bigdata/, last accessed 27 December 2013.

Kaplan, A., and Haenlein, M. (2010) Users of the world, unite! The challenges and opportunities of Social Media, *Business Horizons*, 53 (1), pp. 59–68.

Knowledge Networks (2011) Social Media Now Influences Brand Perceptions, Purchase Decisions of 38 Million in US http://www.knowledgenetworks.com/news/releases/2011/061411_social-media.html, last accessed 6 July 2014.

Koum, J. (2013) 400 Million Stories. WhatsApp Blog. http://blog.whatsapp.com/index.php/2013/12/400-million-stories/?lang=de&set=yes, last accessed 27 December 2013.

Manyika, J., Chui, M., Bughin, J., Dobbs, R., Bisson, P., and Marrs, A. (2013) Disruptive technologies: Advances that will transform life, business, and the global economy. http://www.mckinsey.com/insights/business_technology/disruptive_technologies, last accessed 6 July 2014.

Nicholson, B., Owrak, A., and Daly, L. (2012) Cloud Computing Research. Retrieved from http://www.rackspace.co.uk/sites/default/files/whitepapers/Rackspace_Cloud_Report_Economic_FINAL.pdf, last accessed 27 December 2013.

Schwartz, E.I. (1999) *Digital Darwinism*. New York: Broadway Books.

Solis, B. (2013) 4 Signs Your Stock Won't be a Digital Age Winner: Companies That Ignore Innovation Will be its Victims. *MarketWatch, The Wall Street Journal*. http://www.marketwatch.com/story/4-signs-your-stock-wont-be-a-digital-age-winner-2013-04-16, last accessed 14 July 2014.

Tesco (2011) Home plus subway virtual store. Retrieved from http://dtaylor8blog.files.wordpress.com/2013/09/tesco.jpg, last accessed 27 December 2013.

Vermesan, O., and Friess, P. (2013) *Internet of Things – Converging Technologies for Smart Environments and Integrated Ecosystems*. Aalborg: River Publishers.

Webb, J.W., and Romano, R.M. (2010) *Disrupting the Future – Uncommon Wisdom for Navigating Print's Challenging Marketplace*. Harrisville, RI: Strategies for Management.

Westerman, G., Tannou, M., Bonnet, D., Ferraris, P., and McAfee, A. (2012) The Digital Advantage: How digital leaders outperform their peers in every industry. http://www.capgemini.com/resource-file-access/resource/pdf/The_Digital_Advantage__How_Digital_Leaders_Outperform_their_Peers_in_Every_Industry.pdf, last accessed 14 July 2014.

Chapter 2

Digital Capability Framework: A Toolset to Become a Digital Enterprise

AXEL UHL, MATTHIAS BORN,
AGNES KOSCHMIDER AND TOMASZ JANASZ

2.1 Overview

The future of technology looks *smart, mobile, cloudy, social,* and *big.* The actual impact of technology differs between companies and between industries, although the general planning and transformation process follows similar patterns. The success of digital transformation does not depend on just introducing a new technology. Companies need to carefully investigate and analyze the possible usage, the benefits, and the risks of the new technological trends. Like any business transformation, this includes the people, the culture, the strategy and the processes.

In this chapter we introduce the Digital Capability Framework as a new approach which guides you along the transformation path and supports you to successfully achieve a digital transformation and to become a Digital Enterprise. The foundation for digital transformation requires a complete understanding and holistic analysis of internal and external possibilities, feasibilities, strengths and weaknesses. In order to provide such a holistic view, the Digital Capability Framework integrates the Business Transformation Management Methodology (BTM²) (Uhl and Gollenia, 2012).

A company needs to question whether it is ready to implement new technologies, and whether it has defined a quality strategy to ensure a high return on investment. Potential benefits and risks of a digital transformation need to be carefully studied and assessed prior to undergoing a digital transformation.

The Digital Capability Framework consists of four individual building blocks. First, it is built on six core Digital Capabilities, which are the foundation of a successful Digital Enterprise. Second, it defines Digital Capability Maturity Models, which are used to measure the degree of maturity for each Digital Capability. The maturity models support the analysis of the 'as-is' situation and provide instruments for planning the prospective 'to-be' scenario. The third building block consists of Digital Use Cases, which describe how to reach a targeted to-be state. Finally, the fourth building block of the framework describes a six-step approach to define the roadmap for a Digital Enterprise.

Objectives of this chapter:

1. Understand the concepts of the Digital Capability Framework including its four building blocks: Digital Capabilities, Digital Capability Maturity Models, Digital Use Cases and Digital Roadmap.
2. Consider digital transformation as a holistic approach and understand the benefits of integrating the Business Transformation Management Methodology (BTM²).
3. Learn the principles of transforming into a Digital Enterprise.

2.2 Introduction to the Digital Capability Framework

In order to become a Digital Enterprise, a company needs to identify the business benefits, as well as the risks, of investing in new technology. The promise of new technology is not simply to automate processes but in fact to provide new ways of doing business (Bonnet et al., 2012). IT is becoming the enabling component. More and more companies see the need for digital transformation, however, they struggle in driving the transformation process (Westerman et al., 2012).

In this section, we introduce the Digital Capability Framework, which supports companies to transform themselves into Digital Enterprises. We explain the individual components of the framework and show how companies can benefit from it.

2.2.1 WHAT IS THE DIGITAL CAPABILITY FRAMEWORK?

Every company can transform itself into a Digital Enterprise. This digital transformation process requires certain skills and abilities in order to succeed. Maybe some companies and the responsible workforce are more gifted than others, but these skills and abilities can be acquired by everyone. The success depends rather on the interplay of the individual components, the overall strategy and a holistic view of the transformation process.

We can compare digital transformation with a team sport like football: Individual skills and team tactics are required to play an effective and successful game. Although the initial aim is as simple as to score more goals than the opposition, an experienced coach knows exactly what the key capabilities of successful teams are and his training focuses on improving those.

The Digital Capability Framework is a toolset that helps companies to analyze the as-is situation and to identify new business cases which are enabled by technology trends. The framework consists of four different building blocks (see Figure 2.1).

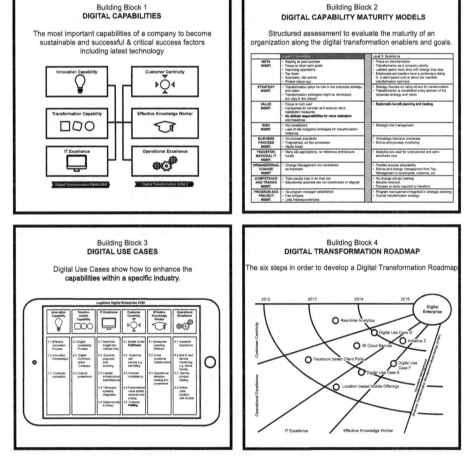

Figure 2.1 The four building blocks of the Digital Capability Framework

The first building block of the framework defines the six core capabilities that a company requires to become a Digital Enterprise. Companies which perform strongly in these capabilities are more likely to beat their competitors. Considering a soccer team, important skills are: strong physical fitness, brilliant ball control, quick thinking and excellent team work. A Digital Enterprise will outperform its competitors if it is able to:

- transform and innovate simultaneously,
- leverage the best-suited technology for its business,
- understand and serve its customers in a superior way,
- provide a highly motivated and collaborative working environment that facilitates knowledge workers, and
- operate its business in an efficient way.

The second building block is Digital Capability Maturity Models which enable measurement of the degree of maturity for each capability. Strong maturity indicates that a company knows exactly how to gain the most from the latest technological trends and how to establish new business cases and enter a new market. Based on the maturity models, one can determine the as-is situation and specify the anticipated to-be situation. Again, this is quite similar to the team sport example. Before the season starts the physical condition of every player is measured, and based on the individual fitness level, appropriate exercises are defined.

The appropriate exercises in the context of a Digital Enterprise are called Digital Use Cases, and are the third building block of the Digital Capability Framework. The Digital Use Cases describe best-practice examples, which can be followed to improve the individual Digital Capabilities. The fourth building block of the framework is a Digital Transformation Roadmap that explains the necessary steps in order to become a Digital Enterprise.

Digital Capability Framework – *the Digital Capability Framework is an integrative approach to digital transformation. The framework consists of six Digital Capabilities, six Digital Capability Maturity Models, Digital Use Cases and a roadmap for a Digital Enterprise.*

Before we explain the four building blocks in detail, we explain an important characteristic of the Digital Capability Framework, namely its relationship to the Business Transformation Management Methodology (BTM²) and highlight the major benefits for your organization.

2.2.2 RELATIONSHIP TO BUSINESS TRANSFORMATION

Digital transformation is a specialized type of business transformation where IT plays a dominant role. Companies need to understand and evaluate several factors to determine the best way to transform. Every transformation is a complex and time-consuming process, and is influenced by its environment, such as customers, competitors, government and regulators, as well as other stakeholders. It is therefore a complex and risky undertaking. Less than 40 percent of transformation efforts are successful and sometimes it takes several attempts to succeed. In order to execute a successful transformation, the management of a meta-routine is crucial. A holistic and integrative methodology that supports such a transformation process is BTM^2.

BTM^2 integrates all major management disciplines, such as Strategy Management, Risk Management or Change Management (see Figure 2.2). The methodology provides an overarching frame called Meta Management that is business-driven, value-oriented and integrates three pillars; namely, the individual management disciplines, the transformation lifecycle and leadership principles.

The Digital Capability Framework takes advantage of the BTM^2 components. It is geared to integrate the eight management disciplines defined within BTM^2, as well as the additional Meta Management discipline.

The integration of BTM^2 with the Digital Capability Framework enables a 360-degree view of all related issues for a digital transformation. As a consequence, the Digital Capability Framework does not only consider the 'what' – what should a company do to improve a certain capability – but also the 'how' – how is the company managing its transformation.

A company can only improve its Digital Capabilities if it considers its entire ecosystem. To make this complexity manageable, the BTM^2 management disciplines are the basis for each of the six Digital Capabilities. The application of BTM^2 ensures that the impact for each capability is observed for all aspects of an enterprise. Within the Digital Capability Framework, each BTM^2 discipline is further categorized into three knowledge areas, which describe the key components of the particular discipline (see Figure 2.3).

In the following, we summarize the core aspects of the individual BTM^2 management disciplines and their corresponding knowledge areas.

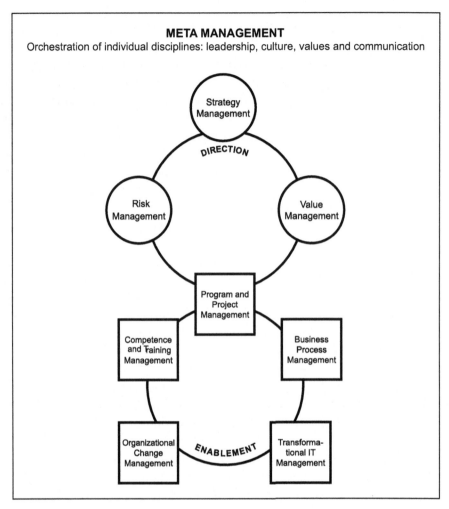

Figure 2.2   The BTM² management disciplines

META	DIRECTION			ENABLEMENT				
	STRATEGY	VALUE	RISK	PROCESSES	IT	CHANGE	TRAINING	PROGRAM
Culture	Vision and Goals	Value Identification	Risk Identification	Governance	Information & Analytics	Change Impact Analysis	Training Need Analysis	Framework
Leadership	Business Model	Value Realization Planning	Risk Management Planning	Methods & Tools	Business Applications	Change Management Planning	Curriculum Development	Organization
Values	Execution	Value Realization	Risk Mitigation	Process Optimization	Communication Technology	Change Management Execution	Training Execution	Execution

Figure 2.3   The BTM² skeleton of the Digital Capability Framework

Meta Management is the overall frame and provides the linkage among the management disciplines, leadership, culture and communication, and allows the digital transformation process to be effective. The knowledge area *Culture* reflects the overall cultural environment of a company. It ensures that all relevant information is communicated appropriately and that all employees have good job satisfaction and are motivated to deliver the best results. It is closely linked to the knowledge area *Leadership*. Managers need to put the right people in the right places and continuously coordinate between the different stakeholders. This includes communication principles such as appreciation, empathy and openness. The knowledge area *Values* describes the concrete value of the activities and how they are incentivized.

The management discipline *Strategy Management* analyzes the needs for and causes of the digital transformation, as well as the level of transformation readiness. The knowledge area *Vision and Goals* ensures that the digital transformation objectives are integrated into the company's overall vision. Furthermore, these objectives need to be considered in the *Business Model,* which is the second knowledge area. It describes the impact of the digital transformation on the company's future ways of making a profit. The third knowledge area *Execution* guarantees that the strategy is executed not only internally but that the digital transformation also includes key partners, suppliers and customers.

Value Management provides techniques for identifying, planning, managing and evaluating the benefits of a digital transformation. The first step is to name and describe the benefits of the transformation. This is part of the knowledge area *Value Identification* and provides the key stakeholders with tools to define the business benefits. Once the potential benefits are identified, a clear understanding of the measurements, responsibilities and required changes has to be created during the *Value Realization Planning*. The last knowledge area – *Value Realization* – ensures that the results are captured and analyzed in order to support future decisions.

Risk Management elaborates on strategic and operational risks, which might jeopardize the success of the digital transformation. The first knowledge area is *Value Identification,* where the potential risks of failure are detected and defined. The risks are not just related to the internal structure of a company but rather monitor the entire ecosystem including customers, suppliers and other stakeholders. Part of the *Risk Management Planning* is to evaluate and rank the identified risks. Not everything can be protected but it is important to establish a risk response plan and know how to deal with the issues once they emerge.

Risk Mitigation is the third knowledge area: It defines how the risk can be mitigated and which steps to take in order to tackle emerging problems.

Business Process Management defines the scope of process changes and the expected improvements in performance. Many companies still struggle to describe their entire process landscape. To make the transformation effort a continuous success the business processes have to be considered from a strategic perspective. The identification of end-to-end business processes and the assignment of responsible process owners is one major task. This is part of the knowledge area *Governance*. In order to document, analyze, implement and execute processes, a company requires the right *Methods and Tools*. This includes company-wide process-thinking and a sufficient level of process management knowledge. The third knowledge area *Process Optimization* deals with existing process inefficiencies, with the aim to optimize and also automate processes within in entire value chain.

Transformational IT Management assesses the extent to which IT changes are essential and provides plans to realize required implementation and testing procedures of new technologies. The knowledge area *Information and Analytics* focuses on the quantity and quality of data captured in IT systems. Well defined KPIs and analytic reports are the basis for management decisions. The setup of the IT landscape is part of the knowledge area *Business Applications*. The goal is to avoid multiple silo applications and provide an application lifecycle management, which is continuously optimized. The third knowledge area *Communication Technology* ensures that new technologies are considered as communication channels across the entire ecosystem. In addition, data security is an important topic to consider.

Organizational Change Management identifies the required types of changes and analyzes their impact on various parts of the organization, as well as the external ecosystem. The knowledge area *Change Impact Analysis* covers the identification of the required changes as well as the impact analysis across the entire ecosystem. The required changes need to be planned and also communicated. It is important to respect all individual stakeholder interests during the transformation, explain the consequences and agree on reasonable compromises. All this is part of the *Change Management Planning*. The third knowledge area is called *Change Management Execution*: Here, the goal is to establish mechanisms for monitoring the effectiveness of the implementation and the subsequent organizational performance. In addition, the communication plan is continuously adapted to the changing environment of the ecosystem.

Competence and Training Management focuses on organizational competencies and individual skills as critical success factors for business transformation and future businesses. It is important to identify new or enhanced competences and skills, as well as roles and people required during the digital transformation. These activities are reflected in the knowledge area *Training Need Analysis*. The actual planning of the new training activities is part of the knowledge area *Curriculum Development*: Here, the relevant resources, necessary facilities and material are determined in order to support staff and other stakeholders. The knowledge area *Training Execution* includes the actual carrying out of the training activities, as well as their continuous monitoring and enhancement.

Program and Project Management considers the program governance structure, roles and team structures, and reporting relationships, to enable 'best-practice' program and project management approaches and techniques to be deployed in order to ensure a smooth execution. The management discipline consists of the knowledge areas *Framework, Organization*, and *Execution*. The first area specifies the program and project management methods and tools which are used within the entire ecosystem; the second area includes the planning for how the overall program can be delivered through a manageable combination of projects that make the most effective use of available resources, and finally, the *Execution* considers how costs, quality and time will be monitored, controlled and improved.

All those disciplines must be addressed to ensure the success of a transformation. The complexity of coordinating different interest groups and aligning different management disciplines with their different goals is challenging. Therefore, the integration of the BTM² disciplines is the central basis of the Digital Capability Framework and provides tremendous value. It ensures that all the important business disciplines, as well as concepts such as culture and leadership, are examined in relation to each Digital Capability. Other existing digital frameworks do not offer such a holistic approach.

2.3 Digital Capabilities

Digital Capabilities specify the key functions and skills that are required to become a Digital Enterprise. These Digital Capabilities are classified into two categories (see Figure 2.4).

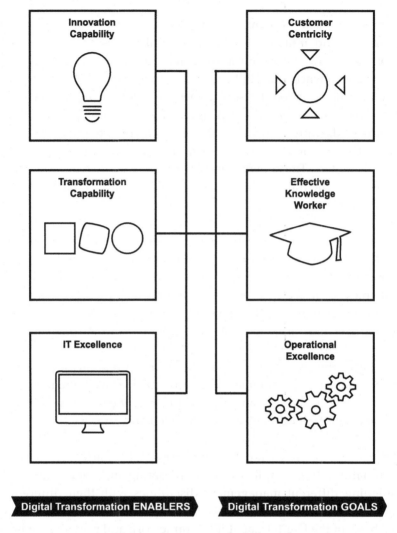

Figure 2.4 The six Digital Capabilities of the Digital Capability Framework

The first category is called *Digital Transformation Enablers*. Companies must be able to transform and innovate simultaneously, while leveraging the best-suited technology for the business. Digital Transformation Enablers comprise three Digital Capabilities, namely 1) Innovation Capability, 2) Transformation Capability and 3) IT Excellence. They have to reach a certain level of quality and maturity before it makes sense to tackle a digital transformation. The *Digital Transformation Enablers* are not the initial reason why a company wants to transform into a Digital Enterprise, rather, they build the stable basis required to enable the transformation.

Once a company has the appropriate skills for digital transformation it can pursue the desired *Digital Transformation Goals*. For Digital Enterprises these goals are to achieve high-level skills in understanding customers and have a close relationship with them, to be able to provide highly motivated and collaborative working environments, and to ensure process execution in the most effective and efficient way. These skillsets are reflected in the three Digital Capabilities: 4) Customer Centricity, 5) Effective Knowledge Workers and 6) Operational Excellence. Successful Digital Enterprises perform excellently in these capabilities, which are also the basis for financial success.

2.3.1 INNOVATION CAPABILITY

Innovation Management – is the capability of managing innovation-related business processes. It enables the company to generate, identify, assess, and realize new products, services and processes facilitated or driven by digital technologies and management practices.

Being innovative means having the ability to continuously transform ideas into new, beneficial and profitable products and services (Lawson and Samson, 2001). A recent study from Shelton and Percival (2013) shows that 'leading innovators have grown at a rate 16 percent higher than the least innovative'. These top innovators also predicted a growth rate over twice as large as the global average and compared to the least innovative companies more than three times higher. Thus, innovation is a competitive necessity for Digital Enterprises.

This skill enables a Digital Enterprise to continuously think about new business opportunities and leverage the latest developments in technology to improve important areas of its business. Successful Digital Enterprises embed the spirit of innovation into all aspects of the company and include the Innovation Capability in the company's vision and goal setting. The culture of Digital Enterprises supports employees to pursue new ideas, to think outside of the box and to communicate and brainstorm with each other. Leaders acknowledge the innovation engagement, and work together to identify the most promising potentials. Considering innovation management from all perspectives also requires setting up a team, which is responsible for analyzing and assessing ideas. This includes having an understanding of the benefits and the potential risks from a business perspective. The cost of realizing the new ideas has to be weighed against the impact, the benefits and the risks. For the ideas worth following, corresponding programs and projects are created. Innovation is important but you also need a strategy for how to transform ideas into business values.

Challenges of the Innovation Capability:

1.   Set up a team, which is responsible for analyzing and assessing innovative ideas.
2.   Leaders acknowledge the innovation engagement and work together to identify the most promising potentials.
3.   Have a strategy to learn from failures.
4.   Include innovation in the company's vision and goal setting.
5.   Provide a strategy for how to transform ideas into your business.

2.3.2 TRANSFORMATION CAPABILITY

Transformation Capability – is defined as the holistic management of extensive, complex changes on which the organization's future success strongly depends.

Becoming a Digital Enterprise means transformation. The changes involved usually have a great impact on the entire organization, and the transformation does not stop when certain areas have been improved. New and unforeseen influences are constantly emerging and companies have to react to them. Thus, the ability to transform is critical for Digital Enterprises. It requires a culture that is open to change and an understanding that this is a complicated idea as many changes have a negative impact on stakeholders. Leaders need to communicate the reasons for the change and its impact on the company as well as on the individual employee. Furthermore, leaders need to listen to their team, solve issues of resistance and take care of employees' and other stakeholders' concerns. One possible approach to overcoming resistance is to involve employees more closely in the change process and give them the opportunity to be part of the transformation and to contribute their own ideas. Digital Enterprises engage employees early in the transformation and manage to align strategy, talent and execution. In order to keep employees motivated, Digital Enterprises should avoid making frequent, uncoordinated, jerky movements, which are driven solely by external factors. Instead, a Digital Enterprise has to provide a clear vision and a business strategy; where it wants to be in five to ten years. In addition, leaders and employees have to understand the impact of the transformation on the long-term strategy. The transformation capability also requires a company to build a team of transformation experts, who know how to use the best-practice transformation methodologies and supporting instruments. Furthermore, the transformation team manages all the different stakeholders' interests and establishes an open communication within the company.

Being able to change also implies being flexible which requires establishing more agile processes which are easy to adapt to new requirements.

The Transformation Capability gives the company the power to implement changes and bring everyone in.

Challenges of the Transformation Capability:

1. Involve stakeholders closely in the transformation process.
2. Clearly communicate the impact of the transformation on the long-term strategy.
3. Manage the resulting complexity and make use of methods like BTM^2 in order to handle this issue.

2.3.3 IT EXCELLENCE

IT Excellence – is the usage of new technologies (such as mobile connectivity, cloud computing, big data and social media) to enhance 'business technology' and, as a consequence, the business. This includes, but is not limited to, real-time insight into important company data, stability, agility, security and dynamic plug-and-play functionality.

The success of the digital transformation heavily depends on IT Excellence which is not simply about implementing new software systems. Companies should not buy new technology because it is trendy and everyone does it. A detailed understanding of the possible usage, benefits and risks is necessary. For example, the Internet provides new sales channels and may change the business model. Technology is not a nice-to-have thing but rather a key driver for the entire business, which requires proper analysis and communication of the changes and benefits, properly designed and executed program and project management and continuous training. Although many IT departments have solid solutions in place they often operate in silos, each with its own data definitions, processes and building blocks. The configuration and functions are usually tied tightly to concrete and fixed requirements and mature technologies, not taking into consideration emerging digital technologies and practices, however, technology trends like mobile technology or social media require fast and iterative methods to continuously test and learn what will work in the market or workplace (Bonnet et al., 2012, p. 10).

Challenges in IT Excellence:

1. Understand the benefits and also the risks of new technology devices and software solutions.
2. Use fast and iterative methods to continuously test and learn what will work in the market or workplace.

2.3.4 CUSTOMER CENTRICITY

Customer Centricity – is defined as the capability of focusing on the most valuable customers by using modern technologies. Thereby, one aims at reaching strategic advantage and increased long-term profits through the alignment of one's products and services with the wants and needs of the 'right' customers.

An organization that aims to become a Digital Enterprise listens to and focuses on their customers. Many industries are still focusing on a product-centric strategy, one that aims to manufacture superior products and achieve high market shares, however, digital technology provides exciting new ways to understand and collaborate with customers. Mobile devices and social media enable an interactive, direct and lively dialogue between customers and companies (Bonnet et al., 2012, p. 20). Digital Enterprises embed customer service into their organizational goals and missions. Their leaders demonstrate how a great customer experience helps the company to achieve its mission. The culture is about the customer and the employees are excited and motivated to provide awesome services. Furthermore, the employees need be trained to understand the shift to customer centricity and the culture of the company should value what it means to provide customers with a great experience. Considering these new channels requires adapting the business processes and IT applications. For example, Customer Relationship Management (CRM) systems are updated to 'Social CRM' systems. Such changes require thoughtful planning and excellent program management. Furthermore, the business processes and IT infrastructure need to be designed to service customers.

At the same time, Customer Centricity is more than just 'focusing on customers'. The two concepts are sometimes confused with each other. To focus on customers means offering a consistently great and relevant experience. It urges companies to treat the customers correctly and it should be the overarching principle for every company. However, being a customer centric company means understanding which customer segments provide the highest profit and enables the company to focus its major marketing and communication efforts on them (Fader, 2012). Essential to Customer Centricity is dual-value creation (Boulding et al., 1993), defined as the simultaneous creation of value for the customer and for the company (Shah et al., 2006). Every business activity must be carefully balanced against the benefits and the risks for the company, as well as the value for the customer. This also includes defining key performance indicators for the different business activities.

Challenges in Customer Centricity:

1. To transform traditional product-centric value chains into customer-oriented process chains with the customer as the basis.
2. To focus on the right loyal and profitable customers and serve them well.
3. To understand which customer segments provide the highest profit and to focus major marketing and communication efforts on them.

2.3.5 EFFECTIVE KNOWLEDGE WORKER

Effective Knowledge Worker – means that employees are the main resource for companies to be competitive. Areas of effective knowledge working are collaboration, work teams instead of hierarchies, knowledge sharing, coaches instead of managers, managing by objectives.

Digital Enterprises require the skill to utilize digital technology in order to enhance the satisfaction of their employees. The working environment impacts on the productivity of knowledge workers (Skyrme, 1999). The workplaces of Digital Enterprises are designed in a way that creativity is encouraged and fostered among employees. Knowledge workers need a flexible workplace: worldwide, anytime and anywhere. The effective knowledge worker is only as good as the organization's culture and its choice of training and competence-building. The competence of knowledge workers can be improved by providing continuous learning and training services (Drucker, 1999). The definition of performance measures can support the engagement and motivation of employees. For instance, employees can achieve a certain bonus for every patent idea they submit. Also, skill gaps hamper digital transformation (Fitzgerald et al., 2013). Setting up a collaborative and creative work atmosphere offers the opportunity for employees to become more loyal, independent, and self-confident. A well-implemented platform for capturing ideas and having a feedback forum are just two examples of how to foster close interaction among employees, however it is important that these platforms are maintained and that employees are indeed receiving constructive feedback. Management of the internal processes and IT systems are equally important as excellent management of programs and projects otherwise employees might get the impression that nobody is listening to them. Changing the way people work also raises the risk of frustration, disillusionment and perceptions that management are being arbitrary in their changes. Thus, great leaders work together with their team and treat team members as humans not as machines.

Challenges in Effective Knowledge Worker:

1. To understand their current workforce, what their employees think and what the difficulties that the team is facing are, and also sharing the great successes that they have achieved.
2. To set up a collaborative and creative work atmosphere.
3. To align the IT systems and the workplaces of knowledge workers in order to provide continuous feedback.

2.3.6 OPERATIONAL EXCELLENCE

Operational Excellence – operational excellence means managing business processes in an organization, so that their performance is outstanding. It is a central capability for any organization that wants to compete. The objective of operational excellence is to realize efficient and effective business processes through continuous improvement and innovation.

It is a key requirement to use a standardized method to assess the capability and maturity of business processes. Naturally, Operational Excellence is closely connected to process management. Mission-critical KPIs and processes need to be defined and monitored closely. Process maturity can also be rated with the ISO/IEC 15504 standard for process assessment (SPICE) (ISO/IEC 15504).

It is important to understand that Operational Excellence requires continuous analysis of benchmarks. As the saying goes, 'if you can't measure it, you can't manage it' (Kaplan and Norton, 1996). Nevertheless, decisions should not only be based on pure numbers. It is important to consider the entire ecosystem, including strategic alignments and cultural change. Modern process and IT infrastructures support the analyses and capture of the relevant information. Supplier qualification and monitoring are also drivers for Operational Excellence. Operational Excellence is a driver for IT Innovation, but IT operations must be properly defined in order to support innovation (Evensen and Rasmussen, 2011).

Challenges in Operational Excellence:
1. To devise fully integrated processes and data as a foundation for operational performance, particularly in global organizations.
2. To manage business processes from a holistic perspective, including aspects such as strategic alignment and cultural change, as well as methods and IT.

2.4 The Digital Capability Maturity Models

The journey towards a Digital Enterprise is complex and time-consuming. Each transformation project is unique and involves numerous individuals, activities, technologies and objectives. In this section, we explain how companies can use the Digital Capability Maturity Model to support their digital journey.

2.4.1 WHAT ARE DIGITAL CAPABILITY MATURITY MODELS?

The general concepts of maturity models can be traced back to Watts Humphrey and his colleagues at IBM in the 1980s, who began to develop a maturity model for software processes. Active development of the maturity model started when Watts Humphrey joined the Software Engineering Institute, a research and development center sponsored by the US Department of Defense, at Carnegie Mellon University in Pittsburgh. The researchers were focusing on a sound method to assess the capability of software contractors. Their efforts culminated in a Capability Maturity Model for software, known as CMM, the first version of which was published in in 1991 (Neuhauser, 2004 and Paulk, 2009). The implementation of CMM raised many problems. Therefore, the CMM Integration (CMMI) project was initiated, to address these questions.

With the release of CMMI a variety of different maturity models followed. For organizations the maturity model provides a benchmark indicating their distance from competitors. Process performance is evaluated based upon individual criteria (capabilities).

A *digital* maturity model measures the maturity of the digitalization process of an organization. Several digital maturity models were proposed in the past. For instance, the digital maturity model developed by MIT's Center for Digital Business and Capgemini Consulting considers digital maturity as a combination of two dimensions: *Digital Intensity* (the level of technology investment directed towards changing how a company operates) and *Transformation Management* Intensity (Bonnet et al., 2012 and Westerman et al., 2012). Both dimensions are considered as x and y coordinates that span a quadrant. Depending on the intensity of both dimensions, companies are characterized by high digital and transformation management intensity (Digirati), low digital and transformation management intensity (Digital Beginners), or a mix of the two (Fashionistas or Conservatives).

The Digital Capability Maturity Models, presented in this book, are based on the measurement principles introduced by CMM and support the analyses of digital maturity from a holistic 360-degree view. The integration of BTM^2 allows us to assess all important business angles for each Digital Capability.

The maturity is classified on a scale from 1 to 5. Each level evaluates the criteria in terms of an evolutionary path from ad-hoc, chaotic processes (initial) to mature, disciplined processes (excellence). A higher level indicates that the activities can reliably and sustainably produce the required outcome. Table 2.1 describes each level.

It is important to understand that the maturity of the Digital Capabilities is not set in stone. Instead, a company has the possibility to continuously improve its Digital Capabilities.

The Digital Capability Maturity Models are supported by a set of assessment tools which allow for the evaluation of the company's situation compared to leading (digital) companies. These assessment tools provide questionnaires to analyze the current as-is situation and identify the anticipated to-be scenario. Performing a Digital Capability Maturity Assessment is the first step towards becoming a Digital Enterprise. The gap between the as-is and to-be scenario uncovers potential improvement areas and enables a step-by-step digital transformation.[1]

Table 2.1   Five maturity levels

Level 1 Initial	Level 2 Reactive	Level 3 Defined	Level 4 Managed	Level 5 Excellence
This level is characterized by ad-hoc and chaotic processes. Processes are immature and unstable. No benchmarks are given for judging Digital Capability.	Digital principles are established and communicated to involved persons. Although no organization-wide process is defined, an elementary management control is installed guaranteeing minimal agreement, which allows repeating the success from prior similar projects.	This level is characterized by an organization-internal schema that is imposed on projects. A documented and intra-organizational standard process is established, which allows for project-related customization.	Process standardization is given and quantitative statistical techniques are used to predict (digital) product quality.	Processes of projects are running routinely. Processes are continuously improved. Problems are analyzed systematically and future asset values are identified.

---

1   See Digital Transformation Roadmap, this chapter for more information.

Digital Capability Maturity Model supports the evaluation of the as-is situation in each of the six capabilities of the Digital Capability Framework. The Digital Capability Maturity Model is a generic evaluation model which incorporates the BTM^2 phases in order to support holistic analysis. Furthermore, the Digital Capability Maturity Model provides an instrument to investigate the transformation needs for each capability for a certain to-be scenario (e.g., which level can be reached using a certain technology).

2.4.2 STRUCTURE OF THE DIGITAL CAPABILITY MATURITY MODEL

In order to evaluate the maturity for each of the six Digital Capabilities, we define a generic structure of the individual maturity models. This generic Digital Capability Maturity Model is tightly integrated with the nine BTM^2 disciplines (see Section 2.2.2). Each BTM^2 discipline is broken down into three knowledge areas. Together they form the generic structure for each of the six maturity models. This ensures a consistent, complete, adaptable and repeatable analysis for each capability.

Each individual Digital Capability is then evaluated based on a corresponding maturity model, which is derived from the Digital Capability Maturity Model (see Figure 2.5).

Figure 2.5   The Digital Capability Maturity Model

Table 2.2   Digital Capability Maturity Model – Meta Management

	Level 1 – Initial	Level 5 – Excellence
Culture	The Digital Capability is not recognized as important or relevant and not part of the culture. In addition, failure and negative feedback are seen as poor experience inside the company.	The Digital Capability is recognized as an important aspect and the progress of enhancing the Digital Capability is continuously measured, reviewed and improved. The status is communicated to the entire organization.
Leadership	The Digital Capability is not an important topic amongst leaders. No or few steps are taken to align specific initiatives with the core ideas of the Digital Capability.	Leaders continuously assess and improve their effectiveness in aligning everyone with the shared understanding of the Digital Capability. Their goal is to become best in industry concerning the Digital Capability by involving the ecosystem.
Value	The Digital Capability is not valued and measured in the organization. Lack of value identification, planning and realization for the Digital Capability.	The value of the Digital Capability and its benefits are seen as strategic objectives. Periodic revisions of established KPIs to value the Digital Capability guarantee an improvement of the incentives.

Basically, each knowledge area can now be evaluated for each Digital Capability based on the five digital maturity levels. Table 2.2 shows an example – an extract of the assessment for the Meta Management discipline and the related knowledge areas: Culture, Leadership and Value.

As each Digital Capability has its own characteristic, the actual content of the maturity models for each Digital Capability might differ, however, the general structure of the maturity model is the same, including the BTM^2 disciplines and its knowledge areas. This ensures that all Digital Capabilities are examined from all business perspectives.

2.5 Digital Use Cases

Once you know where you are and where you want to go the question arises: how do you get there? How do you actually achieve a higher maturity for a certain Digital Capability? This is where Digital Use Cases fit in. In this section, we explain the concepts behind a Digital Use Case and introduce a few examples.

2.5.1 DEFINITION OF A DIGITAL USE CASE

In software and system engineering the term 'use case' describes how a user interacts with a system to accomplish a particular goal. Typically, a use case is described using visual models, and identifies the features of a system component.

In the context of the Digital Capability Framework use cases also describe how to reach a particular goal, namely the goal of enhancing a Digital Capability.

Digital Use Cases are practical scenarios, which exemplify the enhancement of the maturity of a certain capability within a specific industry. The scenarios show appropriate uses of the capabilities where Digital Enterprises can gain competitive advantages.

Throughout this book we provide a first set of such Digital Use Cases. Typically, a Digital Use Case contains a description, gives information about the current situation, meaning the maturity level from where it starts, and the value proposition, meaning the targeted maturity level. In addition, the case might also describe outcome opportunities and benefits and the risks related to it.

The potential benefits of digital technology differ greatly between industries, companies and their business models. For example, the introduction for retailers of online sales channels has a different impact than for consulting firms. Although both types of companies can profit from online business, the actual business benefits and potential risks, as well as the importance of the new online channel to the business are difficult to compare.

Consequently, every company needs to define its own relevant Digital Use Cases and carefully analyze the impact of the new technology.

At the same time, best-practice Digital Use Cases enable you to get a better understanding of how technology can be used inside your business and provide a great basis for further development of ideas.

The next section introduces some general examples of Digital Use Cases.

2.5.2 EXAMPLES OF DIGITAL USE CASES

The examples in Tables 2.3–2.7 provide a generic and partial view on the possible application areas of new technology. The actual impact differs between companies, and the list of benefits and risks depend on the actual type of business.

Table 2.3   Insurance Use Case – Claim Handler

Description	Value proposition
Mobile claim handlers receive all necessary information in real-time, such as customer and detailed contract information and payment status, to most efficiently capture and directly settle claims on the road.	Enable faster and market-leading claim settlement process at the customer site.
Current situation	**Benefits**
Often, claim handlers on the road need to process claim data via paper-based or mail-based environments with no access to backend information such as coverage, payment status, and so on, which leads to incomplete data and delays in claim processing.	• Improve the efficiency of your mobile claim handler and shorten claim settlement cycles. • Reduce claim handling cost through complete integration. • Increase customer satisfaction and customer loyalty.

Table 2.4   Healthcare Use Case – Electronic Medical Record

Description	Value proposition
Electronic medical record provides healthcare professionals instant access to the electronic medical record of their patients.	Physicians working in hospitals (who are mobile workers by nature) have all relevant information instantly without having to search in a paper-based patient record.
Current situation	**Benefits**
Doctors need patient related information at the patient's bed. Critical information is often not available when needed.	• Electronic medical record supports physicians by offering up-to-date information such as vital parameters, images (X-rays, CT, etc.), progress notes, contact information, diagnosis and problems. • Improve the efficiency of the method of treatment. • Increase customer satisfaction.

Table 2.5   Oil and Gas Use Case – Incident Management

Description	Value proposition
Mobile incident management enables anyone to capture initial information related to incidents, near misses, or any safety observation from anywhere at any time. Stakeholders are alerted when an incident or near miss occurs. Observations synchronize with existing safety systems. It also provides safety trend insights by location and incident type to help mitigate future risk and implement process safety changes.	The use of mobile technology improves reporting capture, accuracy, and timeliness, which enhances the safety culture.

Current situation	Benefits
Most incident management processes today are paper-based, with no immediate access to safety systems, and capturing of incidents is delayed.	Prevent incidents by transforming from reactive monitoring to proactive management of risks.

Table 2.6   Customer Relationship Use Case – Online Service Department

Description	Value proposition
Mobile devices and online services redefine the customer relationship. Customers communicate with the service department via the Internet and their mobile devices. Some possible functions are: Customers can chat online with the service department to solve potential problems or retrieve information about the portfolio. Customers can search the database for known issues and potential solutions. Customers post a service request using a mobile phone. Customers can provide feedback about their experience and satisfaction.	Increase customer satisfaction and lower the cost of customer service.
Current situation	**Benefits**
Customers either talk to third-party call centers or send paper-based or electronic mail.	• Customer service can be centralized and the communication can be parallelized. • 24/7 availability. • Avoid personally answering unnecessary questions about small problems, as they can be resolved using the search functionality.

Table 2.7   Retail Use Case – Sales Analysis

Description	Value proposition
In retailing, where margins are slim and shopper behavior is unpredictable, it is important to maintain a close view of the profitability of individual products or ranges according to different purchase channels or customer groups.	Real time analysis of sales data allows retailers to promote low performing products immediately and to attract shoppers with individual offers if necessary.
Current situation	**Benefits**
The volume of point-of-sales data and other important information required to determine the performance of individual products causes delays in making available this important information.	Tighter control of sales performance, faster understanding of revenue streams and better decision making in defining the right assortment in the right channel. Increased sales through real time visibility and through increased service levels.

2.6 Digital Transformation Roadmap

Digital transformation means executing and managing a large and highly complex program. This requires a solid digital transformation strategy and lays the foundation to becoming a Digital Enterprise. In this section, we describe how such a digital transformation strategy can be derived in terms of a six-step approach (see Figure 2.6).

The first step is to establish a general awareness of the importance and benefits of digital technology. The Digital Capability Maturity Models provide the foundation to discovering the current situation of the company and planning the future scenario. On the one hand, the company's abilities to innovate, transform and implement IT systems, that is, the Digital Transformation Enablers, are analyzed by carrying out structured interviews with the responsible managers of the business and IT departments. On the other hand, the maturity levels of the three Digital Capability Goals must be assessed and potential improvements have to be identified. As we have pointed out, the assessment is conducted for the as-is and to-be scenario alike. This activity gives stakeholders new ways of thinking and supports future idea developments. It clearly reveals the gaps, not only between the as-is and to-be digital maturity, but also between the rating and the mindset of different stakeholders. This leads to invaluable discussions and joint solutions. Based on the assessment, the second step is the development of Digital Use Cases for new technologies and the processes under consideration. These use cases aim to define scenarios to show how a company can reach the anticipated to-be state. This exercise usually reveals a large number of optimizations.

The next three steps (see Figure 2.6) resemble well-known management methods: in order to evaluate the alternatives, one performs a benefit analysis (step 3). The next step involves estimating the transformation efforts and costs related to each Digital Use Case. Based on these results, a portfolio can be drawn (step 4). The most promising Digital Use Cases are obviously the ones that are easy to implement while creating high business benefits ('quick wins'). To implement the top-priority projects, a strategic road map is then developed (step 5) while especially bearing in mind the company's current ability to transform. BTM^2 is recommended as the implementation method. As the sixth and last step, business cases need to be drafted in order to justify the investments needed. This includes calculating one-time and ongoing costs, describing the benefits and associated risks as well as the input of technical and human change. The result of the six-step approach is the digital transformation strategy that provides the direction to become a Digital Enterprise.

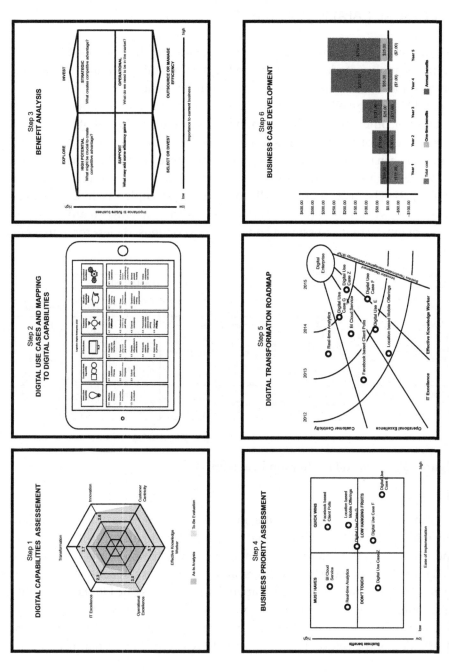

Figure 2.6   Six steps to becoming a Digital Enterprise

In the following section, we explain the different steps in more detail.

2.6.1 DIGITAL CAPABILITY ASSESSMENT

As a first step, the company requires a good understanding of how it leverages digital technology today. Based on the Digital Capability Maturity Models, it can position itself against well-defined industry benchmarks. Every Digital Capability is assessed with a predefined survey, which allows managers, IT, business or other experts to determine the current level of digital maturity. Based on the collected information, the degree of maturity for each Digital Capability can be summarized using a heat map (see Figure 2.7). The structure of the heat map is aligned to the structure of the BTM^2 components (see Figure 2.3). The heat map visually depicts the strengths (white/light grey boxes), the weaknesses (dark grey boxes) and the average maturity (grey boxes) of the current assessment and delivers a condensed view for managers.

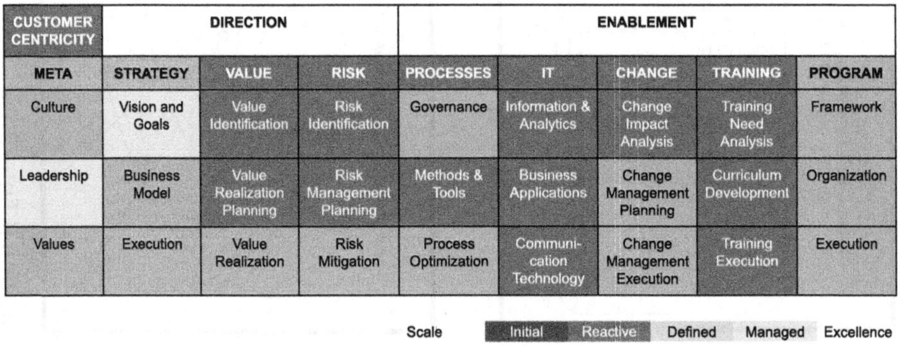

CUSTOMER CENTRICITY	DIRECTION			ENABLEMENT				
META	**STRATEGY**	**VALUE**	**RISK**	**PROCESSES**	**IT**	**CHANGE**	**TRAINING**	**PROGRAM**
Culture	Vision and Goals	Value Identification	Risk Identification	Governance	Information & Analytics	Change Impact Analysis	Training Need Analysis	Framework
Leadership	Business Model	Value Realization Planning	Risk Management Planning	Methods & Tools	Business Applications	Change Management Planning	Curriculum Development	Organization
Values	Execution	Value Realization	Risk Mitigation	Process Optimization	Communication Technology	Change Management Execution	Training Execution	Execution

Scale   Initial   Reactive   Defined   Managed   Excellence

Figure 2.7   Digital evaluation heat map

The complete analysis results in six heat maps, one for each Digital Capability. This 'helicopter-view' provides companies with a good understanding of today's situation and allows them to plan for future scenarios. The management leaders and experts now specify the targeted level of maturity for each Digital Capability using the same Digital Capability Assessment tools. Once both assessments are finalized the results can be compared with each other (see Figure 2.8). This allows planning and prioritizing of the relevant steps in order to reach the higher maturity levels.

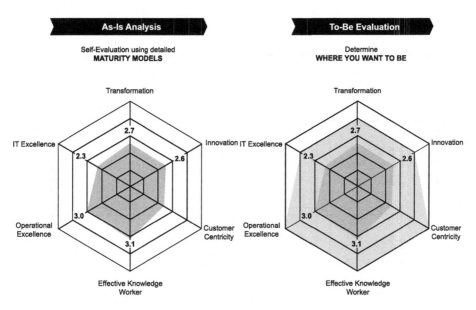

Figure 2.8   Analysis of the digital maturity

2.6.2 DIGITAL USE CASES AND MAPPING TO DIGITAL CAPABILITIES

Technology plays a key role for all six Digital Capabilities, however, the use of each technology has a different impact on the maturity level of the Digital Capabilities. The definition and specification of Digital Use Cases supports companies to improve their Digital Capabilities. Based on the results of the digital maturity analysis, the relevant Digital Use Cases need to be defined. The Digital Capability Framework offers a set of best-practice Digital Use Cases which can be used as a basis for the concrete definition of how to increase digital maturity.

In this step, a team consisting of business and IT leaders comes together and discusses potential application areas for digital technology. During this process, the Digital Capability Framework supports them to get a better understanding of how the different application areas impact the digital maturity of their business. Each Digital Use Case is mapped to the maturity level of the Digital Capabilities, which provides transparency of the possible improvement areas (see Figure 2.9).

The identified Digital Use Cases are the basis for the definition of projects within the digital transformation program.

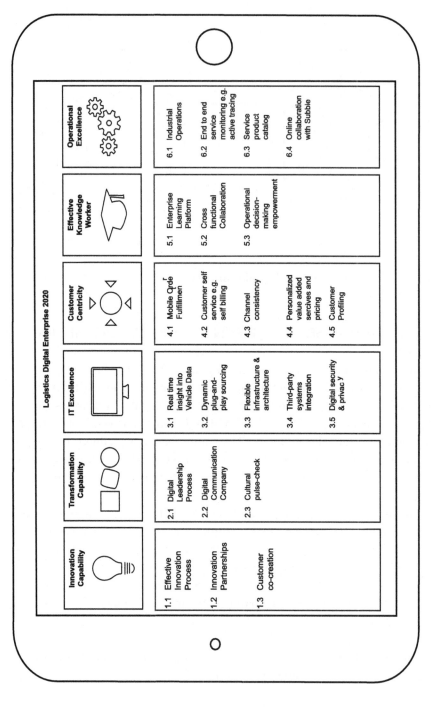

Logistics Digital Enterprise 2020

Innovation Capability	Transformation Capability	IT Excellence	Customer Centricity	Effective Knowledge Worker	Operational Excellence
1.1 Effective Innovation Process	2.1 Digital Leadership Process	3.1 Real time insight into Vehicle Data	4.1 Mobile Order Fulfillmen	5.1 Enterprise Learning Platform	6.1 Industrial Operations
1.2 Innovation Partnerships	2.2 Digital Communication Company	3.2 Dynamic plug-and-play sourcing	4.2 Customer self service e.g. self billing	5.2 Cross functional Collaboration	6.2 End to end service monitoring e.g. active tracing
1.3 Customer co-creation	2.3 Cultural pulse-check	3.3 Flexible infrastructure & architecture	4.3 Channel consistency	5.3 Operational decision-making empowerment	6.3 Service product catalog
		3.4 Third-party systems integration	4.4 Personalized value added serclves and pricing		6.4 Online collaboration with Subble
		3.5 Digital security & privac y	4.5 Customer Profiling		

Figure 2.9   Mapping of the Digital Use Cases to the Digital Maturity

2.6.3 BENEFIT ANALYSIS

Once the Digital Use Cases are defined, the impact of the transformation needs to be analyzed. Every Digital Use Case should provide answers to the question 'why do we need to change and why now' and identify possible consequences of not changing at all. This activity should be part of every transformation project (Uhl and Golenia, 2012).

The Digital Use Cases are classified according to their overall impact and the nature of the business and organizational changes. In general, we can differentiate between changes that solve problems or overcome constraints, and innovations that provide and exploit new capabilities or opportunities. The different types of transformation projects can be classified using the benefits matrix (see Figure 2.10).

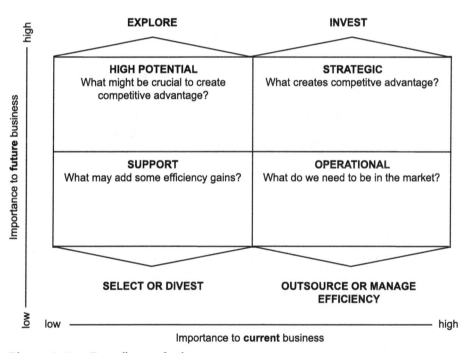

Figure 2.10   Benefits analysis

Digital Use Cases are either primarily *Strategic*, focusing on innovations, or *Operational*, solving problems to remain competitive, or a combination of both. *Strategic* Digital Use Cases may include *High Potential* components, which have to be explored and might provide a competitive advantage in the future.

Operational Digital Use Cases may include *Support* elements, which reduce inefficiencies and costly processes. Some Digital Use Cases include elements of all four types (Ward et al., 2012).

2.6.4 BUSINESS PRIORITY ASSESSMENT

Each Digital Use Case provides different benefits to the organization. Some have a huge impact while others solve smaller issues. The next step is to define the priorities for the digital transformation. Based on the business priority matrix (see Figure 2.11), the business benefits are balanced against the implementation costs.

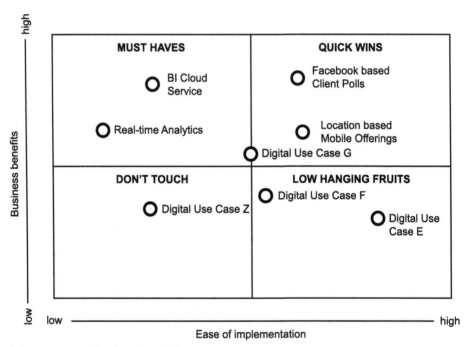

Figure 2.11   Business priority assessment

Digital Use Cases which provide only a small benefit and require a huge implementation effort should not be touched at all. In contrast, digital use cases resulting in major business benefits and involving minor implementation activity are 'quick wins' and should be realized as soon as possible.

Digital Use Cases, which require major implementation activities and provide major business benefits, are important cases and need to be carefully planned and executed.

The fourth part addresses Digital Use Cases, which are easy to implement, however, they do not provide a significant business impact. These digital use cases should only be realized if the resources are available and are not required for any other more important project.

2.6.5 DIGITAL TRANSFORMATION ROADMAP

Having a clear understanding about the benefits of the individual Digital Use Cases and their business impact and implementation efforts, the next step is to define the digital transformation roadmap for the next three to five years. The roadmap provides an overview about the realization timeframe of the individual Digital Use Cases and their impact on the Digital Capabilities (see Figure 2.12).

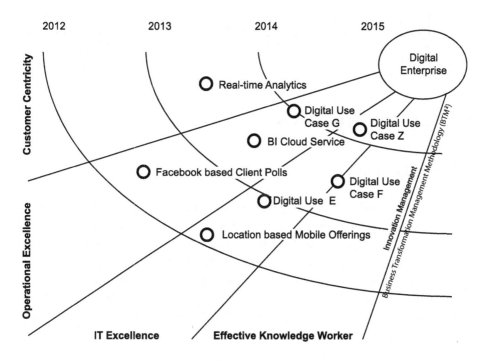

Figure 2.12   Strategic digital transformation roadmap

2.6.6 BUSINESS CASE DEVELOPMENT

The last step is to develop and calculate the actual business cases for the Digital Use Cases which should be realized. The business case (see Figure 2.13) explains the value of the planned investment and has to provide adequate evidence that the value can be achieved. A financial evaluation of the benefits as well as the costs of the changes provide the foundation for the executive management team to take the final decision whether the investment is appropriate and they believe the objectives can be achieved (Ward et al., 2012).

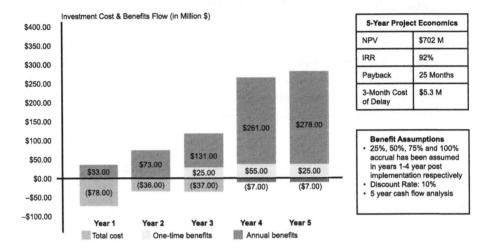

Figure 2.13   Digital business case

2.7 Conclusions

The Digital Capability Framework guides companies along their digital transformation journey. Companies benefit from a holistic viewpoint and a careful consideration of all important transformation aspects. The six Digital Capabilities of the framework are key to establishing a successful digital transformation. The strengths and weaknesses for each individual Digital Capability can be analyzed and compared with each other. This is possible due to the integration of the BTM[2] components. In addition, the integration of BTM[2] ensures that all aspects of the transformation are captured, planned and executed.

Digital transformation is not a 'big-bang' project, meaning that everything has to change from one day to the next. Instead the Digital Capability Framework enables companies to transform step-by-step towards a Digital Enterprise: Not everything needs to be improved at once. Companies start by establishing a thorough understanding of where they are today. Based on this, they can identify the weakest components. The reflection of the BTM[2] management disciplines and the breakdown into knowledge areas allows a detailed picture for each Digital Capability.

References

Bonnet, D., Ferraris, P., Westerman, G., and McAfee, A. (2012) Talking 'bout a revolution. *Digital Transformation Review*, 2(1). http://www.capgemini.com/resources/digital-transformation-review--edition-2, last accessed 6 July 2014.

Boulding, W., Kalra, A., Staeling, R., and Zeithaml, V.A. (1993) A Dynamic Process Model of Service Quality: From Expectation to Behavioral Intentions. *Journal of Marketing Research*, 30(1), pp. 7–27.

Drucker P.F. (1999) *Management Challenges for the 21st Century*, Oxford: Butterworth-Heinemann.

Evensen, O. and Rasmussen E. (2011) Preparing for Operational Excellence and Improvement. PwC Whitepaper. PricewaterhouseCoopers International Limited.

Fader, P. (2012) *Customer Centricity: Focus on the Right Customers for Strategic Advantage*, 2nd edition, Philadelphia, PA: Wharton Digital Press.

Fitzgerald, M., Kruschwitz, N., Bonnet, D., and Welch, M. (2013) Embracing Digital Technology: A New Strategic Imperative. http://www.es.capgemini-consulting.com/resource-file-access/resource/pdf/embracing_digital_technology_a_new_strategic_imperative.pdf, last accessed 14 July 2014.

ISO/IEC 15504–5:2012. An exemplar software life cycle process assessment model. ISO/IEC JTC 1/SC 7.

Kaplan, S. and Norton, D. (1996) *The Balanced Scorecard: Translating Strategy into Action*. Boston, MA: Harvard Business Review Press.

Lawson, B. and Samson, D. (2001) Developing Innovation Capability in Organizations: A Dynamic Capabilities Approach. *International Journal of Innovation Management*. 5 (3): 377–400.

Neuhauser, C. (2004) A maturity model: does it provide a path for online course design? *The Journal of Interactive Online Learning*. Issue 1.

Paulk, M.C. (2009) A History of the Capability Maturity Model for Software. *The Software Quality Profile*. 12 (1).

Shah, D., Rust, R., Parasuraman, A., Staelin, R., and Day, G.S. (2006) The Path to Customer Centricity. *Journal of Service Research*. Vol. 9, No. 2. 113–124.

Shelton, R. and Percival, D. (2013) Breakthrough innovation and growth: Top innovators expect US$250 billion five-year revenue boost. PwC, http://www.pwc.com/innovationsurvey, last accessed 6 March 2014.

Skyrme, D.J. (1999) *Knowledge Networking: Building the Collaborative Enterprise*. Butterworth-Heinemann.

Uhl, A. and Gollenia, L.A. (2012) *A Handbook of Business Transformation Management Methodology*. Farnham: Gower Publishing Ltd.

Ward, J., Rennebaum, T., and Amling, S. (2012) Value Management, in *A Handbook of Business Transformation Management Methodology*. Edited by A. Uhl and L. Golenia. Farnham: Gower Publishing Ltd.

Westerman, G., Tannou, M., Bonnet, D., Ferraris, P., and McAfee, A. (2012) The Digital Advantage: How digital leaders outperform their peers in every industry. http://www.capgemini.com/resource-file-access/resource/pdf/The_Digital_Advantage__How_Digital_Leaders_Outperform_their_Peers_in_Every_Industry.pdf, last accessed 14 July 2014.

Chapter 3

Innovation Capability

NORIZAN SAFRUDIN, MICHAEL ROSEMANN,
RUEDIGER JUNG AND AXEL UHL

3.1 Overview

In recent years, the nature of innovation has undergone dramatic changes in the majority of industry sectors. Innovation has become much more open, global, more frequent, unpredictable and also collaborative in nature involving often a diverse network of partners in highly distributed innovation processes (Chesbrough, 2003; Nambisan and Sawhney, 2007). The role of IT is expanding in providing the capability to innovate in businesses, and can be characterized as an enabler of innovation (Nambisan, 2013).

The focus of this chapter is to showcase how enterprises can innovate with digital technologies. We present some Digital Use Cases to show how contemporary, digital technologies such as mobile, cloud, social media and big data can enable a digital transformation. However, it is imperative for a Digital Enterprise to have a high level of maturity in innovation as a Digital Capability. We therefore propose a Digital Capability Maturity Model for the Innovation Capability, where we demonstrate its application to a leading Digital Enterprise that specializes in converging the digital and physical experience of users – Samsung SDS, a subsidiary of the renowned innovative corporation, Samsung Group.

Objectives of this chapter:

1. Characterize innovation management as a Digital Capability.
2. Describe how to manage innovation holistically for digital transformation.
3. Present the validity of the Innovation Capability Maturity Model in Digital Enterprises.
4. Showcase how Samsung SDS manages its innovation with digital technologies.

3.2 Status Quo

3.2.1 DEFINITION AND CLASSIFICATION

Innovation is the process of turning opportunities into new, value generating ideas, and positioning those ideas into widely used practice (Tidd and Bessant, 2009). The need for survival through self-renewal and embracing changes is the fundamental capability of any living system, including organizations, which can be identified as socio-technical[1] systems. In this regard, innovation can be considered as 'fitness for adoption', and is referred to as one of the world-class assets of organizations (Kanter, 1999). That said, there are different kinds of innovation (Luxembourg, 2005) to achieve strategic advantage. These can be classified in per Table 3.1.

Table 3.1   Different types of innovation

Type of Innovation	Description
Product Innovation	The introduction of new or improved products or services to the market (Propris, 2002)
Process Innovation	Changes to the sequence and nature of the primary process of the firm (Propris, 2002) in terms of its products and services that assist in the creation of competitive advantage, such as organizational improvements to achieve differentiation in terms of quality, time-to-market, after-market support, and so forth (Essmann, 2009)
Organizational/Strategic Innovation	The implementation of new organizational methods (mission, vision, policy, business models) in a firm's business practices, workplace organization or external relationships (Luxembourg, 2005)
Technological Innovation	Changes to technical systems or features leading to product and/or process innovation (Samsung SDS, 2012a)

The different types of innovation can have different degrees of impact ranging from relatively small changes, viz. *incremental innovation*, up to *radical innovation*, which implies major changes in organizations (Adams, Bessant and Phelps, 2006; Essmann, 2009). This presents a continuum of innovation on which an initiative can be mapped (Essmann, 2009). This important definition defines disruptive innovation as a kind of radical change enabled by contemporary technologies, which strongly influences the future trajectory of the adoption and use of digital technologies (Lyytinen and Rose, 2003).

---

1   Organizations embody socio-behavioral systems, i.e. human element, and technical systems, work operations and technological elements.

Regardless of the type of innovation, it is imperative for enterprises to harness the digital technologies for innovation. However, this is easier said than done, as many challenges exist in order to innovate in Digital Enterprises.

3.2.2 CHALLENGES AND BENEFITS

Organizations face several challenges when trying to manage and utilize their Innovation Capability. They might have to deal with reluctance or fear within their workforce, inflexible processes, inappropriate organizational structures and strategic problems of organizational leadership (King Abdulaziz Center, 2014). A study by McKinsey (2008) identified some of the key challenges in Digital Enterprises to be: 1) accountability of digital assets; 2) matching speed and agility of companies that are born digital; and 3) building digital skills across the entire value chain of an enterprise. As such, they offer three recommendations, where the first is to truly understand the value of leveraging digital technology investments, such as applying automation throughout the entire value chain of an organization, which includes sizeable opportunities to significantly reduce costs. The second is to prioritize a digital portfolio as it is very easy to get side-tracked by the plethora of digital possibilities such as data from social media platforms, sensor information or the digital communication channels. The third recommendation is to have an end-to-end view to ensure a consistent experience along the entire business process, thereby making sure that all functions are working harmoniously together. This requires awareness for the enterprise's portfolio of businesses and an understanding of what impact digital technologies may have on the value of the firm and its assets, subsequently allowing them to focus on the required capabilities to proceed forward, and even re-balance the business portfolio as a whole if needed (Kanter, 1999).

Research shows that an organization's capability to effectively innovate can result in improved firm performance (King Abdulaziz Center, 2014). In a rapidly changing environment receptive for digital disruption, the best or perhaps the only way a business can prosper (or survive), is to innovate. This, however, requires that innovation itself can be organized as a well managed corporate capability. To overcome these challenges and to help managers to effectively utilize the power of innovation, many frameworks and innovation management models have been developed, with different measures proposed to assess the performance of the innovation process in the organization.

3.2.3 RELATED WORK

Managing Innovation Capability

Managing and measuring the Innovation Capability of a Digital Enterprise is central to IT as it provides a basis for judging whether firms are ready to initiate digital technologies. Classically, Innovation Capability refers to the ability to continuously transform knowledge and ideas into new products, processes, services and systems for the benefit of the firm and its stakeholders (see application in Section 3.5 on Samsung SDS case study). Innovation Capability itself is not a separately identifiable construct; the capability is composed of reinforcing practices and processes within the firm. These processes serve as a key mechanism for stimulating, measuring and reinforcing innovation. However, quantifying and benchmarking Innovation Capability is a challenge for many contemporary organizations. The various approaches for firms to innovate has made the development of an integrated measurement model a difficult task (Adams et al., 2006), which stimulate the development of a Digital Capability Maturity Model for the Innovation Capability (see details in Section 3.3).

Requirements for Innovation Capability

Managing and measuring innovation distinguishes Innovation Capability, innovation results and innovation excellence (Dervitsiotis, 2010). In this regard, Innovation Capability is considered as the measure of effectiveness of the innovation system, while innovation results are the benefits realized from innovation projects for the firm's key stakeholders. Innovation excellence is defined as a combination of capabilities and results that leads to tangible and intangible benefits for firms. The key elements central to managing innovation are: an organizational culture with an appetite for innovation, leadership and strategy for innovation, internal and external resources, participation from customers, employees and suppliers, and having processes for generating new ideas, innovation project portfolio management, development of new products and effective commercialization. This innovation process provides a more reliable approach to measure and monitor innovation, to compare innovation performance among competing enterprises and to identify more clearly which enablers of innovation have the greatest potential to leverage corporate performance. The need to benchmark an enterprise's innovation capability has brought about many new streams in Innovation Capability frameworks, with a particular focus on maturity models.

Mainstream and Innovation Stream

In our study we identified several approaches to conceptualize innovation. A case study on CISCO (2012b) identifies the following elements within the (innovative) firm: Vision and strategy, harnessing the competence base, organizational intelligence, creativity and idea management, organizational structure and systems, culture and climate, and management of technology. Innovative firms leverage these elements to integrate and manage the company's resources, which can be devoted to the identification, creation of value for customers (new stream), and main activities (mainstream) in an effective manner. Hence, Innovation Capability is about synthesizing two prominent operating paradigms, i.e. innovation stream (exploration) and mainstream (exploitation), to influence the configuration of new and mainstream activities leading to continuous product, process and systems innovation.

A Process Perspective of Managing Innovation

It is imperative to note that innovation does not always mean using the latest, cutting-edge technologies. Innovation encompasses the entire process, starting from a kernel of an idea, continuing through all the steps to reach a marketable product that changes the economy (Schumpeter and Fels, 1939). Still, many tools and approaches have been suggested that can be applied in different stages of innovation to facilitate innovation (Hidalgo and Albors, 2008), which include (but are not limited to) knowledge management tools, market intelligence, cooperative and networking tools, human resource management tools (Hidalgo and Albors, 2008). A high level approach to managing the process of innovation is depicted in Figure 3.1. Generally, the process of innovation can be classified into four key phases (Tidd and Bessant, 2009):

Search Phase: Involves monitoring the operating environment regarding the likelihood for transformational change, including shifts in market requirements and customer demand, changes in rules, regulations or legislations, increasing rivalry, and/or new technological opportunities. It is in this phase that companies take notice of the new and emerging IT trends that have the potential to be part of future mainstream work operations.

Select Phase: Concerns narrowing down the previously identified opportunities, and making sure they align with the business strategy and the environment of the enterprise, including identifying which innovation path will yield the biggest benefits for the enterprise, and eliminate opportunities with significant risks.

Implement Phase: Involves enacting the innovation, (re)using established and scalable project management tools, product lifecycle management approaches and relevant marketing capabilities. Irrespective of the industry that the enterprise is operating in, having a mature, agile ICT infrastructure such can enable scalable innovation and fast prototyping.

Capture Phase: Entails evaluating the benefits realized from the innovation initiative via performance management and measurements, which can range from new revenue streams, innovative efficiency gains, to non-monetary benefits such as improved employee morale and creativity to patents, reputational gains and entire new customer experiences.

Wider adoption of collaborative technologies enables companies to operate and establish their presence across physical boundaries allowing for a more rapid time-to-market. New trends in manufacturing such as the rise of the 'maker movement' and additive manufacturing (such as 3D printing) have lowered the threshold to bring innovative solutions to market. Social media and mobile technologies have proven their ability to transform the way people connect with one another.

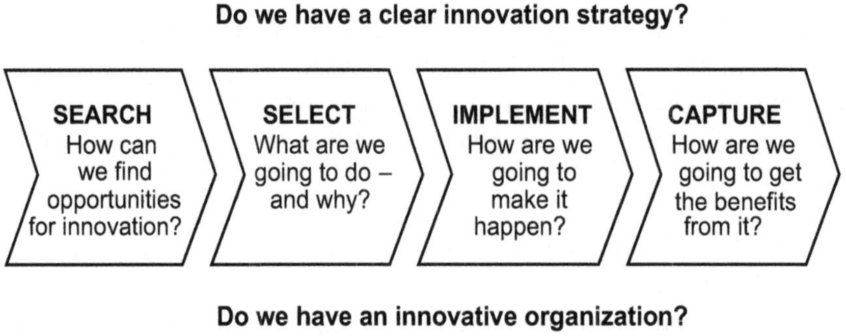

Do we have a clear innovation strategy?

SEARCH	SELECT	IMPLEMENT	CAPTURE
How can we find opportunities for innovation?	What are we going to do – and why?	How are we going to make it happen?	How are we going to get the benefits from it?

Do we have an innovative organization?

Figure 3.1   An approach to managing the process of innovation
Source: Extracted from Tidd and Bessant, 2009.

What's New?

Although organizations are aware of the importance of innovation, there appears to be a lack of consensus on what approaches can help businesses to assess and manage the innovation process (Dervitsiotis, 2010). A holistic approach is necessary to manage innovation specifically with regards to digital transformation. A useful point of reference in this context are the eight management disciplines of the BTM^2 framework (see Uhl and Gollenia, 2012), namely: Meta, Strategy, Value, Risk, Transformational IT Processes, Organizational Change, Training and Competence, plus Program and Project Management. These eight disciplines are crucial for managing innovation in Digital Enterprises as they provide an overview of the critical elements to consider for digital transformations. In the following section and also later on in this chapter, we present how such an approach can be applied to assess the maturity levels for Innovation Capability in a Digital Enterprise.

3.3 Innovation Capability Maturity Model

Table 3.2 shows what constitutes a Digital Enterprise that is low in Innovation Capability (Level 1) and what is considered as high maturity (Level 5).

Table 3.2   Outline of the Innovation Capability Maturity Model (contrast between a low vs. high maturity level)

Discipline	Level 1 – Initial	Level 5 – Excellence
Meta Management	Risk-averse culture Boundary-spanning leaders are not acknowledged	Recognize the value of innovation Embrace the constant, environmental changes by having transformational leadership is identified as having a high level of maturity
Strategy Management	Neither innovation nor the business model are included in the company's vision and goals	Aspiring enterprise vision aiming towards an innovation leader position by including the ecosystem as part of its business model and continuously executing effective and agile innovation initiatives

**Table 3.2   Outline of the Innovation Capability Maturity Model
(contrast between a low vs. high maturity level) – Continued**

Discipline	Level 1 – Initial	Level 5 – Excellence
Value Management	Little to non-existent explication, planning and realization for the value derived from innovation-related initiatives	Identified innovation KPIs Distributed planning within and across the ecosystem of the enterprise Established a framework for measuring qualitative and quantitative benefits derived from innovation-related initiatives
Risk Management	No consideration of risks associated with innovation initiatives No planning for risk mitigation activities	Strategic risk management for innovation-related initiatives for the entire ecosystem
Business Process Management	Little to no governance structure, methods and tools, or KPIs for optimizing business processes	Review and improve existing innovation-related processes Utilize established methodologies and KPIs to manage processes related to innovation initiative
Transformational IT Management	Lack of knowledge management and awareness of leveraging analytics for big data Lack of alignment with IT strategy and not leveraging relevant mobile and social technologies	Knowledge sharing and improvement is integral to the enterprise Utilize IT strategically and creatively via an extended IT platform with its ecosystem
Organizational Change Management	No definition of change impacts No planning for change management activities and communication avenues	Detailed understanding of the change impacts across its entire ecosystem with plans and communication structure in place, which are to be executed on a continuous basis
Competence and Training Management	Little to no understanding of current and future needs pertinent to innovation No training needs analysis Lack of knowledge transfer programs for innovation-related initiatives	Understand the competences required by building innovation capabilities in their workforce and relevant third parties in their ecosystem Recognized leader in talent management for innovation

Discipline	Level 1 – Initial	Level 5 – Excellence
Program and Project Management	No program governance No coherent portfolio of innovation projects Innovation projects are typically not recognized as such, and have no overview of the stages, metrics and status associated with innovation projects	Innovation management is a dedicated business function where the portfolio is reviewed and improved continuously via established planning processes and advanced methods for managing innovation-related initiatives

Once the level of maturity for Innovation Capability is identified, companies can then start to consider converting the digital opportunities into a number of potential value propositions in the context of the company-specific environment.

3.4 Digital Use Cases for Innovation Capability

Digital technologies play a crucial role in enabling innovation strategies towards a digital transformation. In addition to the solutions that companies have become familiar with over the years such as ERP software, contemporary technologies such as cloud computing, data analytics, mobility and social media are reshaping the future of how enterprises perform current work differently, or perform different work altogether. They can have significant implications for existing best practices, and also for the design of digital business models. Table 3.3 describes potential digital technologies that can be employed to enable innovative solutions with respect to each phase of the innovation process.

Having presented several instances where digital technologies can assist in the innovation process, the next section showcases the case study that utilizes those technologies, and the maturity level required for the Innovation Capability of a successful Digital Enterprise.

Table 3.3   Potential Digital Use Cases for Innovation in Digital Enterprises

Phases of Innovation	Mobile	Big Data	Social Media	Cloud
Search	Geo-tag or location-based information can provide evolutionary details of a particular inquiry Observation on evolution of competitors' mobile apps that may inform (evolving) customer requirements	Data analytics can be used to identify trends from primary data, e.g. POS, clickstream, mobile data, sensors, etc. in real-time In-memory processing from secondary data, e.g. social media channels, websites, for a 360° customer view	Source of customer sentiments (e.g. via Instagram, Twitter, YouTube) Source of trending discussions and potential leads for future demands (e.g. FaceBook, LinkedIn, Pinterest) Direct dialog with customer	Archive of existing customer data from organizations distributed across various regions
Select	Access and collaboration among stakeholders across various locations	Customer segmentation via automated cluster analysis, including behavioral attributes Predictive analysis based on customer behavior for precise targeting and risk management	Affordances of social media platforms (e.g. Yammer) can facilitate conversation among stakeholders, leading to selection via crowd-voting	Collaboration among internal and external clients anytime and anywhere, e.g. virtualization
Implement	Channel for marketing based on geo-tag features, i.e. push information when customer is within the proximity of business and/ or affiliates Augmented reality can enhance customer experience	Broad decision support and automation that increases time-to-market Identifying potential network opportunities can not only promote B2C, B2B but also C2C	Direct customer communication and interaction for marketing, B2C influencing B2B Leads from 'friends' (following/ followers) can also lead to C2C engagement	Real-time data processing, access and storage of information on as-needed basis (PaaS, HaaS) Re-purpose existing softwares/ licensing (SaaS) to allow for scalable innovation and fast prototyping
Capture	Direct accessibility to customer anytime, anywhere	Real-time analysis of customer sentiments and behavior, e.g. visualization of results	Source of customer sentiments (positive/negative) Enhancement to CRM practices	Storage and distribution of information with stakeholders in ecosystem

3.5 Case Study Research

In this section, the Innovation Capability Maturity Model is applied to Samsung SDS. Samsung SDS is a Digital Enterprise that reflects the innovative characteristics of its parent company, Samsung Group. In this chapter we aim to address the following research questions:

RQ1. How does Samsung SDS innovate with digital technologies?
RQ2. How does Samsung SDS rank in the Innovation Capability Maturity Model

---

Before proceeding with our case study findings, we first outline some background information about Samsung Group, and the selected case study, Samsung SDS.

3.5.1 ABOUT SAMSUNG

Historical Overview

On 1 March 1938, Samsung was founded in Daegu, Korea. Samsung translates to 'three stars' in Korean, and was founded by Byung-Chull Lee, who initiated the business primarily on trade export. The establishment used to sell dried Korean fish, fruit and vegetables in China and Manchuria; then in 1951 the Samsung Corporation was established with diversified expansion strategies. Over the next three decades the corporation ventured into numerous areas including insurance, securities, food processing, textiles, and retail. Samsung entered the electronics industry in the late 1960s, followed by the construction and shipbuilding industries in the mid-1970s, which were key drivers of the corporation's subsequent growth. Kuh-Hee Lee, son of Byung-Chull Lee, succeeded as the new chairman following his father's death in 1987 (Samsung, 2014). The large Lee family is known to have kept Korean journalists busy for a quarter of a century with its conflicts, rows and political influence (Lankov, 2011), yet the Samsung Group has embedded a reputation as a highly regarded establishment not just for being at the top of Korea's business hierarchy, but as a family conglomerate that thrives in the most difficult of times.

The Game Changers

Samsung has also been constantly transforming itself, shifting its position from being risk averse via a number of re-engineering initiatives (Choi, 1995). Among the notable strategic moves is enacting the Samsung Hybrid System (Khanna, Song and Lee, 2011) which blends the Western system with its traditional Japanese system – this allows for diversification of culture, minds and ultimately a diverse portfolio of innovative products and services.

The evolution of Samsung's market stance over the years demonstrates how the conglomerate has transformed from being a risk averse 'fast follower', that is, *an Enforcer*, to being more risk tolerant that is, becoming an *Ambassador*. To-date, Samsung is seen as *a Game Changer*, reflecting characteristics of global market leaders (see Figure 3.2). Being a *Game Changer* presents Samsung with a key challenge, which is to continuously retain its status quo. Thus, knowing where an enterprise stands in terms of the maturity of its digital capabilities among its rivals can ensure a clear view of what needs to be ramped up in order to be a successful, sustainable Digital Enterprise that is agile and innovative.

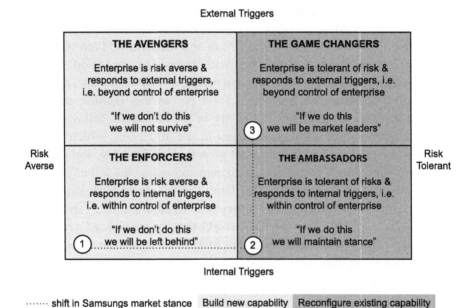

Figure 3.2   The Enterprise Transformation Matrix: How Samsung shifted from being one of the *Enforcers*, to one of the *Game Changers* from 1993–2013

Having described Samsung's position in the global market, we focus our investigation on one of Samsung's thriving business affiliates – Samsung SDS.

3.5.2 ABOUT SAMSUNG SDS

Samsung SDS (herein known as SDS) was established in 1985 as a subsidiary of Samsung Group and provides Information and Communication Technology (ICT) services. These include consulting services (Business Strategy and Discrete IT and Network Consulting); technical services (Packaged and Customized Application Integration, Hardware and Software Implementation and Support, and IT Education); and outsourcing services (Business Process Outsourcing, Application and IT Infrastructure Outsourcing and Network Infrastructure Management). In 2013, the reported revenue for Samsung SDS was USD 6,678 million. The company has been witnessing a steady climb in its revenue since its inception, particularly after the progressive introduction of contemporary digital technologies (such as the establishment of a Cloud Computing Center in 2009), and also after forming strategic coalitions with corporations such as Microsoft in 1997. SDS has been establishing education centers since 1988, as well as multiple research institutes since 1985. Samsung SDS now has over 17,570 employees operating across 11 offices and data centers in 11 countries.

SDS has a vast client portfolio, spanning various industries including those in the public, financial, manufacturing and service sectors. Their innovative solutions are also provided to users within Samsung Group that are serving both local and international business operations, for example to:

- Incheon Airport, ranked as one of the top three airports in the world (World Airport Awards, 2014), was provided with a state-of-the-art electronic passport based immigration service system (part of SDS 'Smart Town' services) that synthesizes the passenger's biometric and travel information (camera for facial recognition, finger print and e-Passport reader). The comparison between the digital information has saved the passenger – and the airport – an average of 15 seconds throughout the document inspection process (Samsung SDS, 2014b);
- Seventeen companies of the Samsung Group are utilizing the Smart Learning Platform (Samsung SDS, 2014a) to nurture talent and to adopt Samsung's 'Creative Business Management'. This was enacted by establishing a Creative Intelligence Campus to facilitate group learning between instructors and employees in a digital classroom, as well as a Creative Intelligence Store that allows for self-directed learning.

The digital classroom embodies the sharing of digital textbooks and various learning materials, such as 5–10-minute video content, accessible via any device with a virtual environment at any time (for example, via PCs, tablets and smart phones). The satisfaction rate of job training at Samsung Electronics, for instance, has increased by 52 percent, and the paperless education resulted in cost savings of 8.4 million Won in collective learning textbooks, or 105 million sheets of paper saved (which would have cost 10 billion Won);

- The King Abdulaziz Center for World Culture (Samsung SDS, 2014c) in Saudi Arabia, chose SDS as its 'Smart Convergence' technology solutions provider based on its success in deploying the Digital Space Convergence (DSC) business model. The landmark Centre has been established with a vision to become a world *knowledge park* that contributes to human development by inspiring a passion for knowledge, creativity and cross-cultural engagement (King Abdulaziz Center, 2014). Visitors to the 220,000m² knowledge park will be able to revel in a seamless user experience between the digital and the physical space. For instance, the connectivity of smart mobile devices across wired/wireless networks allows for real-time alerts on events of interest at any one of the multimedia theatres, or where motion sensors trigger the transmission of audio-recorded information about an art installation when a user sets foot within the proximity of a gallery. Winning the tender for this project strengthens SDS' global market stance, strengthening its Game Changer reputation in the realm of Digital Convergence.

A Global Ambition – Leader in the Convergence Era

SDS was chosen as our case study based on its proven capabilities in managing innovation in the digital economy. SDS takes pride in its vision to provide world-premier ICT services, with a particular emphasis – and strength – in converging the digital and physical experience of its customers. A handful of successful digital business models emerge as a result of innovating, together with the global partners of SDS, in the convergence area that utilizes 'Smart' technologies. Those 'Smart' technologies include leveraging the affordances of contemporary digital technologies such as mobile (smart phones, tablet PCs, digital TVs), cloud infrastructure solutions (HaaS, PaaS, SaaS) and M2M communication, whereby various types of automatic services are applied by communicating via wireless or wired networks machine-to-machine and machine-to-human. Several instances include: Smart Factories (business processes + M2M), Smart Building (Intelligent Building System + M2M), Smart Environment (environmental data + M2M), Asset Management (engineering/

rent + M2M), Smart Grid (energy + M2M), Smart Home (Home electronic appliances/security + M2M), Telematics (Car + M2M), and Smart Logistics (logistics + M2M), among others (Samsung SDS, 2014d).

SDS has also demonstrated its capability of applying innovative Enterprise Social Network Services (SNS) for its clients. The application of social media platforms allows for real-time collaboration and exchange of innovative ideas, such as in the case of Cheil Worldwide, the largest advertising company in Korea, ranked 15th largest in the world. SDS implemented Enterprise SNS to address the need for a common communication channel among Cheil's employees' mobile devices that not only allows for proposal of ideas in real-time, but also stimulates a heightened user experience via gamification. Employees at Cheil can review, reply and reward the creative works, hot topics or items of interest with 'idea money' (Samsung SDS, 2014c). Additionally, avatars or characters with personalities and nicknames are used to represent the employees, which encourages free communication and a conducive digital environment for ideation. As a result of implementing this solution, corporate profits have been earned through new business and process innovation ideas, all through the convenience of a mobile phone.

The key objectives of the aforementioned solutions include the creation of new business opportunities via M2M platform and solution offerings, service differentiation, customer experience by offering convenient mobile applications and cost reduction by making the business operations efficient.

Smart Convergence – SDS Successful Digital Business Model

One of the key aspects of the SDS innovation strategy is the use of an innovative and emerging IT business model (Frost and Sullivan, 2012), such as that of the Digital Space Convergence (DSC). In line with its vision to become a *world-premier leader in providing ICT services in the convergence era*, SDS recognizes 'Smart Convergence' as a rapidly growing field of business, which is being applied to facilities such as libraries, exhibitions, museums and multiplex shopping malls (Samsung Village, 2012). The DSC is dedicated to implementing a futuristic space that merges both the digital and the physical world, where SDS provides the services that cater to the emotional space design and user experience. Enabled by digital technologies such as smart mobile devices, sensors, social media platforms and cloud technology, the intent is to stimulate the user's senses in ways that add value to their experience by improving the user's quality of life in a futuristic fashion, all crafted via the convergence of IT and construction. In other words, several key aspects are critical to the enactment of the Smart Convergence digital business model: digital spatial design, user interface of the smart device, and integration of systems to enable the digital convergence experience.

3.5.3 INNOVATION CAPABILITY MATURITY MODEL AT SAMSUNG SDS

SDS is leveraging their digital technologies to enable the development of innovative digital business models. The use of digital technologies for the 'Smart Convergence' concept is a noteworthy initiative that indicates a high level of maturity of the Digital Enterprise. The list of awards granted to SDS by globally renowned institutions such as Carnegie Mellon University and Gartner is substantial. Other forms of awards earned by SDS, including the German iF Design Award and recognition as Asia's Most Admired Knowledge Enterprise, indicate that the company is known for initiatives that contribute to its high level of Innovation Capability.

In line with the vision of its parent company, SDS is committed to having global standards in conducting its day-to-day business operations. Management at SDS is committed to continuously monitor, assess, redefine and improve the state of the organization and processes to support its business operations.

Innovating 'Samsung Style'

In our interview with a senior executive at SDS, who was highly experienced in conducting numerous transformation initiatives prior to joining the company, she highlighted how SDS has a distinct culture for innovating work practices, known as 'Samsung Style'. Every year, the various organizations develop new products or services to achieve better business performance. This is embedded in Samsung's culture and is regarded as Samsung's way of life. Another executive we interviewed stated how SDS is relatively swift to catch up on new and innovative services. All business divisions in the Samsung Group play a role to initiate innovation projects internally. The executive at SDS states that innovation is on the agenda of every business leader, whereby a dedicated agenda for innovation is in place, which was instigated with Six Sigma initiatives. SDS also employs a systemic approach to innovating with digital technologies, such as the use of the Open Innovation Framework, and collaborates with both internal and external partners within its ecosystem, be it from cross-industry including their clients, as well as academic institutions such as Carnegie Mellon University.

INNOVATION CAPABILITY AT SAMSUNG SDS								
INNOVATION	**DIRECTION**			**ENABLEMENT**				
META	**STRATEGY**	**VALUE**	**RISK**	**PROCESSES**	**IT**	**CHANGE**	**TRAINING**	**PROGRAM**
Culture	Vision and Goals	Value Identification	Risk Identification	Governance	Information & Analytics	Change Impact Analysis	Training Need Analysis	Framework
Leadership	Business Model	Value Realization Planning	Risk Management Planning	Methods & Tools	Business Applications	Change Management Planning	Curriculum Development	Organization
Values	Execution	Value Realization	Risk Mitigation	Process Optimization	Communication Technology	Change Management Execution	Training Execution	Execution

Scale   Initial   Reactive   Defined   Managed   Excellence

Figure 3.3   Results of the maturity assessment for Innovation Capability at Samsung SDS

SDS seeks out external domain expertise for areas the company wishes to venture into, but does not have long experience or deep expertise in, such as the Insurance and Banking industry. In terms of internal collaboration, SDS plays a selective role in facilitating the development of strategies. SDS turns to specific levels of involvement from pertinent consulting teams, as well as external partners such as SAP. Furthermore, programs such as the sGen EcoNetwork endeavor to provide comprehensive assistance in terms of resources that would realize the sGen's ICT-related technology ideas/dreams. The Head of SDS Strategy and Marketing, who is also chairing the sGen program, states (Samsung SDS, 2012):

> *Providing support for startups through the sGen Eco Network will not only result in creating high-quality jobs and stimulating the economy, but it will also play a positive role in cultivating the strong supporters needed for Samsung SDS to become a global enterprise [...] Under this program, Samsung SDS has introduced the 'Creating Shared Value' (CSV) concept in order to move a step forward to becoming a social enterprise.*

Although SDS perceives itself to be more geared towards continuous rather than disruptive innovation, the successful execution of the DSC business model proves that SDS has the capability – and a high one at that – to disrupt the market. They are in fact rather aggressive innovators; whether the general public is ready to embrace the Smart Convergence concept is a different story. Still, companies like Saudi Aramco and Cheil have demonstrated their faith in SDS with the provision of digital innovative solutions that subsequently boost their position in the market.

Improvisational Risk Management

Our interview findings highlight how SDS has established procedures for two kinds of risks: 1) Risks that should be managed and planned at the operational (project) level; and 2) Risks that should be planned and mitigated at the strategic level. Digital Enterprises such as SDS striving to retain their market leader reputation in innovation do need to be risk tolerant in order to not constrain innovation activities by having thorough risk management and mitigation plans; yet it is equally important to be risk aware and taking calculated strategic and operational risks. Executives at SDS are well equipped with the necessary skills and competences to manage innovation-related risks, as they are active in undertaking further education and training programs. Business Transformation Professional Training is one instance of such executive training, whereby, after undertaking the training, the participants felt that a formal risk management methodology need not always apply. Still, they do conduct risk identification and review at project review meetings with managers or senior executives. The reviews take place at least every quarter when the innovation projects are assessed for their progress, which ultimately determines the business performance based on the performance scores. SDS obtains feedback from its customers to assess reputational implications at the corporate level. As such, in spite of not utilizing Key Risk Indicators (KRIs) at the corporate level, checklists are used instead to identify major risks at SDS, while each business division has its own innovation group that manages the risks at the project level.

Our interview also reveals how there is no one, specific methodology used to develop strategies for innovation at SDS. Those strategies developed are based on Samsung's experience, however, those experiences are then complemented with a Business Process Reengineering Process Improvement approach, which is a brief version of a strategic planning approach. While this approach is not documented or defined explicitly at the initiative level, management at the corporate level have step-by-step activities in place to outline how to achieve those strategies by utilizing templates as opposed to having fixed guidelines. This reflects the improvisational nature of SDS in product innovation, which is a known attribute of highly innovative companies (Kamoche and Pina e Cunha, 2001) as they are able to strike a balance between both structure and flexibility, to manage the contradicting demands of control and creativity faced by enterprises in highly competitive environments. Existing research on organizational change and development (Weick and Quinn, 1999) suggests that successful corporations do not rely on purely mechanistic or organic structures and processes. Instead, successful enterprises have well-defined managerial responsibilities, richly connected communication systems (formal and informal), and clear project priorities while simultaneously allowing for design processes to be highly adaptable, improvisational and continuously changing, all of which reflect the characteristics of SDS.

Going Back to Basics

Today, SDS is taking a 'back to basics' approach, which very simply, implies focusing on designing products that cater for the customers' needs. This is based on the observation that SDS is highly competent in having technical-related skills, such as lean management, and project management skills. As such, the company realizes the importance of focusing on design-led innovation skills to complement those technical skills. One of the strategies to foster such competence is by establishing an Innovation Academy to educate all business leaders in developing new approaches to achieve business growth, as the Senior Executives at SDS also indicate how the business has an enterprise-wide understanding (Choi, 1995; Yang, Choi, Hyung Jin, Suh and Bongsug, 2007; Yun and Chua, 2002) of best practices.

The evaluation of current processes for innovation initiatives has led SDS to the decision to go 'back to basics'. This is due to the complexities that have arisen from the increased level of sophistication in today's technology. SDS is therefore reverting to its original business characteristics, which are to satisfy customers' needs and requirements. Based on this realization, SDS has (re) defined the backbone structure or fundamentals of its business, and seeks to explore the next level of innovation from there on. The intent of doing so is to ensure that SDS employees will not be confused by the current complex environment that encompasses emerging digital technologies.

'Back to Basics' at Samsung SDS

About five years ago, Samsung SDS has tried to expand their business to achieve growth. At that time, given the limited human manpower, they deduced that they need ramp up the capabilities and competencies of their consultants'. Project management skills were emphasized heavily instead of systems or process design competencies. After several years, having acquired mainly management skills, Samsung SDS found themselves short of the actual expertise to design processes and systems. The lack of development in systems and process designs has lead to errors in the final IT system that is delivered to the customers, which was largely unknown and rather ironic. This subsequently required Samsung SDS to seek external resources such as subcontractors. Therefore, Samsung SDS have now opted to change their corporate notion of going "back to basics" by:

- Minimizing the hiring core designers by developing those capabilities in-house,
- Focus more on designing systems and business processes.

Measurable Outcomes

One of our interviewees stated that success is considered via a defined strategy and its relation to the business processes at SDS. At the end of the day, the success of a company is defined by how much of the business value is realized. SDS identifies specific goals and measurements of an innovation initiative prior to establishing such projects. Then, according to that goal, the success of the initiative is measured via process effectiveness or cost savings, every six months. According to our interviews, there are KPIs defined for innovation-related initiatives at SDS, where both quantitative and qualitative measures are in place. This includes those for employees, who would typically work in SDS projects for two-three years, gaining both professional and personal incentives. On a personal level, individual employees have opportunities to increase their Innovation Capability, which is perceived to be a great reward in itself. Their efforts are reflected in their annual performance evaluation and made known to management.

3.5.4 Innovation Challenges at Samsung SDS

Even though SDS has demonstrated a high level of maturity in its innovation capability, the leading innovator is not without challenges. Our interviews suggest that its current challenges lie in the ability to retain its Game Changer reputation in its industry. Like similar businesses that strive to keep up to speed in a dynamic environment, SDS is always working towards managing the socio-behavioral and technological challenge for those within and beyond its ecosystem.

Overcoming Socio-Technical Inertia

In order to manage the socio-behavioral and technical challenge, SDS is constantly investing its resources in new product development, where they endeavor to utilize digital technologies, such as cloud technologies. The key is to foresee and empathize with the needs of users in both the digital and physical world, and to bridge this gap for a seamless user experience. The senior executive interviewed states how the employees at SDS face both technical and socio-behavioral challenges in the early stages of innovation projects. Management, therefore, has to deal with employees' levels of comfort with adapting to the change, and in other instances, the required upgrade of particular functions due to the change in work environment. The employees at the transactional level, particularly, find the initiatives challenging, however, top-level management finds these initiatives to be positive. To overcome such challenges, a great deal of communication by top management is carried out to mitigate those issues: From the earlier stages of implementing innovation projects meetings with C-Level executives, particularly with the CIO and CFO, are held to check project progress and identify what kind of changes are made at the front-level worker environment. This reflects how management is well aware of the necessary changes and there have been no reported significant issues in terms of resistance.

During our interview, SDS made reference to the managerial practices of its highly successful affiliate, Samsung Electronics. Samsung Electronics was the first company to introduce SAP ERP in Korea, representing the most successful cases in terms of utilizing best practices in the industry. Having also implemented SAP in Samsung Fire and Marine, as well as Samsung Life, the goal is to spread the experience to the manufacturing, chemicals and distribution and financial industry. One of the key challenges and opportunities is to penetrate the financial industry, which is known to be conservative and risk averse. However, SDS sees the potential to utilize digital technologies, as a natural progression after SAP industry solution adoption, focusing on the adoption of industry specific solutions for insurance. The issue of conservativeness also extends to its current customers who are less receptive to disruptive innovation services from SDS. In order to overcome this inertia, SDS aims to be the proactive trendsetter, and not a reactive follower.

Industry Breakthrough

Another current industry opportunity for SDS is to venture into providing digital services in the hi-tech manufacturing industry. This endeavor is in line with the goals of its parent company, Samsung Group, which plans to be a leading competitor in general manufacturing industry by leveraging its extensive manufacturing experience. The establishment of Samsung Biologics and Bioepis in the biotechnology and pharmaceutical industry is forecasted to be a promising opportunity for Samsung Group, however, they have the capability to achieve this based on their proven track record of manufacturing electronic devices (for example, MRI, CT or Ultrasonic Scan). Therefore, expanding from the electronic manufacturing technology to medical devices appears to be an organic progression for the conglomerate. Although this is a risky initiative, other companies that produce generic medicine have already sought Samsung Biologics to mass-produce those medicines, which highlights the confidence of other businesses to invest in the corporation. It is this strategic alliance that enables the corporation to achieve and to mature its digital capability in innovation management. While this is the current stage of the business,

Samsung Group sees the necessity to eventually evolve into producing generic medicines or designing medical devices. This is where SDS, as an IT service provider, will need to support those corporate business innovations.

Market Expansion

SDS opts for a calculated-risk approach when venturing into the global market. They consider it risky to adopt a rapid expansion approach to developed regions, as they will be competing with other companies in those markets. With SDS's proven capability in the Middle-East with the successful deployment of its digital business model (that is, the DSC) however, SDS is leveraging its mature innovation management digital capability to design IT instruments with software in buildings, thereby increasing the demand for construction-related IT development from SDS. The company's high maturity level in Innovation Capability will also be a strength to leverage in the Chinese market, based on its proven experience in developing business strategies for Samsung Group's business portfolio and business processes.

3.5.5 THE WAY FORWARD

Implications for Senior Management at Samsung SDS and Digital Enterprises

The key challenge identified in our interview with one of the Senior Executives involved in the strategic planning of SDS, is to come up with radical digital business models, viz. disruptive innovation into the market that is embedded with various types of social inertias (Besson and Rowe, 2012). One of the guiding recommendations was derived from our findings via a focus group (or World Café method) conducted with various senior executives and managers at the 2013 SAP Global Business Transformation Summit in Washington DC. We discovered that there are elements of dualities (Van Looy, Martens and Debackere, 2005) in carrying out innovation-related, decision-making processes. There are *general* versus *specific managerial competences* that require consideration when managing innovation initiatives, explained in the following.

The first element of competences[2] to consider when managing innovation in Digital Enterprises is the *general (managerial) competences*. Digital Enterprises

---

2 Competences differ from capabilities in that an organization's *competence* refer to its capacity to deploy resources, typically in combination with organizational processes, to effect a desired end, while *capabilities* refers to the firm's ability to carry out a set of coordinated tasks, using organizational resources to achieve a particular end result (Ashurst, Doherty and Peppard, 2008).

General Competences

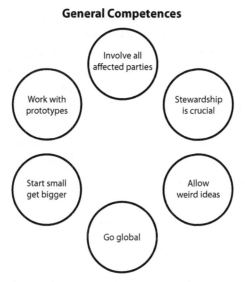

Figure 3.4 **General managerial competences for managing innovation in Digital Enterprises**

carry out the tasks and activities as outlined in Figure 3.4. These essential tasks and activities contribute to the strategic development of innovative digital business models, enabled by digital technologies as described in our case study on SDS, for example, Smart Convergence digital business models.

In addition to the general competences, findings from the World Café also suggest that Digital Enterprises require *specific competences* in deciding to embark on a digital transformation via innovative digital business models. Figure 3.5 summarizes the description on the *specific competences*.

Based on Figure 3.5, our analysis and findings from the focus groups identify how innovation-related initiatives depend on the following as well:

1. **Activity level** of innovation initiatives: Problem-oriented vs. opportunity-oriented;
2. **Approach** taken for innovation initiatives: Deterministic (established methodologies, frameworks, approaches) vs. Non-linear (reconfigure approaches and capabilities);
3. **Triggers** for innovation initiatives: Internal drivers (for example, lack in scalability of ICT infrastructure, losing market share to competitors) vs. external drivers (for example, changing market demand, technological and legislative changes, economic fluctuations);

4.   **Decision-making** for innovation initiatives: Confidence-driven ('gut feeling', tacit knowledge) vs. evidence-driven (empirical based, explicit knowledge);

5.   **Success measurement** for innovation initiatives: Perception (based on face value, external to stakeholders beyond immediate ecosystem) vs. scorecard (for example, risk management KRIs, and other performance indicators KPI for business processes.

The decision-making factors to be considered by senior management also includes the question of where will such decision making occur in the innovation management process?

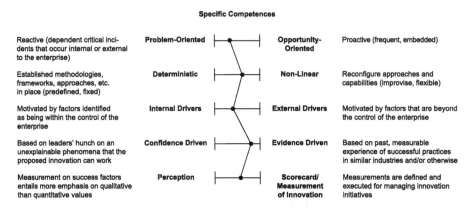

Figure 3.5   Specific managerial competences required for decision-making for innovation management in Digital Enterprises

Minimizing Innovation Latency at Samsung SDS

One of the considerations for SDS is the use of digital technologies as part of the IT management for innovation initiatives. In particular, the process of collecting data and analyzing them for decision-making purposes, prior to embarking on innovation initiatives, can be minimized with the use of information and analytics resources that SDS is offering to its clients. Leveraging SDS's existing digital technologies can assist in minimizing the data collection and analysis latency period via predictive analytics for big data, sentiment analysis on qualitative data via contemporary social media platforms with affordances widely used by the general public and/or targeted market segments, deriving personas for design thinking practices (see Brown, 2008) and so forth. Figure 3.6 illustrates the value that is lost via innovation latency.

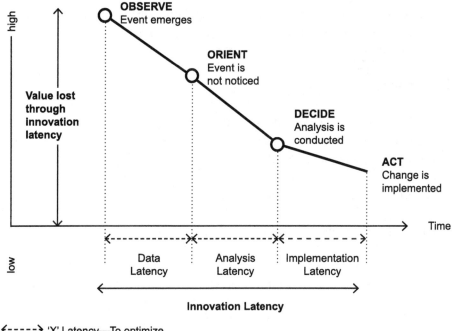

Figure 3.6 Digital Enterprises to consider innovation latency to derive desired value from innovation initiatives

3.6 Conclusion

Innovation Capability in Digital Enterprises refers to the ability to develop not just novel ideas, but to position those ideas into widely used practice that adds value for the end user. The Innovation Capability Maturity Model provides a holistic approach to managing innovation-related initiatives in Digital Enterprises. The case of Samsung SDS demonstrates the execution of unique and rapid adoption of many creative digital business models that are enabled by contemporary digital technologies such as mobile, social media, sensors, cloud technologies and so forth. The key strength of Samsung SDS lies in its ability to leverage and reconfigure its Innovation Capability, by merging information from both the digital and physical world via its Smart Convergence digital business model, in order to create a truly distinctive and seamless user experience.

Acknowledgement: We would like to thank our partners from SAMSUNG SDS for their cooperation. Website: www.sds.samsung.com.

References

Besson, P. and Rowe, F. (2012) Strategizing information systems-enabled organizational transformation: A transdisciplinary review and new directions. *The Journal of Strategic Information Systems, 21*(2), 103–124.

Brown, T. (2008) Design thinking. *Harvard Business Review, 86*(6), 84.

Choi, C.J. (1995) Samsung: Re-engineering Korean style. *Long Range Planning, 28*(4), 6–80.

Frost and Sullivan (2012) Digital Space Convergence (DSC) an Emerging IT Business Model. http://www.frost.com/sublib/display-market-insight.do?id=260711076, last accessed 6 July 2014.

Kamoche, K. and Pina e Cunha, M. (2001) Minimal Structures: From Jazz Improvisation to Product Innovation. *Organization Studies, 22*(5), 733.

Khanna, T., Song, J. and Lee, K. (2011) The Globe Strategy and Competition: The paradox of Samsung's rise. *Harvard Business Review, 89*(7–8), 142–147.

King Abdulaziz Center (2014) *Our Story.* http://en.kingabdulazizcenter.com/explore/about-us/our-story#.U8PEo_mSzHR, last accessed 14 July 2014.

Lankov, A. (2011) *Lee Byung-chull: founder of Samsung Group.* http://www.koreatimes.co.kr/www/news/issues/2014/05/363_96557.html, last accessed 17 June 2014.

Samsung (2014) *History – About Samsung.* http://www.samsung.com/us/aboutsamsung/corporateprofile/history04.html, last accessed 17 June 2014.

Samsung SDS (2012) *Samsung SDS launches sGen Eco Network to support startups.* http://www.sds.samsung.com/aboutsds/pr/newsView.jsp?idx=9qCHQI8U3ek~/YRHgBqf8ac~&number=140&p=1, last accessed 7 July 2014.

Samsung SDS (2014a) *Best Practices – Establishment of Samsung Group Smart Learning Platform.* http://www.sds.samsung.com/bizintro/work/BestView.

jsp?idx=jwGtgpjCQDs~vIw/5SGRyX0~&p=1&part_c=fOCygvh2YfY~Z
KOXcSR9LlI~&search_cate=tUOhgthZ/8Q~HRUmhFFaKnY~&search_
cate2=Oyt4gjhrGqc~HLklyfJOqmY~, last accessed 28 May 2014.

Samsung SDS (2014b) *Best Practices – Immigration Inspection Improvement Pilot Project for Incheon International Airport.* http://www.sds.samsung.com/bizintro/ work/BestView.jsp?idx=vD1kgZZNGUw~53uRG/CZenI~&p=1&part_c=qRx qgfYBOgc~oxbCFb7PgnM~&search_cate=f10Ugtdw7jk~xwPSAcxXvz0~&se arch_cate2=8iPxgZc2Ktc~gGoJTtaKwV0~, last accessed 28 May 2014.

Samsung SDS (2014c) *Best Practices – Mobile i-pub Implementation Project of Chiel Communications.* http://www.sds.samsung.com/bizintro/work/BestView. jsp?idx=J7L0gHXqq2g~IcKkzdQzIRU~&p=1&part_c=mnjRgDWw5wU~ hEh1AY61mjY~&search_cate=09u/gBWThdQ~E5SVsloqOuU~&search_ cate2=wLrFgHVHpo8~KESExHX4DQs~, last accessed 28 May 2014.

Samsung SDS (2014d) *Machine To Machine (M2M).* http://www.sds.samsung. com/popup/service/convergence/M2M.jsp, last accessed 7 July 2014.

Samsung Village (2012) *Samsung SDS Advances Into Middle East With 'Smart Convergence'.* http://www.samsungvillage.com/blog/2012/05/08/ samsungblog-samsung-sds-advances-into-middle-east-with-smart-convergence/, last accessed 7 July 2014.

Van Looy, B., Martens, T. and Debackere, K. (2005) Organizing for Continuous Innovation: On the Sustainability of Ambidextrous Organizations. *Creativity and Innovation Management,* 14(3), 208–221.

Weick, K.E. and Quinn, R.E. (1999) Organizational change and development. *Annual Review of psychology,* 50(1), 361–386.

World Airport Awards (2014) *The World's Best Airports 2014.* http://www. worldairportawards.com/index.htm, last accessed 28 May 2014.

Yang, H.M., Choi, B.S., Hyung Jin, P., Suh, M.S. and Bongsug, C. (2007) Supply chain management six sigma: a management innovation methodology at the Samsung Group. *Supply Chain Management,* 12(2), 88.

Yun, J.-Y. and Chua, R.C. (2002) Samsung uses Six Sigma to change its image. *Six Sigma Forum Magazine* (pp. 13–16).

Chapter 4

Transformation Capability

NILS LABUSCH, ROBERT WINTER AND AXEL UHL

4.1 Overview

Digitalization can focus on improving operational processes by use of innovative technology, however, the Digital Transformation as it is being discussed in this book causes far-reaching changes across the entire enterprise and eventually can affect the entire value chain of a company.

In order to tackle such structural changes, organizations require the ability to adapt as market and technological conditions change. These skills are different from those required to manage business-as-usual operations. As a matter of fact the experiences of successfully running the business can considerably constrain transformation. Therefore, envisioning, engaging, implementing and leading corporate transformation calls for a specific set of skills. Ultimately it is the experience of knowing how to apply these skills that will support successful transformation into a Digital Enterprise.

Many well-known and successful companies go out of business after a couple of years – others survive by constantly changing their business models, adapting to the market environment, and refreshing their inner structures. Companies survive because they have developed a mature Transformation Capability. Thus, together with the other capabilities presented in the Digital Capability Framework, the Transformation Capability is an important enabler of becoming a digital enterprise. Therefore, we start with a discussion about what a transformation is and how it can be managed. We go on by illustrating how transformation pertains to the company's performance and what modern transformation management approaches are available.

This is followed by a discussion of how new technologies can help to improve the company's Transformation Capability. A core issue here is how social media, cloud computing, mobility or big data processing can improve a company's transformation.

We explain the Digital Capability Maturity Model as it applies to the Transformation Capability. The Maturity Model helps to assess how well the company does concerning the Transformation Capability.

Finally, we provide an illustrative case study of a company that can be regarded as a leader in long-term, fundamental, and successful transformation: IBM. Being born in a merger of three independent companies, one of IBM's major strategic goals for more than 100 years has been to improve its transformation capability.

Objectives of this chapter:

1. Analyze 'Transformation' as a phenomenon and explain how it can be managed.
2. Provide an overview of the Digital Capability Maturity Model for the Transformation Capability.
3. Illustrate a case of a very successful Transformation Capability.

4.2 Status quo

4.2.1 DEFINITION – WHAT IS TRANSFORMATION?

Transformation refers to major changes that are not routine, but fundamental, and that substantially alter an organization's relationships with its key constituencies. Transformation can involve new value propositions or changes to the structure of the enterprise (Rouse, 2005). Furthermore, transformation may mean providing old value propositions in fundamentally new ways. The transformation concept is also known as 'business transformation' (Stiles and Uhl, 2012), 'organizational transformation' (Dixon et al., 2010) or 'enterprise transformation' (Baba and Rouse, 2006). Transformation addresses radical, enterprise-wide changes and not incremental or local changes.

Transformations are usually conducted within a period of about two years (Romanelli and Tushman, 1994), however, transformations can take longer or, when very well managed, less time. Examples of fundamental transformations are significant changes to the business model, mergers and acquisitions, or introductions and replacements of enterprise IT systems.

Transformations need clear direction. Lahrmann et al. (2012) conducted a study to investigate how transformations need to be managed in order to be successful, and identified three different approaches to transformation management. The *Value-Driven Approach* was present in 57 percent of the companies examined and is characterized by target-driven planning and comprehensive benefits management. The *Un-Governed Approach* was present in almost 25 percent of the companies and is characterized by minimal governance of people and technology. The *Change Driven Approach* was present in 18 percent of the companies and is characterized by sophisticated people and technology governance, holistic change management and commitment to transformation.

The study showed that holistic approaches that cover a wide variety of management disciplines and areas of business transformation, have a greater probability of succeeding.

4.2.2 THE CASE FOR A TRANSFORMATION CAPABILITY

Without appropriate transformation management making major changes to a complex company is almost impossible. The transformation process is influenced by many parts of the organization as much as the environment (Uhl, 2012). In addition, transformations are rarely limited to a single company, but instead affect the whole value network. But why are companies conducting transformations?

Labusch et al. (2013) based on the work of Rouse (2006) identify four main triggers for transformations: First, the revenue opportunities of emerging markets or new technologies are initiators of transformations. For example, the rise of mobile applications has completely changed some businesses and the value propositions of companies, which has made it necessary to transform processes, technologies and strategy (Basole, 2005). Second, market threats are causing transformations. Faced with the danger of anticipated failure, fundamental changes are necessary. Third, transformation initiatives by main competitors drive transformations. Sometimes, changes in the environment become visible only if a major competitor adapts itself and suddenly performs better or attracts more customers. Finally, internal crisis within the enterprise forces transformation. Examples of crises include eroded performance, steadily declining market performance or cash flow problems.

Transformations involve different stakeholders, disciplines and topic areas and therefore cumulate in a great deal of complexity and uncertainty (Elliot 2011). This difficult environment leads to many failures. Kotter (1995) identified typical reasons for these failures: a sense of urgency is not established, a powerful guiding team does not exist, a vision is not created and/ or not communicated, insufficient planning is conducted, improvements are not consolidated, and new approaches are not institutionalized.

Indeed, many transformations still miss the mark. Ward and Uhl (2012) find that almost 30 percent of transformations fail while only 30 percent are considered a full success. Therefore, even if much research has already been conducted, the topic still requires new and innovative approaches in order to increase the overall success rate.

4.2.3 RELATED WORK

Different approaches exist in order to support transformations. The Business Transformation Management Methodology (BTM^2) for instance comprises four transformation phases (envision, engage, transform, and optimize) and integrates discipline-specific technical and methodological expertise from several areas. BTM^2 provides a base to integrate contributions from management disciplines as diverse as strategy, value, risk, IT transformation, program and project, change, process, and competency management. While strategy, value, and risk management set the course for business transformation, other disciplines enable the transformation process. The discipline of Meta Management is put in place for orchestrating the various work streams (Stiles and Uhl, 2012).

Another prevalent approach, developed at the Massachusetts Institute of Technology (MIT), is the Enterprise Strategic Analysis for Transformation (ESAT), an integrated, analytical framework for diagnosing and improving overall enterprise performance. Similar to BTM^2 it includes an understanding of the enterprise value streams and considers value flows between key stakeholders and the enterprise. The ESAT framework further aims at setting up appropriate governance as much as designing an actionable transformation plan. The development of the method was strongly influenced by the defense sector, for example, Boeing and Lockheed. Another publicly available approach, which is mostly driven by the Canadian government, is the Business Transformation Enablement Program (BTEP). This approach is structured as a circle with eight steps that claim to cover the entire transformation. However, as opposed to BTM^2, the approach does not explicitly provide guidance on how to integrate existing specific management disciplines.

A related discipline to transformation management is enterprise architecture management (Winter et al., 2013). Enterprise architects and transformation managers share many important skills, deal with many common artifacts, use many similar techniques and tools, have some common users and stakeholders, are both concerned with transformation, and are both involved in change projects. However, differences exist with regard to the prioritization of the necessary skillsets and prioritization of activities the two disciplines need or conduct.

In conclusion, existing literature provides some guidance on how to transform organizations and how to measure transformation readiness, however, it neglects the latest impacts of modern and game-changing technologies and it usually lacks a holistic perspective or fails to sufficiently integrate specific management disciplines.

4.2.4 SUCCESSFUL TRANSFORMATION AS A PERFORMANCE DRIVER

Being successful in conducting transformations is very important for the performance of the company. In the worst case, if transformation management is non-existent or wrongly conducted, the company may fail.

It is dangerous to manage transformation by looking only at financial figures. Many factors that are relevant during transformation have an effect on performance in the long run, but not in the short run. Keller and Price (2011) emphasize this issue by calling the company's ability to align, execute and renew itself faster than its competitors 'organizational health'. Health is positioned next to financial performance, which is important in order to satisfy stakeholder groups such as shareholders. Robust health should, however, also be maintained in order to stay competitive in the long run. Studies show that good health (and thus a strong transformation capability) also has a significant impact on financial figures like EBITDA. For example, companies in the top quartile of organizational health are 2.2 times more likely than lower-quartile companies to have an above median EBITDA (Keller and Price, 2011).

4.3 Today's and Tomorrow's Technologies as a Transformation Enabler

Modern technologies such as social media, big data, cloud and mobility should be applied to leverage the Transformation Capability. According to BTM², Transformations can be broadly distinguished into four phases (Stiles and Uhl, 2012): 1) envision (create a case for change and sense of urgency), 2) engage (empower people to act on the vision and plan the effort), 3) transform (change behavior, processes, technology, culture and values) and 4) optimize (internalize, institutionalize and optimize transformation, create stability). Table 4.1 illustrates how modern technologies can be leveraged during these different phases.

Table 4.1   Modern Technologies in the context of the
Transformation Capability

	SOCIAL MEDIA	BIG DATA	CLOUD SERVICES	MOBILITY
Envision	Create sense of urgency	Collect and analyze customer data	Provide quick insights into new technologies and their applicability	Use data from local devices to plan transformation effort
Engage	Collect and address feedback and explain the transformation			
Transform			Govern transformation uncertainty	Gamification
Optimize	Collect open issues and potentials for optimization		Refine processes and prevent costs	Use data from local devices to optimize transformation effort

4.3.1 ENVISION

Social Media

During the envision phase it is important to create a sense of urgency and to make everybody understand that the transformation is necessary. This can be achieved by applying the principles for social media campaigns (David, n.d.):

- Make it personal – try to explain the transformation in a way that addresses the people being affected personally and not in a generic manner. Try to look at it from the point of view of the transformation stakeholder: What does the transformation mean to him/her?
- Make it frequent – vary the message but send it often. Explain the transformation whenever possible.
- Create a sense of urgency – include an urgent call for action. Make it clear that the company needs to be among the first to catch up. If the company is the last in a market undergoing transformation, failure is very likely.
- Encourage sharing – ask colleagues to share their posts and discussions with colleagues – and colleagues of colleagues. Do not forget to share and retweet or repost their thoughts on the transformation (especially, of course, if these posts can help promote the transformation).
- Make it remarkable – describe the transformation in a way that is special.
- Do some research – try to figure out the right times to communicate the transformation. You should be able to react to posts and hit people in

the right mood. Thus, would it make sense to start communicating the transformation the day before Christmas? Probably not.

- Budget – keep in mind that social media marketing is not free and professional results need a professional budget.

4.3.2 ENGAGE

Social Media

During the engage and transform phases, social media in particular can be used to collect feedback and to explain the transformation again and again. Social media allows everyone to post their thoughts about the transformation, and directly communicate with many other people. While some managers would consider this as a high risk, we see it differently: It allows issues to be openly addressed.

Big Data

Big data allows the processing of all the data that can be collected from sensors, social media platforms, tweets, and so on. Thus, it is a package of technology that can prove especially useful in the engage phase.

Companies nowadays have the chance to collect lots of data to prepare their transformation, however, this data needs to be processed and analyzed. Consider an energy company that can predict power consumption by using 350 billion meter readings from 20 million households; or an insurance company that settles legitimate claims 70 times faster than competitors (Bhambhri, 2012).

Thus, big data can be used extensively to keep the most important transformation stakeholder in mind: the customer. Big data analytics help to predict and analyze customers' needs and their behavior after the transformation.

Cloud

The usage of cloud services can leverage digital transformations especially in the engage, transform and optimize phases.

During the engage phase, the cloud can be used to provide quick insights into new technologies and allow the company to assess the possibilities of modern technology. Thus, the cloud is an important tool in order to set the vision. For example, if an insurance company plans to set up a modern web platform to sell and configure its products, cloud services can be used to present a first mock-up.

Mobility

The term 'mobility' summarizes the availability of manifold technologies such as tablets or smart phones that allow users to work from everywhere at any time. This has impacts on the management of transformations in terms of challenges and opportunities.

Formerly, special action was required in the 'envision' and 'engage' phases to communicate the necessity of change and the path that should be followed. In order to address many employees, central road shows, meetings etc. have been used. In a world of mobility, transformation managers need to consider that employees are not necessarily available at their office location but can be traveling anywhere in the world or in their home office. In consequence, transformation managers need to use mobile technology to communicate the transformation to all the employees in their home offices and around the world.

In order to plan the transformation, depending on the business model, mobile technology can provide valuable information. For example, assume a logistics company wants to start a digital transformation and needs to become aware of their most important routes and the challenges for truck drivers. In the past they would have had just a rough idea of the trucks' locations and the current road situation. With mobile devices in place, it is now easy to track and collect the required information. Such information helps to identify the key challenges of the business and to integrate them into the transformation plans.

4.3.3 TRANSFORM

Cloud

Cloud services can reveal most of their potential during the transform phase. In this phase, uncertainty needs to be governed and the cloud can be used to govern this uncertainty in manifold ways (following paragraphs based on Labusch (2011)). If for example, the company is less experienced in certain technologies and is not aware of technical design requirements, cloud computing is a governance mechanism for this kind of uncertainty. Because of its flexibility, users can change very quickly to other technologies and adopt these (Böhm et al., 2011).

Very often, the resources that will be needed during a digital transformation are hard to predict. For this problem, cloud technology can offer the perfect solution due to its flexible, demand-driven price model: you pay for what you consume. The general concept of cloud computing assumes an almost unlimited availability of resources on the provider side and a level of high flexibility for the client (Böhm et al., 2011). Switching from one provider to another is considered to be easy if standard interfaces are used (Youseff et al., 2008).

Cloud computing can also prevent the transformation initiative from vendor lock-in. If standards are used to connect the cloud service provider, it no longer matters which vendor provides the service in the background (assuming that multiple vendors provide the same quality of service and data security).

Mobility

Mobility also affects the transform phase. Managers need to change many routines and cultural aspects of the company. Mobile devices can provide new ways to foster this change for example, by working with gamification which means motivating people to do certain things by making use of their natural desire to play. Consider for example the Nike Plus running app that makes you go running by allowing you to earn cheers from your friends on Facebook, and provides reminders and motivation to move (Alba, 2012). Another example is RedCritter Tracker, where employees earn points whenever they finish work packages on a project. When transformation managers are able to incorporate such new approaches for motivating transformation stakeholders, the likelihood of a successful transformation increases significantly.

4.3.4 OPTIMIZE

Social Media

During the optimization phase, social media could be used to collect ongoing issues and optimization potentials. Thus it can be used as a corporate history of transformation experiences.

Cloud

In the optimization phase of a transformation, the cloud can be used to refine processes and reduce costs. For example, one could think about sourcing not only applications from the cloud but whole processes (referred to as 'business process as a service' – 'BPaaS').

4.4 The Transformation Capability Maturity Model

It is essential to mention that on no account should the digital transformation be limited only to the topic of IT transformation. Without addressing the business site and the identification of their business needs and capabilities digitalization might be doomed to failure. Therefore, we propose to consider the topic of Transformation Capability from a far more holistic perspective. We propose using the Transformation Capability Maturity Model to assess the level of companies' transformational abilities. For setting up a holistic assessment model we used nine BTM^2 management disciplines as outlined in Chapter 2. In Table 4.2 we set out the essential skills and experience with respect to Transformation Capability. For better comprehension we compare the weakest level 1 (initial state) with the highest level 5 (excellence in Transformation Capability).

Table 4.2   Outline of the Transformation Capability Maturity Model (contrast between a low vs. high maturity level)

Discipline	Level 1 – Initial	Level 5 – Excellence
Meta Management	• Culture that is completely against transformations • Employees do not understand the need to transform • Management does not support initiatives to improve the transformation capability • Leaders are neither educated nor interested in guiding transformation activities	• The corporate culture considers transformation as its strategic objective that ensures the future competitiveness of the company • Being a Thought Leader in transformation is key to the company's activities • Best practices in learning and sharing transformation knowledge from inside as well as outside • Leaders are engaged directly; they are open to external and internal feedback • Employees and leaders have a continuous dialog in a team-based culture about the manifold transformation activities
Strategy Management	• Transformation Capability plays no role in the corporate vision • Transformation Capability is not taken into account while changing business model • Transformation strategies might be developed, but 'stay in the drawer'	• Transformation is considered a key element of the corporate vision • Transformation Capability as a core competence when changing the business model • Strategic transformation projects are set up with partners in order to improve transformation capability across the entire value chain • The execution of the transformation strategy includes key partners, suppliers and customers

Discipline	Level 1 – Initial	Level 5 – Excellence
Value Management	• Companies do not plan and execute value realization measures • No defined responsibilities for value realization and baselines • Lack of value measurement tools • The benefits of a transformation remain unknown	• Value identification for transformation initiatives is considered a company KPI • Planning of value realization is a standard procedure within the company or ecosystem • Framework for measuring quantitative and qualitative benefits of the transformation initiatives is defined and mandatory for all transformation initiatives
Risk Management	• Transformations are run without any consideration of potential risks • Lack of risk mitigation strategies for transformation initiatives	• Risk is considered a strategic topic and well-discussed by top management • Formal risk planning for strategic and operational risks is in place • Top management is involved in order to plan mitigations for strategic risks • Risk mitigation is executed on strategic as well as on operational levels
Business Process Management	• Processes run in silos and no governance or ownership is in place • No up-to-date, formal process documentation, no standards and process management knowledge • Lack of process optimization measures – unrecognized issues and process inefficiencies	• There are company- and eco-system-wide process management established for supporting the transformation initiatives • The application of process management methods is mandatory for all transformation initiatives • Process improvements focus on quality • Processes are highly automated and quantitatively monitored
Transformational IT Management	• Analytic requirements and data quality are not considered for transformation initiatives • Many silo applications, no reference architecture model • No application lifecycle management is connected to the transformation programs	• Analytics are used for unstructured and semi-structured data • Data sources are integrated into the transformation processes and security levels for transformation programs are defined • Implementing new technologies like cloud technology or social media in order to communicate the transformation efforts
Organizational Change Management	• Stakeholders are not identified and no stakeholder analysis is conducted • Communication needs are not analyzed	• Detailed understanding of change impacts and the communication needs are analyzed for all relevant stakeholder groups • Professional organizational change management planning is an integral part of all transformation initiatives across the entire business ecosystem

Table 4.2 Outline of the Transformation Capability Maturity Model (contrast between a low vs. high maturity level) – Continued

Discipline	Level I – Initial	Level 5 – Excellence
Competence and Training Management	• Training needs are not directly associated with the transformation initiative • Educational activities are not coordinated or aligned • No training for the transformation is provided and conducted	• Excellent understanding of the required skills • Curricula are differentiated between stakeholder groups • Participation in trainings is mandatory for all affected employees and leaders track progress • The evaluation assesses whether training results are transferred to daily work
Program and Project Management	• No program and project management frameworks are applied • Transformation initiatives are not managed as a program or not even as a project	• Methods and tools for program and project management are in place company-wide • The organization structure for program and project management is in place and is seen as a career opportunity • Communication and knowledge exchange is fostered between the different projects • All transformation initiatives in the company are integrated across the company; inter-dependencies between different transformations are managed

The Transformation Capability Maturity Model is based on the assumption that the maturity increases if a company considers the following aspects:

- Developing the transformation strategy is considered as one of the most important top management activities;
- Transformation is not restricted to IT and the business is strongly involved in transformation activities;
- Benefits of the transformation efforts are continuously managed and measured;
- Transformation governance, methods, tools and processes are in place;
- Strategic transformation projects are set up with partners across the entire value chain.

Companies which resolve to undertake the digital journey place greater emphasis on excellence in Transformation Capability. They consider it as a holistic approach that connects all relevant management disciplines and coordinates them. Moreover, these companies maintain a strong relationship to their business network and include their customers and business partners in the transformation endeavor.

4.5 Case Study: IBM – Mastering a Fundamental Transformation Journey

The International Business Machines Corporation (IBM) as a long standing, well-known global brand is our lighthouse-example for Transformation Capability. The company emerged from a transformation (merger of three companies) and has reinvented its business model many times. This chain of re-invention allows the company to continue to be successful – in contrast to most of its competitors, many of whom have gone out of business. Transformation is one of the most important components of IBM's business model. Since 2000, the company has acquired more than 140 companies in order to increase its portfolio of products and offerings. In 2012 IBM's revenue was $104.50 billion with more than 430,000 employees (IBM, 2012).

We have prepared this case study based on publicly available material that we identified during an extensive literature review. IBM's transformation journey is used to illustrate the Transformation Capability of the Digital Capability Framework.

4.5.1 IBM'S TRANSFORMATION JOURNEY

As a result of a merger of three companies, IBM was founded in 1911 as a 'computer tabulating recording company' (the journey section is based on Wikipedia (2013)). The three companies manufactured a wide range of products, including employee time-keeping systems, weighing scales, automatic meat slicers, coffee grinders, and punched card equipment. IBM then had approximately 1,300 employees.

The CEO at that time fostered effective business tactics: sales incentives, a focus on customer service as well as a company culture of pride and loyalty in every worker. As the sales force grew into a highly professional and knowledgeable arm of the company, the CEO focused their attention on providing large-scale, custom-built tabulating solutions for businesses. He also pointed out the importance of customer orientation – a paradigm that is still in place at IBM today. The name IBM was established in 1924.

Much later, in the 1950s, the company needed to undergo change again. During the two World Wars, much funding was generated by government military contracts. However, peacetime required changes. The company and the environment were in a phase of rapid technological change – electronic computers, magnetic tape storage, and programming were introduced at this time. The CEO at that time reacted to the challenges by rapidly adapting the structure of the organization and by creating a modern management structure that allowed better oversight of the company. He codified the well-known, but so far unwritten, practices and philosophy into explicit corporate guidance.

IBM has frequently changed its business model and divested itself of elements that were no longer considered to be its core business. As an example, its clock production operation was sold in 1958, after 70 years of building clocks and clock equipment. In addition, IBM invested in engineering and developing new products. Even in the Great Depression, the company did not lay off personnel, but instead continued hiring. IBM always provided benefits to employees that were uncommon in those times, such as group life insurance and paid vacations.

In 1969 IBM needed to conduct another huge transformation – unbundling software and service from hardware sales. Until then, software and services (for example, systems engineering, training, and system installation) were included in the hardware leasing rates. The driver for this transformation was antitrust inquiries resulting from IBM's high market share during this time.

In 1981 the era of the personal computer began, and IBM launched the IBM PC that became the market standard for decades. Even if it was not spectacular compared to what competitors could offer, IBM managed to combine the most desirable features into one small machine. It was not cheap, but it was affordable for businesses compared to other computing machines at that time. IBM changed its internal strategy of producing most parts internally by outsourcing major components to Intel or Microsoft.

Nevertheless, by the late 1980s IBM found itself in trouble. The organization (at that time comprising 400,000 employees) was overly complex; processes were inefficient and core products were under price pressure. People started to buy smaller servers instead of mainframes. Thus, purchasing decisions in customer companies were made by different people than before. No longer were mainframe experts talking to IBM sales clerks but instead IBM was talking to business people – a group of customers with whom IBM did not have good relations. As a consequence, the company adjusted its structure to more vertical lines and to business units with strong leaders in order to compete in the different market segments – for example, network components (competitor Novell), microprocessors (competitor Intel) or disk drives (competitor Seagate). Again, IBM disposed of parts of the company that were no longer considered to be core business (for example, printers or typewriters).

Still, IBM struggled and many jobs were lost. In 1993 a new CEO took the helm and transformed the company again. He continued shrinking the workforce (down to 220,000), sold parts of the company and recognized that one of IBM's important strengths was providing integrated solutions. Thus, he revised the decision to implement independent business units. One year later, the company was profitable again. A global services business was created, that quickly became a leading technology integrator. In 2002 IBM increased the service business significantly by acquiring the consultancy division of PricewaterhouseCoopers.

As a parallel strategic move, IBM heavily invested in software, especially focusing on middleware products and even embracing the brand-new open source development movement.

4.5.2 IBM AS AN EXAMPLE OF AN EXCELLENT TRANSFORMATION CAPABILITY

IBM is oftentimes considered as THE example of continuous transformation excellence. This can be attributed to the transformation-savvy structure, culture and behavior that emerged during recent decades and still evolve today.

We conducted an assessment using the Transformation Capability Maturity Model for IBM based on accessible company data. Figure 4.1 summarizes this assessment which revealed that all knowledge areas are rated as excellent except the ones where we did not find enough background information.

TRANSFORMATION CAPABILITY AT IBM

TRANSFOR-MATION	DIRECTION			ENABLEMENT				
META	STRATEGY	VALUE	RISK	PROCESSES	IT	CHANGE	TRAINING	PROGRAM
Culture	Vision and Goals	Value Identification	Risk Identification	Governance	Information & Analytics	Change Impact Analysis	Training Need Analysis	Framework
Leadership	Business Model	Value Realization Planning	Risk Management Planning	Methods & Tools	Business Applications	Change Management Planning	Curriculum Development	Organization
Values	Execution	Value Realization	Risk Mitigation	Process Optimization	Communication Technology	Change Management Execution	Training Execution	Execution

Information missing   Scale   Initial   Reactive   Defined   Managed   Excellence

Figure 4.1 **Results of the maturity assessment for Transformation Capability at IBM**

Meta Management

At IBM transformations are not managed somewhere and somehow, but instead the transformation management unit reports directly to the CEO. Its current (2014) head, Linda Sanford, is a senior vice president (Center for CIO Leadership, n.d.). From her point of view, strong governance models need to be established in order to overcome silo structures, however, establishing such structures sometimes requires trial and error. IBM is aware that such structures need to be changed from time to time and no transformation leader should be afraid to conduct this change (Sanford, 2010).

In addition, IBM has noted that leaders who are keen on transformation need to be available at all hierarchical levels. In particular, the company has used social networking skills in order to leverage the transformation strategy all over the world-wide business ecosystem. Leadership principles have been established that include thinking in terms of systems and patterns, the ability to handle uncertainty with optimism, openness to different cultures, meaningful collaboration, and a spirit of restless reinvention (Sanford, 2010).

Technology is used to manage the transformations: IBM is running one of the largest private cloud environments in the world. It is mostly used to run manifold analytics that consolidate information from nearly one hundred different information warehouses and data stores, providing IBM teams with analytics that rapidly deliver solutions to clients. Because of the cloud environment, the company expects to realize tens of millions in savings over five years. IBM aimed to have 80 percent of its internal development test activities supported by the cloud by 2010. Optimized IT also delivers substantial cost savings that can be reinvested to further the transformation process. So far, IBM's transformation efforts have been funded in part by the more than $1 billion in IT savings that were gained over the past four years (IBM, 2012).

Strategy Management

IBM has managed to establish goals and visions of transformation and was able to rebuild its internal structure or change its business model (for example, from hardware sales to services and software). Currently the company aims at progressing in markets like Shanghai that grow much faster than traditional markets (Sanford, 2010).

In addition, the company has understood that moving into the future is not only about understanding what needs to be added and invented, but also in which areas they need to divest. Businesses that no longer fit the strategy are discontinued, like the sale of the ThinkPad business to Lenovo. The company claims that without doing so it would be larger – but at the same time less client-oriented and less productive. On the invention side, the company fosters organic investments and growth by acquisitions in higher value segments such as business analytics and cloud computing (IBM, 2012).

In order to be a customer-centric company, IBM has large parts of its workforce directly working at customer sites. Thus, the workforce is highly mobile. Mobility solutions are therefore also supporting IBM's transformation efforts. The company addresses these different needs by providing internal app stores and the possibility to integrate employees' own devices in the corporate infrastructure (Sávio, 2012).

In summary, the strategy focuses on providing a good client experience and this goal is key to all transformation initiatives in the company. The transformation is grounded in the strategy – it is not something done off to the side (Center for CIO Leadership, n.d.).

Value Management

As far as investor relations allow, IBM is measuring the success of its business model and the corresponding benefits over the long term, not in any individual quarter or year. The company's strategies, investments, and actions are all taken with the objective of optimizing long-term performance. The financial benefits of the transformation initiatives are reinvested in initiatives that foster higher growth or higher margins, such as business analytics and cloud computing in addition to improving profitability (IBM, 2012).

By integrating major functions, the quality and efficiency of processes have been improved. The recent economic crisis could be successfully managed. In summary, IBM achieved more than $8 billion in productivity improvements during recent years. This has contributed to earnings-per-share gains (Center for CIO Leadership, n.d.).

Risk Management

IBM has established an enterprise risk management that involves all stakeholders in the company, all the way up to senior management teams. Risk management is seen as an indicator of good corporate governance. Thus, IBM established strategic decisions with an explicit consideration of underlying risks. Part of the enterprise risk management is also to take advantage of experiences that occurr elsewhere in the company. In consequence, risk is not managed in silos (for example, country by country), but holistically. This was achieved by creating a structured risk management methodology and by integrating risk management into all processes (Mattathil, 2011).

Business Process Management

IBM manages and optimizes its processes continuously. As many processes as possible are centralized, for example, IT, human resources, finance, supply chain, marketing and communications, real estate, legal and sales operations. The company has realized $4.2 billion in spending reductions through shared services (Sanford, 2010). The strategic goal was to become a globally integrated company by implementing a consistent set of processes and standards world-wide in order to reduce inefficiencies and to improve collaboration. The company fully standardized its major processes and was able to introduce a new operating model with global resource centers of excellence where they made most sense from a business point of view. This included a shift of resources towards building client relationships and employee skills while positioning the company for new market opportunities (IBM, 2012). In order to realize this goal, technology needed to be used in such a way as to have the information flow seamlessly all over the world (Center for CIO Leadership, n.d.).

One of the principles behind optimizing the processes is radical simplification. For example, the 'opportunity to order' process took much too long from the sales peoples' point of view. The company simplified and optimized the process in order to save about five hours for each seller. During these simplification efforts, it was important to simplify from the view of the user – not from the view of the process owner (Sanford, 2010).

Transformational IT Management

As an IT company, IBM is using technology everywhere. Therefore, the CIO and her team are critical to the company. They are considered agents of change and a well-managed technology landscape is considered to be a big business enabler. It is considered critical that the CIO actively cooperates with other C-level members in order to keep the transformation running. IBM does not just consider its CIO responsible for keeping the data center running. The best CIOs are recognized as business experts as well as technology experts (Center for CIO Leadership, n.d.).

IT architecture-wise, IBM is integrating its business applications horizontally all over the world. The goal is integration across the whole enterprise on a common platform – the SAP Business Suite. This has already allowed IBM to get rid of 900 legacy applications and create major cost savings accordingly (Center for CIO Leadership, n.d.). Apart from that, IBM has simplified and standardized further applications, which in total lead to a downsizing from 15,000 to 4,500 applications – a further reduction by 800 is planned (Center for CIO Leadership, n.d.).

Organizational Change Management

IBM has understood that employees need to be convinced to join the transformation journey. In some situations this is easy: Back in the early 1990s, when IBM was fighting for survival, everyone understood that fast transformation was necessary if the company was to be saved. But even when times are good, the best companies continue to reinvent themselves. This is because IT technology, capabilities and requirements as well as market dynamics are always changing. A famous quote at IBM is 'change is part of IBM's DNA.' According to the company, businesses today are not in a position to choose the technologies they will embrace or ignore. The choice is simple: get on board or get run over (Center for CIO Leadership, n.d.).

In order to create employee buy-in to transformation, different actions can be taken. IBM conducted world-wide online meetings, called 'jams', across the entire company on questions like what are IBM's most basic values. The event took three days, but it was able to bring an impetus to the company that still lasts today. These 'jams' continue to be conducted in transformations and used in order to develop new ideas (Sanford, 2010).

In terms of human resource management, IBM was an early adapter of diversity principles and practices. The company added sexual orientation to its non-discrimination practices in 1984, created executive diversity task forces in 1995, and offered domestic partner benefits to its employees in 1996. The company is often listed among the best places for employees, employees of color, and women to work (Wikipedia, 2013).

Competence and Training Management

Managing training needs and skills is considered very important in the company. Due to the mode of transformation, IBM needs to remix and deepen its expertise constantly. For example, the strategy of focusing on analytics was underlined by hiring more than 8,100 experts with skills in that area (IBM, 2012).

Social media has been used at IBM for a long time. When social media began it was discussed for some time whether using social media at work should be allowed for IBM employees. Finally, the decision was clearly taken that social media should be allowed in order to have people trained in its usage. Back in 2006, the company invited its employees to help write the guidelines for blogging. By collaborating on those guidelines and creating what is called the Digital IBMer, the company demonstrated commitment to sharing expertise with clients and helping them create positive outcomes (Center for CIO Leadership n.d.). This helps IBM to stay in contact with all relevant stakeholders during the transformation effort.

Program and Project Management

IBM changed into a process and project oriented organization more than 15 years ago. It introduced one common standard based on the PMBOK (PMI, 2008) in order to standardize and simplify communications, tools, formats and techniques and to not reinvent things over and over. Furthermore, qualified project managers are assigned to all projects and project performance is measured. Project managers are embedded in a project management community that includes mentoring, teaching and the exchange of best practices (IBM, 2011).

The amount of data in an organization like IBM is gigantic – it is big data. In order to make appropriate decisions in a transformation and utilize the data for project management, it needs to be analyzed comparably fast, so that it can be used effectively. In order to become a smarter enterprise, IBM acknowledged that they need to figure out how to turn the information into insight – in order to take faster and smarter decisions (IBM, 2012).

For example, IBM uses technology for staffing transformation-related projects by matching job profiles of the open position with non-structured data from job postings and résumés. This enables the company to avoid under-utilized personnel and provide better client value faster. The measure of unassigned resources has dropped from 8 percent to 3 percent since this system was put in place. The productivity measured by billable utilization has improved by 18 percent. In addition, the analytical tool set is used for external perspectives on the transformation. For example, math experts from the research section are working on analytical processes to better understand and leverage the market environment (IBM, 2012). In addition, IBM used analytics to optimize the grouping of customers and sales areas and thus to sharpen the goal of the transformation (Mattathil, 2011).

4.6 Conclusions

The Transformation Capability is somewhat special since it both requires all other capabilities to succeed – and is also needed by these others to succeed. Thus, the importance of the capability depends on the context of the digitalization. Are there immediate business needs or, rather, long-term opportunities? Is there a sense of urgency, and a Transformation Capability needs to be established rapidly, or is the capability already sufficiently mature?

In order to build the Transformation Capability companies need to change their structure and incentive systems. The IBM case illustrated that a company that learns to gear all its benefits and incentive systems towards transformation learns how to successfully use this difficult but important capability. Here, the establishment of centers of excellence for transformation and the positioning of transformation at the top of the company hierarchy are key to success. While the broad inclusion of stakeholders into transformation is always difficult, current technologies help to deal these with challenges: big data in order to learn about the affected customers, cloud technology to govern risks, mobility and social media to communicate and collect immediate feedback.

But is this appropriate for every stakeholder? Very likely it is not. Thus, transformation managers need to consider the different stakeholder groups in different ways. For instance, this can be done by addressing different age groups in a different manner. It seems to be a good idea to have social media in place, but also being able to communicate the core of the transformation via more traditional media.

The transformation teams themselves should leverage diversity. Younger employees who want to learn and start their careers should be joined by experienced employees across various disciplinary backgrounds. The infamous business vs. IT conflict should be avoided by any means. Mixed teams are also very important in order to communicate the transformation needs across the entire company and to spread the sense of urgency for the transformation.

The presented Digital Capability Framework and in particular the Transformation Capability Maturity Model provide a holistic assessment and a starting point for identifying gaps in a company's Transformation Capability. It helps to plan a development path for the capability and is thus a major part of the overall move towards a digitalized company.

References

Alba, D. (2012) Top 10 Gamification Apps | Motivate Yourself and Your Workers. http://blog.laptopmag.com/top-10-gamification-apps, last accessed 15 October 2013.

Baba, M.L. and Rouse, W.B. (2006) Enterprise transformation. *Communications of the ACM*, 49(7), p. 66.

Basole, R. (2005) Transforming enterprises through mobile applications: a multi-phase framework. *AMCIS*. pp. 1935–1939.

Bhambhri, A. (2012) How to use big data to transform your company – SmartPlanet. http://www.smartplanet.com/blog/smarter-ideas-insights/how-to-use-big-data-to-transform-your-company/, last accessed 15 October 2013.

Böhm, M. et al. (2011) Cloud Computing – Outsourcing 2.0 or a new Business Model for IT Provisioning? In *Application Management*, edited by F. Keuper, C. Oecking and A. Degenhardt. Wiesbaden: Gabler, pp. 31–56.

Center for CIO Leadership, IBM Senior Vice President Linda Sanford Describes the Company's Transformation of Systems, Products and Processes | Center for CIO Leadership. http://centerforcioleadership.com/?p=400, last accessed 7 July 2014.

David, E. 7 Agency Secrets to Powerful Social Media Marketing Campaigns. http://www.adherecreative.com/blog/bid/152032/7-, last accessed 16 October 2013.

Dixon, S.E.A., Meyer, K.E. and Day, M. (2010) Stages of Organizational Transformation in Transition Economies: A Dynamic Capabilities Approach. *Journal of Management Studies*, 47(3), pp. 416–436.

Elliot, S. (2011) Transdisciplinary Perspectives on Environmental Sustainability: A Resource Base and Framework for IT-enabled Business Transformation. *MIS Quarterly*, 35(1), pp. 197–236.

IBM (2012) *Annual Report*, Armonk, New York.

IBM (2011) *IBM: Keys to Building a Successful Enterprise Project Management Office*, Armonk, New York.

Keller, S. and Price, C. (2011) *Beyond Performance: How Great Organizations Build Ultimate Competitive Advantage*, Hoboken, NJ: John Wiley and Sons.

Kotter, J.P. (1995) Why Transformation Efforts Fail. *Harvard Business Review*, pp. 59–67.

Labusch, N. (2011) Cloud Computing – Governing Uncertainty in Distributed Electronic Business Networks. In *ERCIS Working Paper No. 11 – Network e-Volution*. Münster: European Research Center for Information Systems, pp. 91–111.

Labusch, N. et al. (2013) The Architects' Perspective on Enterprise Transformation: An Explorative Study. In *Practice-driven driven Research on Enterprise Transformation (PRET-6)*, edited by F. Harmsen and H.A. Proper. Utrecht: Springer, pp. 106–124.

Lahrmann, G. et al. (2012) Management of Large-Scale Transformation Programs: State of the Practice and Future Potential. In *Trends in Enterprise Architecture Research and Practice Driven Research on Enterprise Transformation*, edited by S. Aier, M. Ekstedt, F. Matthes, E. Proper and J.L. Sanz. Barcelona: Springer, pp. 253–267.

Mattathil, G. (2011) *IBM's Transformation Journey: Enabling growth, productivity, and culture change*, Available at: http://de.slideshare.net/gmattathil/ibms-transformation-journey, last accessed 9 July 2014.

PMI (2008) *A Guide to the Project Management Body of Knowledge (PMBOK® Guide)*, Newtown Square, PA: Project Management Institute.

Romanelli, E. and Tushman, M.L. (1994) Organizational Transformation as Punctuated Equilibrium: An Empirical Test. *Academy of Management Journal*, 37(5), pp. 1141–1166.

Rouse, W.B. (2005) Enterprises as systems: Essential challenges and approaches to transformation. *Systems Engineering*, 8(2), pp. 138–150.

Rouse, W.B. (2006) Introduction and Overview. In *Enterprise Transformation*. Hoboken, N.J: John Wiley and Sons, Inc., pp. 1–16.

Sanford, L. (2010) *The Road to a Smarter Enterprise: IBM's transformation journey*, http://www.ibm.com/smarterplanet/global/files/se_sv_se_products_the_ road_to_a_smarter_enterprise_.pdf, last accessed 6 July 2014.

Sávio, M. (2012) Enterprise Architecture Governance for an Enterprise Transformation Journey: The IBM Internal Case. São Paulo: The Open Group. http://de.slideshare.net/msavio/enterprise-architecture-governance-for-an-enterprise-transformation-journey-the-ibm-internal-case, last accessed 6 July 2014.

Stiles, P. and Uhl, A. (2012) Meta Management – Connecting the Parts of Business Transformation. *360 Degrees – The Business Transformation Journal*, (3), pp. 24–29.

Uhl, A. (2012) Introduction. In *A Handbook of Business Transformation Management Methodology*, edited by A. Uhl and L.A. Gollenia. Farnham: Gower Publishing Ltd., pp. 1–7.

Ward, J. and Uhl, A. (2012) Success and Failure in Transformation – Lessons from 13 Case Studies. *360 Degrees – The Business Transformation Journal*, (3), pp. 30–37.

Wikipedia (2013) The History of IBM. http://en.wikipedia.org/wiki/History_ of_IBM last accessed 1 November 2013.

Winter, R. et al. (2013) Enterprise Architecture and Transformation: The Differences and the Synergy Potential of Enterprise Architecture and Business Transformation Management. In *Business Transformation Essentials: Case Studies and Articles*. Farnham: Gower Publishing Ltd, pp. 219–231.

Youseff, L., Butrico, M. and Da Silva, D. (2008) Toward a Unified Ontology of Cloud Computing. *2008 Grid Computing Environments Workshop*.

Chapter 5

IT Excellence

NILS LABUSCH, ROBERT WINTER AND AXEL UHL

5.1 Introduction

Managing information technology (IT) is a key differentiator in times of ongoing digital transformations. Business transformations are doomed to fail if corresponding IT transformations are not managed appropriately, whereas excellence in IT management might create huge markets and transformation success potentials can be leveraged.

IT Excellence is seen as one of the three Digital Transformation Enablers (alongside Innovation and Transformation Capability) in the Digital Capability Framework. These enablers represent underlying capabilities which have to reach a certain level before it makes sense to tackle the Digital Transformation. Moreover, the Digital Transformation Enablers are prerequisites for reaching higher maturity levels in other digital capabilities such as: Customer Centricity, Effective Knowledge Worker, and Operational Excellence.

In order to leverage IT Excellence the deliberate management of modern technologies like cloud, social media, big data or mobility solutions is a major differentiator. In order to be able to cope with these technologies, IT departments need to acquire new skills, need to monitor new threads and need to be aware of a faster pace of change in Digital Enterprises.

Therefore, we illustrate the challenges that IT management is facing and show the influence of IT management on corporate performance. We further discuss the most important technology trends and their effects on IT management. We go on by introducing the IT Excellence Maturity Model – a comprehensive model for the assessment of a company's IT Excellence in the context of digital transformation. We further illustrate IT Excellence with a best-practice lighthouse case from the financial industry.

Objectives of this chapter:

1.   Illustrate the challenges for IT management in the context of digital transformation.
2.   Discuss how new technologies pertain to these challenges.
3.   Present the IT Excellence Maturity Model that allows companies to assess and improve their IT Excellence maturity for digital transformation.
4.   Demonstrate by a case study how mature companies manage IT in an excellent way.

5.2 Status quo

5.2.1 DEFINITION – WHAT IS IT EXCELLENCE?

In many companies today, IT can be considered to be the 'shop floor of the enterprise' since many products are already very information prone (for example, insurance products or bundles of machines and services) or become so because of an increase in service orientation of the firm, however, this service orientation also affects IT function or the respective outsourcing provider. While IT expectations were often focused on costs and availability, now IT is expected not only to be cheap and highly available, but also to act as an innovator for the business. This means that IT managers on the one hand need to be able to develop a higher maturity level for mission critical IT components – but on the other hand always need to be monitoring the environment for new and upcoming IT innovations and their business potentials.

Thus, the IT Excellence capability of the Digital Capability Framework is concerned with an IT function that is able to provide excellent IT solutions to the company and to support other Digital Capabilities. Such an IT function might be realized completely in the form of an internal IT unit, or by outsourcing certain functions.

The company's IT function needs to deal with environmental changes such as data in the cloud, smart homes, smart cities and even smarter customers and users. IT management needs to understand when new technologies are mature enough to be applied and needs to understand when 'first mover' risks have sufficiently decreased to leverage new technologies. In addition, managers need to be able to 'look beyond their home turf', and to see relations to the other important capabilities of a Digital Enterprise.

Excellence, according to the Oxford Dictionaries means 'the quality of being outstanding or extremely good.' Thus, the IT Excellence capability of a company not only describes keeping the IT landscape up and running ('run IT'), but also being outstanding in keeping IT services aligned with business needs and business plans ('change IT'). In terms of the Digital Capability Framework, IT Excellence is the usage of new technologies (like mobile connectivity, cloud computing, big data and social media) to enhance 'business technology' and, as a consequence, the business. This includes, but is not limited to, real-time insights into important company data, stability, agility, security and dynamic plug-and-play functionality.

While the 'visible' portion of IT Excellence is often related to new and fancy technologies and gadgets, another crucial component is the 'invisible' portion that deals with, for example, the security concerns and data protection issues that eventuate.

5.2.2 TODAY'S CASE FOR ACTION

Today IT plays an important role in almost every company. Far beyond productivity enhancement, IT controls the most important parts of companies' value chains, however, IT complexity is always growing and imposing management challenges. Flyvbjerg and Budzier (2011) state that on average IT projects have cost overruns of about 27 percent. While this figure is not promising, there is a far more alarming one: there are a disproportionate number of projects that have a cost overrun of 200 percent, on average, and a schedule overrun of almost 70 percent. These 'black swans' are the true threat.

In day-to-day IT operations further issues occur. Whenever statements like 'we in IT know best what is good for the user' are heard, there is imminent danger that exactly the opposite is true. Instead, an excellent IT unit communicates with users, considers their demands and comes up with solutions that can compete with market prices. In addition, IT units need to be respond very quickly – otherwise, users will just build up their own IT, without checking back with the IT unit, without any chance of synergies and without appropriate risk management. Therefore, IT Excellence is user-centric and needs to always think from the perspective of the user of technology.

In order to stay ahead of the competition, IT management needs to address some current challenges in addition to the general ones: These include, but are not limited to Shadow IT, security, technical complexity, staffing and, as always, business–IT alignment.

Bring Your Own Device: IT in the Shadows

For more and more companies it is becoming normal to use platforms and tools that some people consider 'private fun' for leveraging their business. Examples include Skype communication or document sharing within a research team, advertising events on Facebook or LinkedIn, or networking activities with partners. All of this is actually the 'new normal' for many modern jobs and not 'nerd stuff' any more.

However, this needs to be understood by corporate IT management. It is no longer possible to prevent employees using websites or services that they deem useful to increase their productivity. While it might be possible to block certain websites or prevent software installation by employees, the influence of the IT unit ends when the employees use their own smartphone in order to connect with business partners via Facebook.

Security

Utilization of user-owned devices raises major security issues, however, managing the security of the IT landscape goes beyond BYOD. According to Brown and Yarberry (2008) employees are considered a greater risk than hackers. Employees and long-term contractors do not need to break into a company since they are already insiders. The most important risks are computer intrusion, theft of intellectual property, credit card fraud, online extortion and internet fraud, identity theft and money laundering (Brown and Yarberry, 2008).

Technical Complexity

Most organizations use IT platforms and services that have been developed over long periods, acquired through acquisitions or complicated by many waves of vendor consolidation. For these companies, moving forward requires an almost archaeological effort to unearth, understand, and work with all these layers of sedimentary business technology. This journey will go on and IT units need to continue to cope with these issues (Gruman, 2007).

Staffing

It is becoming more and more difficult to attract skilled staff. According to Brown and Yarberry (Brown and Yarberry, 2008), with lowering birth-rates, the exodus of senior, skilled professionals will hit the industry. These people especially need to be retained as long as possible in order to keep expertise about legacy systems in the company.

However, young talent also needs to be attracted into the company. In former times high salaries might have been sufficient, but a recent study (Kane, 2013) reveals that the current generation, called generation Y, has very different work-place expectations. People born in the 1980s are considered to be tech-savvy and thus are used to current technology in their day-to-day activities. They like to trade a few billable hours in order to allow for a better work-life balance; more time to spend on hobbies and/or with friends and family. Generation Y is also quite high attention-craving: feedback and guidance from the employer is expected and this worker generation is not afraid of questioning authority.

Thus, companies need to come up with new flexibility in the design of IT jobs. Organizations need to increase part-time work and flexible project assignments in order to provide work models that are attractive for employees as they reach potential retirement age. They also need to offer similar options to the younger employees. Furthermore, they need to allow their employees to develop themselves. A well-known example is Google, who provide their employees with the opportunity to invest part of their work-time in whatever project they want to.

Business–IT Alignment

Although this topic has driven researchers and practitioners for many years it has not lost its relevance. Chan and Reich (2007) review the literature of the past three decades and distil the most relevant challenges for attaining alignment. First, the problem of common understanding is prevalent – IT does not understand the business and vice versa. In other cases, the business strategy is not known (in worst cases not even by senior management) or formulated in a manner that does not allow for adoption. Alignment therefore is almost impossible. Further, if people in the company do not consider alignment an important issue, this of course is a strong barrier. Some businesses managers do not believe that IT has a strong impact on the company's success and thus do not actively support the process of alignment. Interestingly, the status of the IT and the extent to which it is embedded in the corporate culture are alignment challenges. Fearful managers, in particular, seem not to consider IT as a benign force in the company. Finally, Business–IT alignment is not a (desired) state, but rather a process that needs to cope with the incremental as much as the fundamental changes that permanently shape the enterprise.

5.2.3 THE EVOLUTION OF IT EXCELLENCE MANAGEMENT

There is lots of related work on corporate IT management. During recent decades many frameworks or maturity models have been presented. Many have disappeared, but some can be seen as well established and mature.

The Control Objectives for Information and related Technology (COBIT) (Lankhorst, 2012) provide a standard for IT governance. The framework is particularly based on the provision of 'good practices' that support implementing an IT governance structure throughout the enterprise. The COBIT framework provides guidance for 34 identified IT management processes that are grouped into domains; planning and organization, acquisition and implementation, delivery and support as much as monitoring. Furthermore, COBIT provides critical success factors for achieving optimal control over IT processes, key goal indicators (does the IT process meet the business requirements?) and key performance indicators (how well does the IT process perform concerning its goals?).

The IT Infrastructure Library (ITIL) (Lankhorst, 2012) is a widely adopted reference process framework for IT delivery and support. ITIL is considered to be the de facto standard for IT service management world-wide. It contains a series of documents that provide guidance about the establishment of good IT processes. In addition, ITIL provides guidance on how to measure the quality of the IT service provision in terms of quality. Compared to other frameworks such as COBIT, ITIL is operationally oriented and the (control) guidance provided by COBIT might be implemented by ITIL reference processes.

In addition many highly mature IT departments apply enterprise architecture (EA) techniques like those provided by The Open Group Architecture Framework (TOGAF) (Josey, 2011). While EA is usually concerned with wider topics than IT, it provides a solid foundation for a goal oriented understanding of the organization and IT support potentials. For that purpose, TOGAF provides four types of architecture: Business Architecture defines the business strategy, governance, organization, and key business processes; Data Architecture describes the structure of the organization's logical and physical data assets and data management resources; Application Architecture provides a blueprint for the individual applications to be deployed, their interactions, and their relationships to the core business processes of the organization; finally, Technology Architecture describes the logical software and hardware capabilities that are required to support the deployment of business, data, and application services. These architectures can be constructed and maintained by applying the provided architecture development method. Depending on the purpose, different architectures might be established and institutionalized to an appropriate extent within an organization.

5.2.4 IT EXCELLENCE IMPACT ON FIRM PERFORMANCE

Recent studies indicate that IT Excellence not only influences the costs of the company but, even more, has a significant impact on the firm's performance. Masli et al. (2011) conducted a study where the link between a superior IT capability and firm performance is shown. The winners from 1988 to 2007 of the CIO 100 Award (provided by the CIO Magazine) were analyzed. The authors take different firm performance measures (for example, Return on Assets, Return on Sales or Tobin's Q) and identify whether firm performance is related to winning the CIO 100 Award. This was often the case, however, the study also shows that although around the turn of the millennium it was appropriate to conduct one or two innovative projects in order to stay ahead of the competition, this changed later on. While Carr (2003) controversially argued that IT does not matter any longer and should be managed instead like a commodity, Masli et al. (2011) state that firms need to permanently innovate in order to stay ahead of the competition. Samson et al. (2013) present similar results by stating that seven out of ten award winners outperformed the Dow Jones Industrial Average. Therefore, depending on how it is positioned in the company, IT Excellence as a capability is able to leverage the company's business performance.

5.3 Today's and Tomorrow's Technologies from an IT Perspective

In this section we illustrate the major technology trends; mobility, cloud computing, social media and big data guided by the COBIT categories planning and organization, acquisition and implementation, delivery and support, and monitoring. The new technologies offer huge business opportunities. Although they create huge challenges, IT units can develop into innovation drivers and provide business leaders with their knowledge (see Table 5.1).

Table 5.1   Modern technologies in the context of IT Excellence

	Mobility	Social Media	Cloud	Big Data
Planning and Organization	• Device and Operating System Management • Application Architecture and Lifecycle Management	Social Media Integration User Credential Management	• Rapid technology adaption • Vendor Relations	• Big Data Architecture
Acquisition and Implementation	• App Development • User Interface	• New platforms • Bandwidth issues	• Application Migration • Application Integration	• Big Data Integration • Management of unstructured data
Delivery and Support	• Organizational Skills • Role business vs. IT	• Role business vs. IT	• Service Quality • Organizational Skills • Role business vs. IT	• Organizational Skills • Role business vs. IT
Monitoring	• Data security • Device security	• Fraud detection	• Availability • Data security	• Data Governance • Log File Analysis

5.3.1 PLANNING AND ORGANIZATION

Mobility

Planning and keeping the application landscape under control is an important challenge in this regard. While in the past, IT departments could decide which mobile phone solution should be used in the company, nowadays different models need to be handled at the same time. Thus the lifecycle management needs to be ensured even with different smart phone operating systems (for example, iOS and Android) at the same time. The roll-out management is even worse when considering the manifold versions of a phone operating system that are used within one company. Specialized tools exist in order to coordinate those processes, however, companies need to realize that the tools are needed.

The policies to acquire new software need to be adjusted in a similar way. The support of different devices and platforms creates architectural issues: the consolidations of application landscapes that drove IT departments during the last few decades are becoming messy. The software zoo returns – but now it's mobile. This, of course, is the worst case scenario which occurs if the development of new mobile applications is not conducted thoroughly. A solution for this issue is a segmentation of the manifold application into pace layers. Pace layering means distinguishing applications in layers like systems of record, systems of differentiation and systems of innovation (Genovese, 2012) and defining architectures and standards for each of these levels. The differences are clear – while a contract management system in an insurance company would be located in the record level, mobile apps belong to the innovation layer. Between the different layers solid integration technology is necessary.

Cloud

Until recently, the cloud was THE hot topic in IT management. Everything and everyone 'went cloud'. Today the cloud is still alive, but has grown up. The cloud's unavoidable challenges are manifold, but its potentials are still considered to be significant.

When it comes to planning IT resources, the cloud is a perfect buffer to deal with uncertainties (subsequent section based on Labusch (2011)). Often it is difficult to forecast the detailed technical design requirements for a new product or service that the business entails; with cloud computing, users can very quickly change to other technologies and adopt these (Böhm, Leimeister, Riedl, and Krcmar, 2011). Cloud customers can also dry-run new technologies very quickly (Anding, 2010), however, finding the necessary technology in the cloud market is a problem – vendor independent platforms that collect different cloud services and provide an overview for prospective customers could solve this problem (for example, cloudbook.net).

While this is the positive side of the cloud, negative aspects also occur. The cloud hinders planning and designing of the IT landscape whenever business departments buy (mostly web-based) services via the cloud – without asking the IT unit. Especially in connection with increased mobility, cloud services became very famous – but cloud companies often do not focus on their users' data security, legal or compliance issues.

For the IT unit, the cloud means losing direct control of resources and software, for example, website infrastructure and operations staff for when they decide to do cloud computing (Motahari-Nezhad, Stephenson and Singhal, 2009). This can cause problems in relation to regulations such as the Sarbanes Oxley Act, which are harder to comply with within the cloud

(Rittinghouse and Ransome, 2009). In particular, whenever companies have to prove their compliance with auditors, some rethinking is necessary because data is not stored statically in one place any longer, but fluidly between multiple servers (Rittinghouse and Ransome, 2009). Many companies already prohibit their collaborators from saving data in the cloud (as part of non-disclosure agreements) or strictly forbid their employees using services such as Dropbox.

When planning cloud operations, the IT department needs to keep in mind lock-in effects with vendors. Even when services are in the cloud, they can be very specific in terms of interfaces and operations, so that a high risk occurs of becoming overly dependent on one vendor, however, by sticking to standards, companies can avoid becoming too vendor dependent. In addition, the problem is becoming less and less important, at least for virtualization, because vendors are interested in allowing their customers to easily move from a competitor to the own company. For example, all major server virtualization companies like VMware, OpenStack or Amazon (Germain, 2013) provide migration tools. When it comes to software-as-a-service, for example, Salesforce.com, the lock-in is more dangerous. In consequence, standardized interfaces should be used whenever possible that allow access to different cloud providers. Further, a hybrid strategy should be chosen where mission-critical applications are run in the internal, private cloud of the company while non-mission critical ones are hosted outside (Germain, 2013).

Social Media

Social media can be seen from two points of view. From an internal perspective, employees are using social media in order to communicate with each other or with customers. From an external perspective, customers use social media in order to communicate with the company or about the company. It is the IT unit's responsibility to enable the company to process and use this data (external perspective) and protect the company from associated threats (internal perspective).

From the IT point of view, implementation and hosting of social media platforms is not the challenge. Standard open source blog systems, chat rooms, etc. are available and can be rolled out on webservers of the company. The challenge is, rather, in harvesting social media data where customers talk about a company. Much planning is necessary in order to achieve this task – companies need to identify the appropriate interfaces (for example, what is the best way to receive data from Facebook?) in order to make use of the data. After that, it needs to be specified how and for what purpose the data will be used, and which regulations might prevent the usage.

Whenever publicly available social media platforms are supposed to be integrated, in enterprise applications the challenge for the IT department becomes huge. More and more applications and web services exist that allow for monitoring and consolidating social media platforms for a professional purpose (for example, hootsuite.com or buffer.com) (Zeevi, 2013), however, these are rather marketing oriented. Solid IT integration is very difficult at the moment starting with harmonizing and managing corporate accounts and passwords for enterprise pages for example, on Facebook. While Facebook offers to use its account name in order to log in to other websites, integration in the other direction (for example, using the corporate mail address as login credentials to Facebook and automatically getting access to the company's resources like a fan page or support group) does not work.

Big Data

With regard to *planning*, big data imposes huge efforts compared to traditional databases. To begin with, staff are required who are able to cope with new technologies such as HANA or Hadoop. Such experts are currently hard to acquire since the technology is quite new. A way to solve this could be offering staff the opportunity of 'playing around' with technology and providing training.

In addition, the data models need to be appropriate. According to Kanaracus (2011) the performance of big data differs greatly depending on the underlying data model. Thus, the conceptual foundation is a very important aspect and needs to be considered in detail.

An important question is about the sources of the data. Collecting much more data than before is at the core of Big Data. For the IT organization this means heavily increasing its knowledge of data integration topics. While in the past, different enterprise IT systems needed to be integrated (and that already is a very difficult task), in a Digital Enterprise many external data sources need to be integrated. The best example is social media. Companies can learn a lot about their customers by involving social media. Integrating those data is difficult due to the manifold interfaces and the unwillingness of social media providers to share all data with the companies (Being able to analyze data for advertisements is their bread-and-butter business, thus they are not willing to give it away).

5.3.2 ACQUISITION AND IMPLEMENTATION

Mobility

Implementation of mobile applications fosters increasing efforts. Currently not many frameworks exist that allow programming for all mobile devices (and the respective operating systems) at the same time (exceptions include Adobe AIR, Unity and Codename One). Instead, different apps need to be developed for Apple systems (IOS), Google systems (Android), Microsoft systems (Windows), etc. While in the past one application was developed that had to run on a single platform (for example, Windows PC) currently many different platforms need to be maintained. This forces developers to strictly stick to programming paradigms like encapsulation or differentiation of data, calculation and presentation. Only companies that are able to manage their development accordingly will be able to cope with today's mobility challenges.

In addition, all of these platforms pose different requirements concerning the look and feel of the apps. A user who is used to the iOS style still wants it for business applications (for example a sales support app). Therefore, programmers are needed who are not only able to implement great algorithms but are also keen on aesthetic aspects. How to find such people? One possible way is screening the app stores for well-designed free (or cheap) apps that are offered by single programmers, and trying to employ them (for example on a project basis). Another way, of course, is motivating and training the existing staff in coping with the new challenges.

Cloud

Compared to outsourcing, the major advantage of cloud services is the price model: Only what is used needs to be paid for. Thus, capital expenditures are replaced by operational expenditures – a true advantage of the cloud. Still, IT units need to be aware of which type of data is processed in which type of cloud. The most well-known are public cloud services like Dropbox, Google Drive, SalesForce, iCloud, etc. The problem is that nobody knows where the data is stored and who has access. After the revelation of, for example, the NSA's more-or-less unlimited access to Google, careful review is needed of which documents can be stored in such clouds, however, with less important documents use of the public cloud is still an option, and convenience and user experience might rate higher than security issues.

Many IT organizations are rather negative about cloud services, however, sometimes these services follow stronger regulations concerning data security than the IT organizations' own data centers. Furthermore, decision makers tend to mix up services that are offered by the cloud providers for private persons (for example, Google Mail) and those for business users. The regulations and procedures followed often differ a lot (for example, concerning the use of stored data or mail for advertisement purposes). One should also not forget that one's own data centers are not proof against data abuse or loss – lists with tax data of clients of Swiss banks were not leaked at an external provider: The leak happened in their own data center. In addition, it might be easier to convince users to avoid storing certain very important documents in the cloud instead of completely forbidding its use. The alternative for companies is to provide internal, private clouds – for example by enabling a data center to provide internal pricing and scalability based on cloud principles.

Nevertheless, often IT units are no longer asked whether certain data should be stored in the cloud or not – it just happens. The decision nowadays is often taken where the budgets are located –usually the business units. In other words, how many SalesForce contracts were initiated by the IT unit? – probably not many. In order be involved in such decisions, the role of the IT department needs to change. A department that only has good arguments for why certain things should *not* be done will be irrelevant sooner or later. An IT department that provides good ideas or even more secure (but also convenient) alternatives for cloud services that the business wants to introduce may even increase its own importance.

Taking the decision on which applications should be sourced to the cloud can have different impacts depending on how the cloud service will be used. The virtualization of a physical server with the native applications running on it can be easy, if it is already a standard system. Sourcing a whole host-based application landscape would require fundamental reengineering, however, traditional enterprise application development is not dead. Instead, the range is extended by integrating cloud elements in these applications. Thus developers need to have a much broader skillset in order to integrate these elements (Beckley, 2013).

Social Media

IT departments need to be able to identify and integrate new social media platforms very quickly. While systems like Outlook or Lotus Notes have been used for decades, social media platforms might become unpopular very fast.

For example, a couple of years ago, MySpace was a famous and well-used platform; today, nobody talks about it, instead, everyone is on Facebook. In fact, so many people are on Facebook that some have already decided to shift to other platforms like Instagram (especially young people who are afraid of being stalked by their parents). Thus, the IT department needs to foresee these trends and needs to be able to react to sudden shifts in user behavior.

Depending on how such platforms are shaped, they might require considerable amounts of bandwidth in the corporate networks. A good example is the well-known messaging tool Skype. This tool is the horror of IT units since it makes its way through almost every network – not caring about the thoroughly planned network routings the company has made. This means, the entire traffic for this application might move through a very narrow connection somewhere at the end of the world, while not being monitored by the network administrators. If a tool such as Skype is not controllable, the IT department should be able to provide alternatives that are perceived by the users as appropriate and simple. Just prohibiting such applications is no longer sufficient.

Big Data

When implementing big data technologies in the company, it is important that current corporate standards and architectural principles are observed. Big data technologies do not affect only one layer in current IT management approaches. It is not just about installing a new database, but instead specific hardware is needed (much more memory than before), and specific platforms, etc. are needed, In addition, IT management needs to (re)design the integration of multiple data sources. While traditional standardized sources (for example, EDI documents) are comparably easy to include, completely new and vendor dependent standards are very difficult. IT management needs to adjust the architectures in such a way that they are flexible enough to connect with (for example) smart watches or other devices of the internet of things that might be necessities for businesses within a couple of years.

Part of this data integration discussion is the ability to process unstructured data. Big data means being able to process unstructured data in order to offer new services. Take Siri, the voice detection in Apple phones that is able to answer questions (Lohr, 2012). It is a good example of machine learning based on big data since it takes the many questions that are submitted daily by millions of users in order to increase its answer space. Many business-related data could be analyzed in addition, like Twitter feeds or sales data, however, in order to integrate these, and to be able to interpret the data in the right manner, the company needs to have knowledge on the technical as much as the statistical side. If the latter is not available, false conclusions may be drawn based on the data harvested (Lohr, 2012).

5.3.3 DELIVERY AND SUPPORT

Mobility

Things are also changing with respect to mobility delivery and support. Helpdesks so far have employed mostly technology specialists, but with mobile devices the support staff should also be innovative and user centric. While the past motto of many support staff was: 'we give the user what we think he needs and at the same time reduce our work load' the motto today should be 'the user needs to trust in our competence in order to follow our recommendations that also reduce our workload.' In the mobile world, installing an app is very easy and conducted very rapidly – so why should the user install the specific app that the IT department wishes him to? Of course, technical barriers could be implemented, but surely trust would be a better option?

The role of IT is also changing since more and more employees will be forced to bring their own devices to work (instead of being provided with devices by the company) (Kaneshige, 2013). For the IT departments this means losing control over their infrastructure, however, it becomes even more important to develop strategies that take into account the inability to plan certain developments that are imposed by the manifold devices.

Cloud

During delivery and support, managers need to consider the specific nature of cloud services (section below based on Labusch, 2011). Since there is no explicit negotiation of the contract, the customer (manager) has to accept the provider's general contract in order to use the service. The problem is, that the customer is in a weak position to rate the quality of the service if he has never used that service before (Jøsang, Ismail and Boyd, 2007). Additionally, the cloud platform itself might be updated faster than the software that is implemented based on it. Thus, more updates are needed than are usually planned for (Rittinghouse and Ransome, 2009) which requires higher support efforts. Support staff need to be very capable of understanding how the various cloud services work.

Thus, the skills of employees need to change when cloud solutions are introduced. It is no longer possible to go to someone in the IT department and ask for a quick fix or a solution for a problem. Instead, some external provider needs to be addressed and it becomes much harder to determine who is responsible for solving the problem. This needs to be guided by service level agreements and guidelines. In addition, the skillset of IT employees as well as other employees in the company needs to change in order to be able to set up contracts and to communicate problems in a manner that is understandable for outside (cloud) providers.

The general relationship concerning the support changes. Business innovation and technology innovation are more tightly coupled in a Digital Enterprise than ever before. Thus, 'support' means being involved in the development of new products services and not just in purchasing new equipment. Thus the IT leadership personnel needs to be able to think in terms of business strategy much more than waiting for direction from other executive levels (Beckley, 2013).

Social Media

Social media is perceived as an area that IT departments are responsible for (Krigsman, 2014). This provides the chance for the IT departments to communicate the necessity to the business side. Clever IT departments thus have already today started to communicate the utility of social media to their business peers.

In addition, IT managers can sell themselves to the business as knowledgeable and information savvy. While, especially in traditional companies, many line managers might have no experience with social media, the IT units can offer to be partners in developing guidelines for social media employee training. In addition, when a 24/7 presence in social networks is expected, support is needed that is able to fulfil these requirements.

Big Data

From a delivery and support perspective, again highly qualified staff are needed. In particular, since big data technologies are (compared to traditional relational database systems) less mature, more patches and updates need to be managed (Kanaracus, 2011). At the same time the support staff as the connecting point to the (internal) customer need to be very sensitive concerning the new business opportunities that big data can create. Thus, the IT department has at this point the opportunity to become a true innovator for the business.

This also includes the ability for IT to extend its task from 'saving money' to 'making money'. While an important focus for IT leaders is to reduce costs by automation here and there, being able to apply big data analytics means that direct contributions to the business can be made. The first important step in this regard is to analyze who the most important sponsors are that could be supported by the big data solutions – and in which regards. Marketing could be addressed by tasks like customer insights or segmentation, management by budgeting or forecasting. Furthermore, supply chain management could be supported as much as customer service, pricing and product strategies (Hollis, 2012).

5.3.4 MONITORING

Mobility

While in the past mobility was mostly limited to providing a mobile phone and a laptop at home, today's smartphones and tablets change the situation in different ways. Users are accustomed to having full control over their devices and being able to download all sorts of apps. These apps, however, impose challenges for IT management. Usually apps have access to the users' phones contacts and are used to exchange messages with others. Thus, external parties might access information via employees' communications. Even worse, these external parties might not apply the same security standards that apply for internal IT. For example, the very famous WhatsApp messenger (which is used to send more than 17 billion messages a day (Fröhlich, 2013)) has already suffered from a few serious security flaws.

What happens for example, if a phone is lost or stolen? This issue needs to be recognized as soon as possible by the IT department. The company needs to be able to delete the critical data on the phone remotely in order to protect its data. The good news is that vendors recognized the problem and all smartphones are supposed to have the functionality of a 'kill switch' by mid-2015 at the latest (Gross, 2014), however, having the functionality is not enough – the IT department needs to be able to use it. For this purpose, special solutions for mobile device management and the appropriate internal processes will help.

Even when the worst case does not occur, data security on the device still needs to be assured. This begins with providing employees with clear guidelines on how to use the mobile device and how to protect data. Such guidelines need to be simple and easy to remember, and include, what data can be shown to people outside the company and which not. In addition, data should be classified in order to simplify dealing with the guidelines. Last but not least, of course, security software should be installed and updated on a regularly basis (Viswanathan, n.d.).

Cloud

Monitoring the cloud is more difficult than monitoring private systems. On the one hand, due to server farms located in different destinations, the availability of the cloud in general is high. On the other hand, even the cloud can go offline. For example, when the Amazon cloud service went offline for 25 minutes nobody knew why (Whittaker, 2013) – something that would not happen in traditional data centers – and should not happen, when critical data is located in the cloud.

Furthermore, problems can occur when cloud services are hosted in other countries or regions. For example, an insurance company located in Europe has problems hosting its customer contracts in the US. These issues need to be analyzed, and solutions (such as tagging data with metadata that provides guidance in which countries it may be stored) need to be identified.

Social Media

Monitoring social media activities is important in order to determine if corporate data security standards are adhered to, or if the activities pose any danger to the company.

However, monitoring is difficult right now since social media providers do not allow direct access to their platforms. In consequence, it is more appropriate to change the behavior of employees and train them on the security settings that social media platforms offer, even for their private accounts. In order to give guidance to employees, a social media policy should be in place.[1]

Big Data

Big data initiatives need to be monitored: On the one hand performance needs to be constantly monitored in order to identify optimization potentials; on the other hand, the quality of the created results needs to be checked on a regular basis in order to avoid incorrect results being provided to the business.

---

1   Examples from large companies can be accessed at http://socialmediagovernance.com/policies/.

In order to ensure the appropriate monitoring and overall management of big data and connecting to business departments in an appropriate manner, the role of a Chief Data Officer (CDO) should be established. According to Lee et al. (2014) leading organizations have established this role in order to leverage their big data initiatives. The authors describe three dimensions that determine how the role of the CDO could be designed in a particular organization depending on the demands. In the first dimension companies need to decide how the role is positioned concerning inward and outward collaboration – should the focus be on internal stakeholders or rather on customers and partners in the value chain?). Second, the data space – should the role focus on traditional or rather on big data? Third, the value impact dimension – should the role focus take a service-oriented or strategic focus? From our perception, a CDO in a Digital Enterprise should be a strategic role that focuses on big data issues concerning internal and external collaboration.

Big data is not only a technology that needs to be monitored, but also one that could be used to monitor other IT systems in order to detect fraud. In particular, log file analysis is a topic that has gained attention. Whenever strange patterns occur in the data, alerts can be created very quickly and the IT unit can take action against the security issue.

5.4 The IT Excellence Maturity Model

With respect to IT Excellence the overall goal is to enable competitive advantage while reducing operational cost and risk. In order to cope with the associated challenges the IT Excellence Maturity Model was developed. The maturity assessment of a company's IT Excellence is guided by the general BTM² approach which holistically considers nine relevant management disciplines: Meta Management, Strategy, Value, Risk, Processes, Transformational IT, Organizational Change, Competence and Training as much as Program and Project Management (for detailed description see Chapter 2). In Table 5.2 the maturity model for IT Excellence is illustrated by comparing level 1 (initial state) with level 5 (excellence).

Table 5.2   Outline of the IT Excellence Maturity Model (contrast between a low vs. high maturity level)

Discipline	Level 1 – Initial	Level 5 – Excellence
Meta Management	• IT seen as not business critical • IT is regarded as a 'necessary evil' that needs to be kept as cheap as possible • Leaders are not aware of the impact of IT and are not skilled accordingly	• IT capability is valued throughout the company and is seen as a major business enabler • The company uses new technologies early on, tests technologies, is an early adopter • IT leaders are tightly integrated into the top management decision processes
Strategy Management	• IT is always reactive and without clear IT strategy • IT use is not planned and no business–IT alignment takes place	• Strategic roadmap for IT Excellence for the whole company and the business network in place • Business model is based on having a mature IT Excellence capability • IT is holistically planned and a sophisticated as well as holistic IT portfolio planning is established • The value network is included in providing feedback and insights about the strategy execution
Value Management	• IT related initiatives are not being evaluated • Conflicting benefits that never become explicit and hinder the company	• Responsibilities are clearly defined and measures are in place that allow for controlling the planning of value realization • Value realization of IT is considered to be of strategic importance and is executed across the entire company
Risk Management	• IT related risks are ignored because of unplanned and reactive IT implementations • Risk planning and mitigation is done on a case-by-case basis, or not done at all • IT Excellence initiatives are hit very frequently by major risks	• Strategic risk identification for IT Excellence is a KPI for the entire ecosystem (partner, supplier and/or customer) • IT-related risks are a topic in the top-management teams • Mitigation strategies are explicitly defined on a strategic level as much as on an operational level • Risk related to data protection, data security or a lack of appropriate skills are covered by senior management
Business Process Management	• No excellence *Governance* standards are defined concerning the management of IT • No documentation of as-is and to-be processes • Lack of process automation and process benchmarking	• Simple, streamlined and measurable IT and business process standards that are applied across its entire ecosystem • Mechanisms are in place that allow for a continuous business process innovation activities in all areas • Processes are regularly assessed, benchmarked and improved over the entire value chain

Discipline	Level I – Initial	Level 5 – Excellence
Transformational IT Management	• KPI and analytic requirements are not driven for IT Excellence • Data quality is unreliable to improve IT Excellence • No management decisions based on analyzed data for IT Excellence • Multiple silo applications • No application lifecycle management in place • No usage of new technologies (like mobile connectivity, cloud computing, big data or social media) • Security is unreliable	• Continuous updates and improvements of KPIs, analytics, data quality and standards • Flexible analysis of un- and semi-structured data • Managed, robust and flexible application architecture • Application lifecycle management processes and tools are optimized to use industry best practices • Continuous consideration of new technologies • Security is an integrated IT Excellence practice
Organizational Change Management	• No change impact analysis for IT Excellence • No attitudes of different stakeholder (groups) and possible interventions defined • No effective communication activities (to create positive attitudes and to increase acceptance levels) for IT Excellence defined • No change management activities executed or they are conducted in an ad-hoc fashion and not much is learned from the experience	• Measured and controlled (with KPIs) change need and impact for IT Excellence • Measured and controlled (with KPIs) stakeholder management and interventions for IT Excellence • Communication across the entire ecosystem for IT Excellence activities • Change execution is professionalized (e.g. by having supporting roles in place) and conflicts are actively managed and solved
Competence and Training Management	• No consideration of training needs associated with IT management • No knowledge management for IT Excellence in place • Lack of standard training curriculum developed and used • No explicit trainings for IT Excellence defined and conducted • No evaluation metric for IT Excellence trainings defined	• Professional training programs developed for the different stakeholder groups • Training covers the whole company perspective and business units are involved in the development process • Knowledge management is measured and controlled for IT Excellence. It is part of employees' individual objectives • Training evaluation includes transfer of knowledge to the workplace
Program and Project Management	• No appropriate project organization established • No dedicated staff that is responsible for the project management	• Applying a professional project management framework for the IT functions to manage IT projects • IT Excellence initiatives are integrated within the company and multi-project management is set up in order to manage priorities

To sum up, the there are some key aspects of IT Excellence which are addressed in the presented maturity model that need to be taken into account if a company sets off on the Digital Transformation journey:

- IT departments need to go beyond the maintenance and operation of traditional infrastructure and application environments. They have to deal with innovative technologies and fundamental changes in the digital world.
- IT managers have to deal with the question of who is responsible for the digital technologies, their costs, their integration and their smooth functioning.
- CIOs must govern a dynamic, resilient, responsive and available IT operation that is secure, compliant and cost-effective.

Companies that are making the effort to reach higher maturity levels in IT Excellence need to consider it as a continuous process and constant innovation. They take advantage of the next new thing in order to reach greater efficiencies and capabilities, however, they do it with deliberation and in close alignment with the business. Strategy, governance processes, performance management, benchmarking, data security and data protection, knowledge management and professional competence management are crucial for successful IT Management. This maturity model provides integrated guidance for CIOs on how to tackle IT Excellence as an enabler for becoming a Digital Enterprise. In the next section we present a case study in order to illustrate the model.

5.5 Case Study Finanz Informatik

5.5.1 INTRODUCTION

Finanz Informatik (FI) is a lighthouse in IT Excellence due to long-term experience in the market, a history of mergers, and transformational experience. This experience is reflected by clear principles such as, having a well-defined architecture aside from a business development vision. FI has been able to combine continuous service extensions with permanent efficiency gains. To achieve this position, the merger of various IT-Organizations within the groupings of the German savings banks was necessary. Otherwise, costs for the development of a modern core banking system would have exceeded the benefits.

Although FI is one of the biggest IT-players in Europe, the company is fairly unknown to the public. FI and affiliates provide IT services for 417 savings banks, eight regional state banks and numerous other banks with more than 245,000 users. FI runs the largest IT operations in the German banking sector.

FINANZ INFORMATIK—COMPANY FIGURES 2013	
Revenue (in mill. €)	1.511
with saving banks	974
with state banks	261
Employees (full-time equivalents)	4.992

CUSTOMERS	
Saving banks	417
State banks + Deka Bank	9
State home loan banks	10
Accumulated balance sheet of supported saving banks (in bill. €)	1.064

Sources DSGV (12/31/2013); German Federal Bank; Others
All figures refer to FI and its subsidiaries.

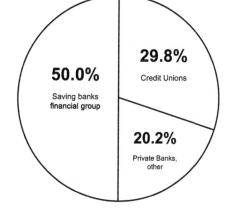

Figure 5.1   Finanz Informatik serves a large part of the German retail banking market

Thus, FI is an ideal case from which to learn how IT Excellence can be achieved: On the one hand, they conducted a large number of mergers and on the other hand, they consolidated the IT platform. With the first merger in 1995 the decision was taken as to which of the six existing core banking IT platforms should be used after the merger. Right from the beginning a best-of-six-worlds solution was excluded from discussions because of the many failures of this approach in other companies. Instead, 'one system' was considered to be the new default. Features that were solely included in the competing systems have been implemented as a 'plus' in this new default system, which was named 'One System plus' or 'OSPlus' from that time. The project to migrate all of the saving banks to 'OSPlus' was one of the largest and most complex IT projects in Europe – and it was finished in time and on budget!

5.5.2 FINANZ INFORMATIK (FI) – A HISTORY OF MERGERS

In order to understand how FI could became a lighthouse in IT Excellence, the history of the company needs to be explained briefly.

FI was founded in 2008 from the merger of two IT-organizations (Finanz-IT and Sparkassen Informatik) within the group of German savings banks and regional state banks: This was the final step of many earlier mergers of local IT organizations.

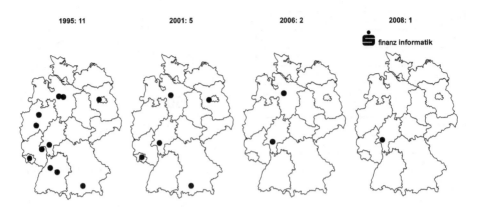

Figure 5.2   Consolidation process

To assure cost efficiency, security and the ability to leverage new technologies, the multitude of IT service providers in the group needed to be consolidated. Due to the federated structure of the public savings and loan banks, this decision could not be taken by a central board, but instead needed to evolve over time – which means that each and every single bank needed to be convinced to merge its own IT service provider with Finanz-IT or Sparkassen Informatik and thus, finally, with FI. This could only be achieved by having one good argument in its favour: being excellent in IT.

FI merged over 13 years from what was formerly 11 companies into one in 2008, and conducted a major journey of mergers along that road (see Figure 5.2). Today the company's head office is located in Frankfurt, Germany. The company and its subsidiaries have more than 4,900 employees and a sales volume of 1,511 million Euros (in 2013). FI is responsible for servicing 125 million accounts. Each year 98 billion transactions are handled. The company is owned by its customers (thus, the banks) – which, as a consequence, leads to a business model that is more focused on cost reduction than on creating new business. Therefore a strategy was applied that focused on realizing synergies, but still being able to improve the existing technology infrastructure. The strategy was balanced in a way that the merger cross-subsidized the development costs of the new technology platform (see Figure 5.3).

FI provides a full range of IT services, including the development and implementation of individual IT solutions, networks and technical infrastructure, as well as data processing centers, consulting, training and support. With the highly efficient 'OSPlus' core banking solution, FI is offering one of the leading IT systems in the German retail banking sector.

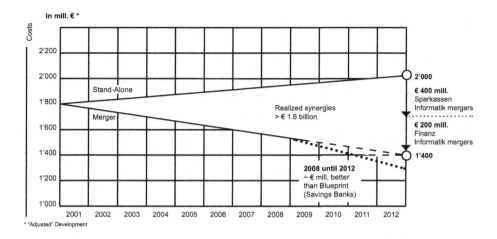

Figure 5.3   Realized synergies

5.5.3 A HIGHLY MATURE PLAYER IN IT EXCELLENCE

We conducted the assessment below with FI, based on the interviews and available material using the IT Excellence Maturity Model. The result (Figure 5.4) shows that the company is truly IT excellent and that the Digital Maturity Assessment is valuable.

IT EXCELLENCE AT FINANZ INFORMATIK								
IT EXCELLENCE	**DIRECTION**			**ENABLEMENT**				
META	**STRATEGY**	**VALUE**	**RISK**	**PROCESSES**	**IT**	**CHANGE**	**TRAINING**	**PROGRAM**
Culture	Vision and Goals	Value Identification	Risk Identification	Governance	Information & Analytics	Change Impact Analysis	Training Need Analysis	Framework
Leadership	Business Model	Value Realization Planning	Risk Management Planning	Methods & Tools	Business Applications	Change Management Planning	Curriculum Development	Organization
Values	Execution	Value Realization	Risk Mitigation	Process Optimization	Communication Technology	Change Management Execution	Training Execution	Execution

Scale   Initial   Reactive   Defined   Managed   Excellence

Figure 5.4   Results of the maturity assessment for IT Excellence at Finanz Informatik

Meta Management

IT Excellence at FI is considered to be part of ongoing leadership, value and culture discussions. To leverage IT Excellence, the company developed a codex that deals with this specific aspect. Managers and senior personnel within the company need to know the codex, and have to be able to break it down into actions for their specific area of responsibility and subordinate employees. The codex contains guidance, for example, on how to lead, and how to communicate with employees and customers.

Strategy Management

Surprisingly, FI's business model does not aim to create profits. Why? FI is owned exclusively by its customers, which means that profits are losses on their side. The company is driven to be as cost efficient as possible, while maintaining an appropriate IT service level. This situation is similar to large internal IT units. The difference, however, is that such internal units report to one CIO rather than to 400+ owners. So, to gain IT Excellence, diplomatic competencies and communication skills are developed by executive training and temporarily hiring specifically-skilled staff.

As well as reducing costs, the business model further includes being an innovator for the banks to allow them to create and sell new and innovative end-products with the OSPlus System. However, innovativeness and agility are not as important in the banking sector as might be the case in other industries – security and stability are more vital. This part of the overall strategy is broken down to the IT strategy. Consequently, to gain IT Excellence, the company first needed a clear business strategy as a foundation. In the second step, the IT strategy was derived to make the overall strategy more tangible and understandable.

Value Management

Benefits are controlled, and the goal is to work with optimal structures, optimal technologies and optimal strategies. This needs to be measured and the measurements need to be perpetually reviewed. The priorities are the following:

1. Security
2. Availability
3. Cost Effectiveness

We can see that an IT service provider in an environment such as financial services cannot concentrate only on cost effectiveness (as is often claimed in different areas). Benefits are comprised of other important factors, in this case security and availability.

The priorities also changed depending on the overall situation of the company. While developing IT Excellence, adherence to schedules was very important. While it still is important, priorities have changed in the phase of running the business (compared to changing, transforming the business).

Risk Management

The banking sector is characterized by many regulations concerning risk management. In consequence, dealing with risks has a long tradition at FI. In the past, the banks that own the company, and at the same time are its customers, mostly ran their own IT infrastructures. Via the wide area network they connected to FI to use all the applications that FI provided. However, most of the management and service tasks concerning workplace IT were handled at the customer's side – customers were running 'fat' clients. Nowadays terminal servers are in place and the customer banks run 'thin' clients that connect to FI. As a consequence, all applications run in FI's private cloud and maintenance efforts were purposefully shifted to FI. While one key advantage is scale effects concerning costs, in addition many risks that come along with operating a decentralized IT infrastructure could be concentrated at FI. This concentration of the operations provided the foundation to introduce an efficient and effective Risk Management that mitigates risks and contributes to achieving the value goals of security and availability.

An additional concept to reduce operational risks is the group concept. Each customer bank is part of a group, based on the region it is located in. Each group is comprised of a similar number of bank accounts. Thus, groups contain fewer large banks or more small ones. The groups are assigned to resources like hardware platforms or virtual machines on a one-to-one basis. This ensures, for example, that failure of a hardware component does not affect all customer banks at the same time, but only one group.

Today, Risk Management is a well-established and regular process at FI, managed by a team that is responsible for driving the process and analyzing risks for the different departments. The departments by themselves (and of course their line managers) are responsible for the specific risks. The risks are regularly assessed and mitigation strategies are documented. This means that at least once a month employees from the risk department talk to the responsible risk owners. Risks are organizational as well as technical.

Business Process Management

Business Process Management is conducted by using defined and standardized process templates. These are even customizable for the customer banks if they believe that their processes need to be implemented individually. The customizations are directly related to FI's core banking systems via workflow engines. This concept positions FI as an excellent IT provider since the company is able to provide (semi)individual solutions to the customer frontend, but at the same time achieves industrialization of the backend. Internal process quality is measured by quality checks as well as market benchmarks.

Transformational IT Management

How does FI use IT for its own purposes? Sophisticated tools and processes for risk management are in place as well as communication tools, for example, for video sessions that are used to introduce new and innovative technologies. The company further introduced an internal social media platform the goal of which was to collect expertise and knowledge that before was redundantly created and hidden in the company. The social media approach helped to bridge different hierarchical levels and locations. The introduction of the platform fostered many discussions since some leaders did not want to allow everyone to know everything due to fear of losing influence. This problem was addressed by making it clear that the social media platform is meant to foster functional discussions, but that the existing leadership and governance structures are not expected to be affected.

During the mergers an electronic information platform called 'FIPlus' was established to communicate important aspects of the transformation process, and provide as much transparency as possible at every stage.

To stay ahead of competition and to leverage efficiency potentials, FI is actively conducting projects in all technology trends that are considered important. Internal rules and processes clearly define when new technology is ready to be used for production purposes.

To leverage these technologies in earlier stages, services based on new technology are often provided by subsidiaries where a faster and flexible development cycle is available, due to the smaller size of the company.

This approach allows, for example, for the timely integration of mobile technologies. Since FI recently developed the OSPlus core banking system that is based on modern service oriented principles and a well-designed architecture, such mobile requirements can be easily implemented. The sales personnel can directly see all relevant customer data on their iPads. This allows for much closer collaboration with the customer than having a laptop screen in between people – or even worse, a stationary PC. In addition, FI offers the technology to manage devices for its customer banks. This includes, in particular, meeting high security standards like data encryption, device deactivation and automatic security policy comparison.

Organizational Change Management

FI is aware of the necessity of organizational change management. For this reason, large-scale changes like the mergers are managed by an explicit project that involves many top level managers. For the endeavor to become IT excellent, this was very important. Top level executives attended a large number of events where employees were informed about changes concerning their positions, and the company's development path. Special 'round table' talks were established where 20 to 25 participants from different departments and from all hierarchical levels participated. These proceedings required considerable effort, however, they created useful discussions with employee representatives, and satisfactory arrangements were found and adopted. In addition, managers and team leaders were given 'master presentations' with the latest news about changes, and these could be used in local or function-based team meetings.

During the mergers, FI always tried to mix senior staff and lower level employees from the merging companies into new organizational units. This was necessary to avoid a strong unit 'taking over' the others, and to create a new integrated company. From FI's experience it was very important to set up and communicate the new company structure at a very early stage of the project. This helped to identify commonalities and to support the integration.

Competence and Training Management

Training is important in order to stay ahead of the competition. The company has plans for prospective candidates concerning important positions. The departments define the necessary skill profile and the HR department takes care of an appropriate announcement. Especially during the mergers where all employees were located in new organizational units, training and skills management was important. Whenever employees were moved to positions that required new skills, training was conducted. Introducing this thorough skills management process was an important step towards IT Excellence.

To increase the competence level in new technologies and to evaluate how far these could leverage the existing business, the company is conducting study tours: Employees visit large vendors like Microsoft or Cisco and attend presentations of prototypes. To build prototypes and get access to such innovations, a specific budget is allocated. Employees have strong relations with vendors, and are involved in networking activities with peers internally and externally. This has helped FI to adapt current technology trends.

A major issue in the area of training management is the increasing number of older employees. Heavy investments are made in education and FI concentrates on teaching modern technology use and programming, and thus provides reasons to stay with the company.

Program and Project Management

FI applies the market standard methods in program and project management, and integrates them within the company. All projects need to be managed according to these guidelines, and this also holds true for innovative technologies.

An example of the rigorous application of program and project management guidelines is a standardized process for big data introductions that includes a sequence of standardized steps: Analyzing potentials for a specific business area (for example, by conducting workshops, analyzing legal topics, analysis of application scenarios); evaluation and proof of concept (development of prototypes, structured result analysis, temporary provision of technical infrastructure); detailed conception (IT and business architecture integration, choice of hard- and software, determination of vendor model) and finally implementation (implementation, go live, training) (Totok, 2014).

To staff the projects appropriately, and to avoid unnecessary assignment of tasks to external partners, a special division – the 'Project and Service Pool' – was introduced. Employees with special skills and knowledge were not laid off during the mergers but instead, were encouraged to move to this division. Having the experts within the company enabled FI to keep their experience, and to utilize it in a quick and flexible manner in numerous projects. Whenever a project manager wants to include external service providers in a project, a request must first be made to the 'Project and Service Pool'. If experts are available that can provide the service internally at a reasonable cost, the task stays internal, and is not offered to an external provider. The internal pool of people has already saved the company more than 6 million euros by eliminating the need to contract personnel from external partners.

A Company That is Able to Leverage Modern Technology

FI has a high maturity in IT Excellence because it developed this skill during a history of mergers. Best practices were institutionalized, and used to convince new customers to merge their IT providers with FI.

Due to the specific banking environment that fosters security and stability rather than fancy and latest technology, the ability to decide quickly and clearly about the necessity of new technologies is an important skill. Internal rules and processes clearly define if and how new technology is ready to be used for production purposes by including all factors like market pressure, integration in existing processes, cost efforts, etc. Apart from these factors, the company also understands how important standardized process and project management structures, as much as efforts in organizational change management, are.

However, FI is still progressing and investing in its IT Excellence capability in order to stay ahead of the competition. The necessity is created by the customer banks whose business models were eroded by the low margins that currently can be earned in the finance market. Thus, further reducing costs, for example, by becoming even more independent from single vendors, is an important future goal for FI. This goal also needs to be considered whenever new technology is introduced.

5.6 Conclusions

From the case and discussions above we learn that an excellent IT capability is an important enabler of digital business models.

An important step in changing perception of the IT department is to run it as a profit center. In the Finanz Informatik case we can learn that an internal IT provider can be cheaper and better than an external one. In this case, internal departments freely choose FI as their prioritized provider.

Much depends on the skills of the personnel in the IT departments. Here it could be a good idea to exchange people from the business side with IT people and vice versa. This enables creating an understanding of business needs on the one side and IT barriers on the other. In addition, it creates relationships within the company and thus helps to prevent or solve problems very quickly.

In order to realize the value of an excellent IT department, qualitative and quantitative measurements should be in place. This can be seen in the FI case, where strong performance control was established since the founding of the company.

The Digital Capability Framework, and especially the maturity model for the IT Excellence capability allow for an assessment of the company's position concerning IT Excellence. It allows identification of gaps in the current IT organization and provides a foundation to develop a roadmap to fix those gaps.

Acknowledgement: We would like to thank our partners from Finanz Informatik for their cooperation. Website: www.fi.de.

References

Anding, M. (2010) 4 SaaS: A Love-Hate Relationship for Enterprise Software Vendors. In *Software-as-a-Service*, edited by A. Benlian, T. Hess and P. Buxmann. Wiesbaden: Gabler pp. 43–56.

Beckley, M. (2013) How the Cloud is Changing the Role of Technology Leaders. WIRED online. http://www.wired.com/2013/09/how-the-cloud-is-changing-the-role-of-technology-leaders/, last accessed 16 May 2014.

Böhm, M., Leimeister, S., Riedl, C. and Krcmar, H. (2011) Cloud Computing – Outsourcing 2.0 or a new Business Model for IT Provisioning? In *Application Management*, edited by F. Keuper, C. Oecking and A. Degenhardt. Wiesbaden: Gabler pp. 34–56.

Brown, E.J. and Yarberry, W.A. (2008) *The Effective CIO: How to Achieve Outstanding Success through Strategic Alignment, Financial Management, and IT Governance*. Boston, MA: Auerbach Publications.

Carr, N.G. (2003) IT doesn't matter. *Harvard Business Review*, 81(5), 41–49.

Chan, Y.E. and Reich, B.H. (2007) IT alignment: what have we learned? *Journal of Information Technology*, 22(4), 297–315.

Flyvbjerg, B. and Budzier, A. (2011) Why Your IT Project May Be Riskier Than You Think. *Harvard Business Review*, 89(9), 23–25.

Fröhlich, C. (2013) SMS-Ersatzdienst: Whatsapp plant auch für iPhones Abogebühren – Digital | STERN.DE. stern.de. http://www.stern.de/digital/online/sms-ersatzdienst-whatsapp-plant-auch-fuer-iphones-abogebuehren-1985496.html, last accessed 1 October 2013.

Genovese, Y. (2012) Accelerating Innovation by Adopting a Pace-Layered Application Strategy. Gartner. https://www.gartner.com/doc/1890915/accelerating-innovation-adopting-pacelayered-application, last accessed 9 May 2014.

Germain, J.M. (2013) How to Avoid Cloud Vendor Lock-In. http://www.linuxinsider.com/story/79417.html, last accessed 8 May 2014.

Gross, D. (2014) 'Kill switch' may be standard on US phones in 2015. CNN. http://edition.cnn.com/2014/04/16/tech/mobile/ctia-phone-kill-switch/, last accessed 16 May 2014.

Gruman, G. (2007) Strategies for Dealing With IT Complexity. CIO Magazine. http://www.cio.com/article/158356/Strategies_for_Dealing_With_IT_Complexity, last accessed 1 May 2013.

Hollis, C. (2012) The Role of the CIO in Big Data Analytics. Chuck's Blog. http://chucksblog.emc.com/chucks_blog/2012/06/the-role-of-the-cio-in-big-data-analytics.html, last accessed 16 May 2014.

Jøsang, A., Ismail, R. and Boyd, C. (2007) A survey of trust and reputation systems for online service provision. *Decision Support Systems*, 43(2), 618–644.

Josey, A. (2011) TOGAF Version 9.1 Enterprise Edition. The Open Group, 1–13.

Kanaracus, C. (2011) SAP's HANA is hot, but still in early days. http://www.networkworld.com/news/2011/091511-saps-hana-is-hot-but-250942.html, last accessed 1 October 2013.

Kane, S. (2013) Generation Y – Characteristics of Generation Y. http://legalcareers.about.com/od/practicetips/a/GenerationY.htm, last accessed 1 October 2013.

Kaneshige, T. (2013) Mobility Brings Changing Roles for CIOs, Workers and Businesses. cio.com. http://www.cio.com/article/739490/Mobility_Brings_Changing_Roles_for_CIOs_Workers_and_Businesses?page=1&taxonomyId=600007, last accessed 19 may 2014.

Krigsman, M. (2014) Enterprise social media: New battleground for CIO influence. ZDNet.com. http://www.zdnet.com/enterprise-social-media-new-battleground-for-cio-influence-7000027244/, last accessed 16 May 2014.

Labusch, N. (2011) Cloud Computing: Governing Uncertainty in Distributed Electronic Business Networks. In *ERCIS Working Paper No. 11 – Network e-Volution* (pp. 91–111). Münster: European Research Center for Information Systems.

Lankhorst, M. (2012) *Enterprise Architecture at Work: Modelling, Communication and Analysis*. Springer.

Lee, Y., Madnick, S., Wang, R., Wang, F. and Zhang, H. (2014) A Cubic Framework for the Chief Data Officer: Succeeding in a World of Big Data. *MIS Quarterly Executive*, 13(1), 1–13.

Lohr, S. (2012) The Age of Big Data. The New York Times. http://www.nytimes.com/2012/02/12/sunday-review/big-datas-impact-in-the-world.html?pagewanted=all&_r=0, last accessed 25 July 2014.

Masli, A., Sanchez, J.M., Richardson, V.J. and Smith, R.E. (2011) Returns to IT excellence: Evidence from financial performance around information technology excellence awards. *International Journal of Accounting Information Systems*.

Motahari-Nezhad, H., Stephenson, B. and Singhal, S. (2009) Outsourcing Business to Cloud Computing Services: Opportunities and Challenges. *IEEE Internet Computing, Special Issue on Cloud Computing*, 10, 1–18. http://www.hpl.hp.com/techreports/2009/HPL-2009–23. html, last accessed 9 July 2014.

Rittinghouse, J. and Ransome, J. (2009) *Cloud Computing: Implementation, Management, and Security*. Boca Raton, FA: CRC Press.

Samson, D. (2013) Do CIO 100 Organizations Outperform the Market? E-Leader Singapore. http://www.g-casa.com/conferences/singapore12/papers/Samson. pdf, last accessed 9 July 2014.

Totok, A. (2014) Big Data. *FI – TS Management Forum* 2014.

Viswanathan, P. What Strategies Should an Enterprise Adopt in Order to Ensure Data Protection? http://mobiledevices.about.com/od/ kindattentiondevelopers/f/What-Strategies-Should-An-Enterprise-Adopt-In-Order-To-Ensure-Data-Protection.htm, last accessed 16 May 2014.

Whittaker, Z. (2013) Amazon.com sites suffer 25 minute outage, cause unclear http://www.zdnet.com/amazon-com-sites-experiences-outage-aws-ec2-unaffected-7000019586/, last accessed 1 October 2013.

Zeevi, D. (2013) 10 Best Social Media Management Tools. http://dashburst.com/ best-social-media-management-tools/, last accessed 8 May 2014.

Chapter 6

Customer Centricity

AXEL UHL AND KIM MACGILLAVRY

6.1 Introduction

Customer Centricity is one of the six key capabilities of the Digital Capability Framework. The Customer Centricity capability plays an increasingly important role in mature markets where differentiation between products and services is relatively low. To avoid falling into the commodity trap companies need to distinguish themselves from other companies or face competing on price, which inevitably results in profitability being reduced. One way of doing this is to develop innovative and distinctive products, however, products can be copied and the competitive advantage can therefore be short lived. In addition to product and innovation excellence it is therefore important for companies to manage the customer experience.

In this chapter, we first outline the foundation of Customer Centricity and explain why IT is important as an enabling component. We also show how customer experience can be improved using the latest technology. We continue by introducing the Customer Centricity Maturity Model, which allows us to measure the maturity level of the Customer Centricity capability. Based on the customer lifecycle, we then discuss some major Digital Use Cases related to the capability. The chapter concludes by introducing the World Disney case study as a lighthouse example for a highly mature company in the area of Customer Centricity.

Objectives of this chapter:

1. Outline the foundation of Customer Centricity.
2. Explain the key components of the Customer Centricity Maturity Model.
3. Explain how Customer Centricity can be improved based on Digital Use Cases.
4. Describe the key characteristics of the lighthouse case Walt Disney.

6.2 Foundation of Customer Centricity

6.2.1 DEFINITION AND CLASSIFICATION

In an environment in which companies can no longer differentiate themselves from their competitors based on pure product characteristics, the relationship to the customer becomes extremely important. Successful companies consider Customer Centricity as a dominant philosophy to enhance the customer's value and ensure economic success. In this context, we define Customer Relationship Management (CRM) as a customer-oriented business strategy which tries to establish long-lasting relationships to profitable customers. It is supported by modern Information Technologies (IT) and holistically combines marketing, sales and service concepts (see Hippner and Wilder, 2011).

CRM differs from traditional, transactional marketing strategies by focusing on building and maintaining customer relationships worthy of loyalty. Basically, the customer is the central basis. In contrast, transactional marketing focuses primarily on promoting and selling products.

Table 6.1   Comparing traditional and customer centric marketing approaches

	Transactional Marketing	**Customer Relationship Management**
Goal	Immediate growth through customer acquisition	Long-term profitable growth by creating customer loyalty and preference
Target object	Selling products	Creating customer relationships
Timescale	Short term returns	Long term returns
Focus	Pre-sales	Entire customer relationship life-cycle
Sales approach	Transactional selling	Needs and solution-based selling
Communication	Broad-scale advertising and promotion, one-way communication	Multi-channel approach, two-way dialogue
Customer	Anonymous	Tailored to and targeted at specific customer segments
Typical markets	Developing markets and commoditized products and services	Mature markets and differentiated products and services

Transactional marketing dates back to an era of permanently increasing demand, as was the case in the 1950s–1970s or at the start of the 20th century in several Asian markets. In these market circumstances it is business critical to capitalize on the intrinsic growth by acquiring as many customer orders as quickly as possible. In this context delivering the right product at the right quality and price is more important for a company than having a long-lasting relationship with its customers based on a superior service experience. As a result transactional marketing is rather short term in nature. Marketing activities focus mainly on the pre-sales and sales phases. The tools used here are product advertising, promotion, and a strong sales team. Table 6.1 summarizes the key differences between transactional marketing and CRM.

CRM is not a sales and marketing discipline alone. Successful companies have adopted a customer centric business model that embeds the voice of the customer across the whole organization; from top management to the work floor, across all functions and countries.

Every customer goes through a number of steps, before, during and after purchasing a product or service. These steps are known as the customer lifecycle. According to the marketing analysts Sterne and Cutler (2000), this customer lifecycle consists of the five distinct steps: reach, acquisition, conversion, retention, and loyalty. In other words, the cycle starts by getting a potential customer's attention, explaining the portfolio to them, converting them into paying customers, and retaining them as loyal ones, who share their satisfaction about the product or service with other prospects (Rouse, 2007). If customers are lost, they still might be willing to renew the relationship in the future.

The lifecycle supports structuring the CRM activities and allows adjusting the marketing, sales and service strategies for each step. For example, potential customers need to be addressed differently in comparison to already existing customers or to lost ones.

From a Customer Centric point of view, we focus on the following four phases of the customer lifecycle: *Information, Offering, Purchasing,* and *After-Sales.*

One important facet along the customer lifecycle is the customer experience. Customer-centric enterprises ensure that all customer interactions are consistent across all touch points throughout the customer lifecycle.

One example is that customers do not want to describe their problem statements over and over again. If a customer calls a service hotline he or she is usually routed through different service personnel and has to explain the matter each time from the very beginning.

Creating a customer centric company takes time; it is an ongoing and continuous process of listening to the customer, learning and improving what you do (see Figure 6.1). To be successful the mindset of the people involved needs to change and everyone needs to integrate this way of thinking and doing into their daily work.

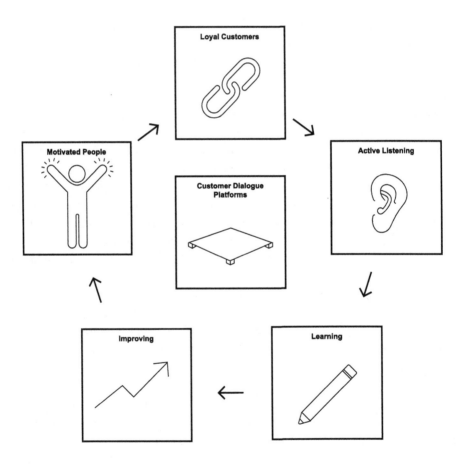

Figure 6.1   **Customer experience management is a way of doing business**

The Customer Centricity capability is, therefore, a management philosophy that involves fully aligning the company with existing and potential customer relationships, and which makes the customer the focus of all business considerations. The core principle is to increase the value of the company and of the customer by managing customers systematically (Rapp, 2002).

6.2.2 IT AS AN ENABLER FOR CUSTOMER CENTRICITY

IT plays an important role for all customer-centric processes. One part of CRM includes information systems that support all phases of the customer lifecycle. The principal benefits are efficient, paperless processes and workflows, central data storage, greater transparency and efficiency in all customer interactions, and a full customer history. Modern analysis tools also enable better customer segmentation and needs-based customer contacts and offerings, as well as improved after-sales service.

In general, we differentiate between three different types of CRM: communicative, operational, and analytical CRM. Communicative CRM encompasses the direct interface with the customer and the associated communication channels (e-mail, SMS, letter, call center etc.). Examples of operational CRM include processing information from analytical CRM, customer evaluations, customer segmentations, and campaign management. Analytical CRM involves, for example, analyzing customer and transaction data, extracting information from customer data, as well as data warehousing and data mining.

A special requirement for current customer centric processes is the on-site integration of all customer interactions, regardless of the type of communication, whether it is a conversation, phone call, fax, letter, e-mail, or social media ('multi-channel management'). The information from all interactions must be recorded to be able to guarantee the best possible service. Such interactions are also an important source of information for identifying customer needs and making appropriate offerings available.

As we mentioned at the beginning of this section, IT supports all phases of the customer lifecycle. In the *Information* phase, market analyses or needs analyses are carried out, or advertising campaigns or sales promotion measures are supported.

In the *Offering* phase CRM systems can help to customize the product or service, and they can support the quotation management process. Price calculations and financing offers are also part of the range of functions.

In the *Purchasing* phase order processing, payment processing, and delivery are among the range of functions, as well as, for example, the installation of a software product.

After-sales service is also supported by complaints management, customer service, customer care, and customer retention functions.

New technologies such as social media, big data, and mobility are becoming ever more important for CRM. From a Customer Centricity perspective, the rapidly increasing numbers of social media and mobility users result in greater reach of marketing measures, improved interaction possibilities, and larger volumes of data for customer segmentation. In turn, big data management allows larger data volumes to be analyzed in real time, which then enables customers to be targeted in the correct manner and companies to be in the right place at the right time with the right product in real time.

Mobile devices become the primary customer interface. The reasons for this are the extremely high level of penetration, the availability irrespective of location, the advanced technology, and the increasing capability of mobile devices to also communicate with machines, thereby becoming a universal device for controlling a wide range of applications.

Although, IT plays a dominant role in enhancing the Customer Centricity capability, we want to stress that Customer Centricity is not just a marketing approach but a complete business model that needs to drive decision making at all levels in an organization. In the next section, we summarize some of the major aspect in regards to customer experience.

6.2.3 ENHANCING THE CUSTOMER EXPERIENCE

Modern information and communication technologies play an increasingly important role in establishing and nurturing profitable customer relationships in the long term through holistic and differentiated marketing, sales, and service concepts (Bruhn, 2002). Ensuring a professional customer experience is one of the major focus areas to ensure a high Customer Centricity capability. Key considerations in this regard are:

Capturing the Voice of the Customer

Companies need to have large amounts of meaningful and accurate customer information so that they can better segment their own customer base, and provide a superior customer experience to everyone. Companies with a strong Customer Centricity capability use a variety of methods and applications that allow them to systematically capture the voice of the customer, and make this available quickly to the appropriate people in their organization. To do this well companies rely on sophisticated CRM tools that allow them to manage all phases of a customer lifecycle, from pre-sales through purchasing to post-sales.

Nowadays the customer journey starts well before a customer contacts a company for a product or service. Often the decision to do business with a company is largely made in the pre-contact phase. So, influencing the customers at a very early stage requires companies to engage with them much earlier than in the past, for example by leveraging social media.

Going Multi-Channel

Another trend is that customers seek a dialogue with companies through multiple access channels. Where telephone contact with a customer service department is still an important channel, some customers prefer to use e-mail, the web, personal contact or alternative means such as mobile devices. Increasingly customers use several access channels, often at the same time. This puts a strain on companies that need to ensure that the interaction is equally satisfying regardless of the channel used. An important complexity that needs to be managed is that all customer entry points need to be kept up-to-date with all the interactions a customer has had with a company, regardless of where and when they have taken place.

Speed is of the Essence

During the sales phase of a customer relationship, speed is of vital importance for modern customers. They expect their business to be valued by the companies they work with, and the pro-activity of a company to be able to respond to queries and complaints efficiently often determines their overall opinion. Failing here risks ruining the entire relationship that was built up to that point. To manage this phase well it is critically important that information is available and shared on a timely basis within the organization. Too often the front line of an organization is unable to manage the customer relationship properly because they are dependent on other parts of the organization, behind the front line, which tend to be more inward focused and slow to react.

Continuous Learning and Improving

Finally, when considering the last phase of the customer lifecycle, companies with a strong Customer Centric capability are very efficient at gathering post-transaction evaluations from customers. It is at this point that the customer will be able to tell a company how the entire, end-to-end journey was experienced and they are only then able to rate the experience in its entirety. Many techniques have been developed to capture the customer feedback. One of the most widely used methods is the Net Promoter Approach where customers are asked how likely they are to recommend your company to friends, colleagues and business partners (Reichheld and Markey, 2011). The outcome needs to be passed on quickly to the right people in the organization who can reach out quickly to the relevant customers and share the root causes with their teams and make improvements. Again, this and other similar techniques require tools and applications to manage the information efficiently.

In the next section, we introduce the Customer Centricity Maturity Model as part of the Digital Capability Framework.

6.3 Customer Centricity Maturity Model

Customer Centricity is a critical capability for an enterprise. Not only in consumer businesses which have developed strong brand marketing expertise, but across all industry types it is quickly becoming vital to have a highly customer centric organization that is able to continuously capture the voice of the customer and build it into their decision making processes across the whole company.

However, having a strong Customer Centricity capability is not just a question of the right technology. Customer Centricity must be considered as a holistic corporate philosophy. Corporate values, management, communication, strategy, processes, key figures, risk tools, IT, employee knowledge and know-how must be geared towards profitable customers to ensure that customers have the best possible experience.

In order to integrate a holistic view, the Customer Centricity Maturity Model is defined by the nine management disciplines of the BTM². Table 6.2 highlights the key characteristics of the maturity model by comparing the weakest level of Customer Centricity with the highest level.

Table 6.2   Outline of the Customer Centricity Maturity Model (contrast between a low vs. high maturity level)

Discipline	Level 1 – Initial	Level 5 – Excellence
Meta Management	• Focus on increasing turnover and market share • Focus on short-term goals • Good salesmanship • Extrinsic motivators • Sales incentives • Focus on operations and sales	• Focus on long-term relationship with profitable customers • Improve customer experience • Build trust with customers • Look for win/win situations • Focus on customer needs and manage change
Strategy Management	• New products and features • New marketing campaigns	• Long-term transformation plan to improve customer centricity • Focus on maximum customer value • Utilize capabilities of full ecosystem to develop new services, products, and solutions
Value Management	• Measure number of new customers and sales	• Measure satisfaction of profitable customers and increase share of wallet
Risk Management	• Focus on competitors and market forces	• Strategic risk assessment for profitable customers and ecosystems
Business Process Management	• Optimize sales processes • Processes fragmented with media breaks and local specifics	• Optimize all processes to maximize customer experience (including back office and non-customer-facing processes) • Defined, integrated, and standardized processes across all departments and entities • No media breaks and consistent quality levels • Process for new media included
Transformational IT Management	• Limited amount of data about customers available • Data quality is unreliable, inconsistent and hard to extract • No data used to improve Customer Centricity	• Continuous updates and improvements of KPIs and analytics for customer centricity • Continuous improvement of data quality and standards for Customer Centricity • Flexible analysis of un- and semi-structured data for Customer Centricity
Organizational Change Management	• Improve sales mentality • Increase willingness to spend	• Culture change towards customer centricity and utilization of new media
Competence and Training Management	• Sales training	• Leadership and behavioral training • Functional training where required to support job enrichment
Program and Project Management	• Customer centricity not considered as a program	• Strategic planning and main element of overall enterprise transformation plan

The Customer Centricity Maturity Model presented here is based on several fundamental assumptions. Customer Centricity maturity increases with the following:

- Increasing knowledge of customers;
- Standardization of the processes and services from a global perspective;
- Increasing integration/harmonization of systems;
- Use of new technologies such as mobility, big data, social networks or cloud solutions;
- Increasing significance of the customer experience and simplicity of working together with customers;
- Integration of the ecosystem.

The highest level of maturity – Level 5 Excellence – can only be achieved once there is a maximum degree of globalism, customer knowledge, process and system standardization, including the companies ecosystem, and use of new technologies.

Companies which perform excellently in Customer Centricity are following a systematic and holistic development process that lasts several years. The underlying maturity model provides important planning assistance because it recommends attainable mid-term goals for all important methodological disciplines.

6.4 Digital Use Cases for Customer Centricity

In order to increase the maturity for the Customer Centricity capability, the latest technology provides unknown opportunities for optimization. Table 6.3 summarizes several possibilities based on the four phases of the customer lifecycle: Information, Offering, Purchasing, and After-Sales. Based on these phases, we will outline several examples of use cases for mobility, cloud, SAP HANA, social networks, and 3D printing, which will be described in detail in the following sections.

6.4.1 DIGITAL USE CASES IN THE INFORMATION PHASE

Mobility

The wide prevalence of mobile devices enables more people to obtain information about products and services than ever before. Companies must prepare themselves for the fact that the mobile device will be the primary means of communication in the foreseeable future. This means that all product information and advertising measures should be distributed primarily via mobile devices.

Table 6.3   Digital Use Cases for different customer centricity phases

Customer Centricity Lifecycle	Mobile	Big Data	Social Media	Cloud
Information	• Access to information via a mobile device • Location-based information • Real-time price changes in the range • Living objects – active communication between products and the mobile device	• Collection and analysis of customer information from social media/Web • Analysis of unstructured data • Automatic reply to inquiries	• Leads from social media (friends) • C2C collaboration • Distribute information via social media channels • Customers share experience, rate products • Build communities to engage with and influence	• Use of the platform from cloud providers, such as social networks or market portals (eBay, Amazon, Apple, and so on) • Customer use of the platform • Push information
Offerings	• Location-based offerings • Personalized offerings • Real-time communication • Support via video conference	• Provide customer profiling • Check solvency of customers • Verify payment • Analyze risks	• Advertising and promotion of new products, services or features • Product documents • Discounts for social media groups	• Offerings via cloud partner
Purchase	• Payment with mobile device in store or on-line • Real-time information about delivery • Quality control of delivery • Elimination of distributers or coordinators	• Expert-finding • Installation guides	• Problem-solving • Payment via social media	• Distribution via cloud provider • Payment via cloud provider
After-sales	• Automatic answering of questions • Improve response time • Provide/obtain customer feedback	• Analyze data to provide solutions before the problem occurs • Monitor goods • Pro-active incidence management	• Collaboration with eco-partners • Provide answers to questions • Capture customer evaluations	• Service via cloud provider's ecosystem

Social Media

Social media are characterized by the fact that they are used to exchange vast amounts of sometimes very personal information. Preferences, interests, activities, and much more is posted, which enables completely new knowledge to be acquired about 'customers'.

Furthermore, the benefit of information on social media is that it does not have to be entered manually, for example, by call center employees or field staff. Usually, it is also available free of charge.

Another opportunity presented by social media is the ability to intensify customer relationships and acquire leads or potential new customers. Many companies establish their own communities in the social media and engage in in-depth conversations with their community members. Customers can ask questions, companies can publish their replies, and vice versa, and further 'friends' can be invited to the platform.

What makes this form of virtual relationship so special is its similarity to real-life social relationships between people. This also enables companies to become more 'human'.

Once the relationships have reached a certain level, social media enable the various parties to learn from one another. This learning takes place not only between companies and customers, but also includes communication between individual consumers. In other words, consumers on social media exchange information about specific topics. We find an interesting example of this in the field of healthcare. At 'PatientsLikeMe', patients can work together with and learn from physicians and other patients on an ad hoc basis.

This can result in new products and services, or the process can also be used to develop specific co-innovations between companies and customers.

Big Data

Whereas in the past it was rather difficult to use unstructured data such as that generally found in social media, big data technologies now provide the opportunity to analyze large data volumes in real time and to use them for the customer information process. The data can initially be used for customer analyses or customer segmentation. Multidimensional customer profiles can be created, which allow us to better understand the complexity of people than segmentations have previously enabled us to do. The present situation of a person can be represented in much more detail. It is the transition from 'what we think the customer wants based on past data' to 'knowing what the customer really wants' (see Figure 6.2).

The collective knowledge from social media can be used as a living reference work in matters relating to products, services, and so on. A new aspect will be the ability to answer questions in an individual context. In other words, for example, questions about 'flight details' will be answered specifically for the respective customer because historical customer data can be linked to the current question in real time. It will also be possible to ask further questions that are needed for the answer, such as 'Where do you wish to fly from?', 'Business or economy?', and 'Do you require a hotel?' In this way, intelligent digital service centers can be set up to enable a highly efficient information process.

6.4.2 DIGITAL USE CASES IN THE OFFERING PHASE

Mobility

Mobile devices also play a large part in the *Offering* phase. For example, customers can be located via a mobile device and they can be sent local offerings that are only valid in the nearest shop.

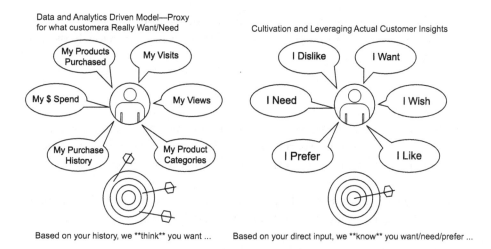

Figure 6.2   Know and understand the customer

Another possibility would be to send specific offers, such as discount vouchers, to customers' mobile devices as soon as they enter a shop. Customers can be identified via their mobile devices and they can be provided with offers that tie in with their preferences.

However, mobile technology also enables additional information about a product, such as who produced it and where, to be displayed on a mobile device. Products 'come alive' and communicate actively with the customer, which completely changes the consumer experience.

Shop prices can also be changed dynamically and in real time, for example, depending on the weather; umbrellas become more expensive when it rains, ice cream costs more when it is hot. In this way, pricing structures can be optimized and adjusted to current demand.

Big Data

Real-time availability of data enables the financial reliability of an existing or new customer to be verified in the *Offering* phase. To this end, search engines can compile structured and unstructured information from a variety of data sources such as social media, credit information, a personal CRM database, or CRM databases on cloud sales platforms, and real-time analyses can define a rating that results in additional discounts, markups, or certain modes of payment being rejected.

For internal risk management purposes, risk analyses can be carried out for an offering portfolio so that a company only ever has a previously defined risk portfolio.

Social Media

Customer Centricity encompasses all customer interactions, and for that reason, social media also play a large part in the *Offering* phase. Social media can provide access to multimedia product information, such as via videos on YouTube.

Another possibility is to set up specific interest groups who, for example, are granted special group discounts or other such privileges.

Offerings can be communicated through the cloud on various social media platforms, which considerably improves Web presence on the Internet and increases sales rates.

6.4.3 DIGITAL USE CASES IN THE PURCHASING PHASE

Mobility

In the *Purchasing* phase, mobile devices can be used to make cashless payments using 'near field communication' or a payment app such as mpax by scanning a QR code.

The *Purchasing* phase also includes delivery. Mobile devices can receive real-time information about the delivery status, including any delays affecting an item. Qualitative information, such as whether a maximum or minimum temperature has been exceeded or not reached, can also be sent via a mobile device in the form of notifications. Furthermore, the quality of a delivery can be rated directly via an app on the mobile device.

In some sectors, mobile devices will also perform an intermediary role and lead to the elimination of coordinators or agents. For example, switchboards that have coordinated customer inquiries and taxi requests to date will become superfluous. Instead of calling a taxi company, the customer places an order via an app. The app registers the coordinates and sends them to the nearest taxi. Registered customers can then also pay directly via an app and receive their receipt online.

Social Media

Social media already play a key role in the *Delivery* phase. In particular, the exchange of knowledge between customers when installing or using products and services is becoming increasingly important. Customers report on their problems and solutions – mostly in a language that is generally easily understood by other customers rather than citing technical specifications. Customers also frequently put helpful videos on the Web as they usually illustrate how to solve problems more clearly than written texts.

6.4.4 DIGITAL USE CASES IN THE AFTER-SALES PHASE

Mobility

In the *After-Sales* phase, apps on mobile devices can facilitate the process of creating tickets in the event of problems with products. This enables problems to be reported and rectified more quickly.

Mobile devices also offer the possibility to get instant customer feedback on their experiences with a company. Traditional methods using market research and surveys take a long time to provide results and are typically very difficult to translate into concrete actions in an organization. Using mobile technology to get on-line and continuous feedback from customers is much faster, and the information can be channelled much more quickly to the right people in the organization. So, follow-up is faster and improvements more tangible for customers.

Big Data

Sensors located in products can send product data (usage frequency, usage duration, load levels, wear and tear, and so on), which can be evaluated using real-time analyses to ensure that problems can be fixed before they even arise.

When capturing the voice of the customer at every touch point, it is critical to have the right means to deal with all the data. Taking the customer's time to collect information can lead to unhappy customers if they don't feel that they are being heard and they don't see that companies improve themselves.

Social Media

A benefit of social networks in the *After-Sales* phase is the provision of information relating to a company's entire ecosystem – customers, suppliers, employees, and partners. A social network can function as an information hub for all parties involved. For example, customers can make suggestions for improvement or express their own wishes, and all of the company's divisions and its partners can contribute to finding solutions.

Specialists from areas such as development, purchasing, or finance, who would not otherwise have any contact with customers, can also be involved in rectifying problems. Why is this important? Because customer satisfaction is influenced by all interactions with a company – even by incomplete invoices or faulty bought-in parts.

Furthermore it is important for companies to use social media to enter into dialogue with customers. Not only do companies therefore have to be able to digest all the customer noise, but they also need to be able to reach out to customers to actively position themselves so that they can positively influence customers' opinions and behavior.

6.5 Case Study Research

Quick facts:

*   The Walt Disney Company is the world's largest media conglomerate, with assets encompassing movies, television, publishing, and theme parks.
*   With more than 300 million likes across all of its Facebook pages, The Walt Disney Company is one of the most powerful brands around, both online and offline.
*   Social media analyst Starcount ranked Disney number two after Google.
*   Within the last ten years, The Walt Disney Company has quadrupled its market value.

6.5.1 INTRODUCTION

Just a few years ago, The Walt Disney Company (commonly known as Disney) was in a difficult economic situation. The parks had several structural problems: Most visitors came on the weekends, which meant that people had to wait a long time to pay their entry fees, use the transport facilities, and in particular, queue for the attractions in the parks; whining children and irritated parents made visiting the parks a frustrating experience, with the consequence that visitors seldom wanted to come back again; sales were falling and the measures that had been implemented to drive profits up were not having the desired effect ticket prices for visitors to the theme parks were at the top end of the scale and it was not possible to further increase the overall number of visitors. In an effort to maximize profitability Disney had lost its customers. This became a downward spiral where the focus on making money off visitors stole the magic that customers were expecting.

6.5.2 CUSTOMER CENTRICITY AS THE WAY FORWARD

Based on these findings the Disney management decided to focus systematically on customer orientation. The value chain starts with Leadership Excellence, which leads to Employee Excellence that delivers Customer Satisfaction and Loyalty and this results in Financial Success. Where in the past the focus was firmly on the bottom line first and foremost, the culture shifted towards providing a great customer experience that would automatically lead the company to profits. This holistic approach embraced the corporate culture, the processes, and a technological realignment. It was a complete business transformation.

Customer satisfaction became the most important company value for all of the managers and employees, and it was firmly entrenched in career plans as well, in goal, appraisal, and incentive systems. Employees became 'Cast

Members' who are personally responsible for the satisfaction of visitors, irrespective of whether or not they have had direct contact with customers. To this end, the employees were (and still are) trained in special programs and prepared for customer interaction.

In another step, employees assumed responsibility for all of the core processes, from ticket reservations to hotel and transport arrangements – either online or via travel agencies. From the customers' perspective, all of these processes were to be integrated and coordinated. Customers were also kept fully informed about additional offerings and discounts.

6.5.3 TECHNOLOGY AS THE MAIN ENABLER FOR CUSTOMER CENTRICITY

The prerequisite for all this was to upgrade the IT, which replaced outdated, separate systems with a modern CRM system. Previously unknown visitors became 'Guests' and the company began to learn more about them – with all their preferences and interests. This also established the foundation for continuous customer communication and Disney could now provide targeted offers.

Information technology also helped to reduce frustration in the parks. Walt Disney World sold a 10½-inch plush Mickey Mouse doll with a very special feature – Pal Mickey was a toy that had a sensor built into its cute little black nose. When he came near an infrared transmitter somewhere in the parks, he vibrated and chuckled. When the visitors heard or felt Mickey chortling, they were supposed to squeeze his belly and he would relay some handy park information. It was a way for the resort to push information to the guest, all in the guise of a plush toy.

Pal Mickey responded to over 400 different infrared transmitters located throughout the theme parks. He would provide interesting tidbits about attractions or specific areas of the parks. He would remind the visitor how soon it was to the start of a parade or show. He would also tell the visitor which of the Disney costumed characters could be found nearby. To make Pal Mickey even more appealing, he was loaded with over 700 different prerecorded sayings. When the visitors were away from the parks, squeezing both of his hands simultaneously would switch him into game mode.

At the very least, Pal Mickey is a nice piece of Disney park history. From a technological perspective, it was cool for the time and it was a first step towards interactive communication technology.

6.5.4 THE NEXT LEVEL OF CUSTOMER CENTRICITY – MOBILE AND SOCIAL FIRST

Pal Mickey has since been replaced by a whole range of mobile apps, which make it even easier for visitors to select the best information.

For example, The Walt Disney World Maps app contains full-size maps for the Magic Kingdom, Epcot, and other Disney theme parks in Orlando, FL.

The popular Disney World Dining app includes full menus for all 160 restaurants, making it easy to determine which restaurants to visit and which to skip.

The Walt Disney World Notescast app contains pretty much everything a visitor needs to know about Disney World. With 300 pages of information and more than 500 photos, the app details coming attractions, parade schedules, important phone numbers, Disney World tips, and the history of the park.

The Mouse Memo is a handy iPhone app that organizes all of the travel information a visitor needs during a trip to Walt Disney World. Users can enter and track hotel confirmation numbers, dining reservations, rental cars, tee times, flights, and more. This Disney World app can help keep vital information organized.

In addition to mobile communication, Disney has also focused on social networks as a communication platform. Social media are complementary to everything the company does to strengthen the emotional ties and the franchise.

Simply put, the engagement on the platforms is centered on two main principles: to reach families and Disney enthusiasts, and to share content that the guests are compelled to talk about and share.

'Oh My Disney (OMD)' is dedicated to original content based on Disney stories and characters. It offers an already loyal audience more of what it wants and is available on Twitter and Facebook. Visitors can also post their own pictures or stories.

'Disney inside' is another page that provides insider content and information about what happens behind the scenes.

Another way of getting visitors involved is Disney's presence on YouTube, with more than 1.5 billion videos viewed. Three and a half million videos have been uploaded by Disney followers.

This is a special form of emotional storytelling and it offers Disney additional touch points with its customers – before and after visiting a park or seeing a movie.

To further enhance the attractiveness of social platforms, Disney offers its fans benefits that are only available on these platforms, such as the chance to see a movie as a 10-day pre-release. The fans need to vote for their city and the city with most votes receives the pre-release.

This way, Disney brings together the past and the present and it gets visitors involved in creating emotions.

Social media are also deployed inside and outside the company to gauge general opinion or as an analysis tool for new ideas. This unique opportunity to obtain representative feedback from employees or followers has led to social platforms becoming a needle mover within the company's strategy. Three hundred million cumulative 'likes' are testament to the success of Disney social media.

Disney invests a great deal of time and staff resources in operating its various social media channels. But Disney has also shown that there is nothing magical about achieving success with social networks; it is much more about adopting an effective communication strategy that is implemented across various social platforms.

6.5.5 EVALUATING THE DIGITAL MATURITY OF WALT DISNEY

This section highlights the results of the overall maturity assessment of the Walt Disney case study. We evaluated the company based on the Customer Centricity Maturity Model. This maturity assessment aims at unveiling both visible and latent aspects of the company that account for its excellence in customer orientation. The assessment reveals the corporate philosophy, values, management, communication, strategy, operations, IT, employee knowledge, and know-how that are orchestrated in a holistic way to ensure best possible customer experience. The assessment is based on an extensive online research, literature review, and qualitative data analysis, in the field of customer orientation at Walt Disney.

CUSTOMER CENTRICITY AT THE WALT DISNEY COMPANY ▽ ▷○◁ △								
CUSTOMER CENTRICITY	**DIRECTION**			**ENABLEMENT**				
META	**STRATEGY**	**VALUE**	**RISK**	**PROCESSES**	**IT**	**CHANGE**	**TRAINING**	**PROGRAM**
Culture	Vision and Goals	Value Identification	Risk Identification	Governance	Information & Analytics	Change Impact Analysis	Training Need Analysis	Framework
Leadership	Business Model	Value Realization Planning	Risk Management Planning	Methods & Tools	Business Applications	Change Management Planning	Curriculum Development	Organization
Values	Execution	Value Realization	Risk Mitigation	Process Optimization	Communication Technology	Change Management Execution	Training Execution	Execution

Scale Initial Reactive Defined Managed Excellence

Figure 6.3   Results of the maturity assessment for Customer Centricity at the Walt Disney Company

The results are summarized in a heat map, which is structured according to the management disciplines and knowledge areas of the Customer Centricity Maturity Model (see Figure 6.3). In summary, our analysis revealed that Walt Disney is having the highest maturity level 'Excellent' for Meta Management, Strategy Management, Risk Management, Transformational IT Management, as well as Competence and Training Management. The other disciplines scored as shown in Figure 6.3.

In addition, to the findings explained in the previous section, we briefly highlight some additional input related to Meta Management, Strategy Management and Risk Management.

Walt Disney, who was the founder of the company, had the vision to bring 'great storytelling to life with immersive experiences never before imagined' (The Walt Disney Company, 2013). Disney is well aware that it needs a competent workforce and strong leadership to achieve what he aspired to. He stated that: 'You can design and create, and build the most wonderful place in the world. But it takes people to make the dream a reality'. To live up to the founder's expectation, the company considers three concepts to motivate and inspire their staff: Vision and Values, Behaviors over Intentions, Purpose before Task (Jeff, 2014).

The strategy of the Walt Disney Company is configured around its core competencies and a business model that complements these competencies.

The core competencies lie in its ability to design and animate its shows, in the perfect art of storytelling, and the operation of its theme parks in an efficient and productive manner (Management Study Guide, 2013). However, the company's strategy has been affected by the expansion of innovative technologies and globalization. Therefore, it has been adapted accordingly in order to meet the new requirements of the economy and the market. In fact, there are three major strategies that The Walt Disney Company has been pursuing: 'create high-quality content for families, making that content more engaging and accessible through the innovative use of technology, and growing our brands and businesses in markets around the world' (The Walt Disney Company, 2013). In the future the company will focus even more strongly on being ready to adapt to rapidly changing customers' wants and needs by expanding its products and services to foreign countries. The strategy is to adapt to the local customs, while maintaining Disney's American flavor (Mclendon, 2013).

The Walt Disney Company pays close attention to the strategic threats that can prevent the company's growth and threaten its financial security (Mclendon, 2013). Several strategic risks were identified in the 2012 Annual Report and Shareholder Letter that is: changing global or regional economic markets, rapidly changing customer tastes, dependence upon disruptive technology, expense of electronically stored data protection, cost of new investments and human resources. Therefore, it is crucial for the company to address these potential threats in order to stay focused on its mission and vision and to provide promising prospects for the future for its customers, stakeholders, and employees.

6.6 Conclusions

This chapter has described the details of Customer Centricity as one of the six key Digital Capabilities. One goal of Customer Centricity is to ensure that all customer interactions are consistent across all touch points throughout the customer lifecycle. Companies that build a strong relationship with their customers tend to grow faster and more profitably than others because their customers stay loyal longer (reducing attrition rates), are more likely to award more business to the provider they like doing business with (uptrading), are cheaper to serve (for example, fewer complaints and claims) and tend to spread positive word of mouth (new business gains).

Therefore, Customer Centricity is a critical capability for an enterprise. Not only in consumer businesses which have developed strong brand marketing expertise, but across all industry types it is quickly becoming vital to have a highly customer centric organization that is able to continuously capture the voice of customer and build it into the decision making processes across the whole company.

References

Bruhn, M. (2002) *Exzellenz im Dienstleistungsmarketing: Fallstudien zur Kundenorientierung, Wiesbaden*: Wiesbaden: Gabler.

Hippner, H. and Wilde, K.D. (2011) Grundlagen des CRM – Konzepte und Gestaltung. Wiesbaden: Gabler.

James, J. (2014) How to Inspire Your Team: Leadership Lessons from Walt Disney, published by Inc.com. http://www.inc.com/disneyinstitute/james/leadership.html, last accessed: 3 June 2014.

Management Study Guide (2013) Strategic Management: Core Competency Theory of Strategy. http://www.managementstudyguide.com/core-compe tency-theory-of-strategy.htm, last accessed 3 June 2014.

Mclendon, N. (2013) The Disney Company: Success Strategies and Risk Factors, http://simondixie.hubpages.com/hub/The-Disney-Company-Success-Strat egies-and-Risk-Factors, last accessed 3 June 2014.

Rapp, R. (2002) *Strategisches Account Management: mit CRM den Kundenwert steigern*, Wiesbaden: Gabler.

Reichheld, F. and Markey, R. (2011) *The ultimate question 2.0. How net promoter companies thrive in a customer-driven world*. Boston, MA: Harvard Business Press.

Rouse, M. (2007) Customer Lifecycle, http://searchcrm.techtarget.com/definition/customer-life-cycle, last accessed 16 April 2014.

Sterne, J. and Cutler, M. (2000) E-Metrics: Business Metrics for The New Economy. http://www.targeting.com/emetrics.pdf, last accessed 16 April 2014.

The Walt Disney Company (2013) Fiscal Year 2012 Annual Financial Report and Shareholder Letter, http://cdn.media.ir.thewaltdisneycompany.com/2012/annual/10kwrap-2012.pdf, last accessed 3 June 2014.

Chapter 7

Effective Knowledge Worker

NORIZAN SAFRUDIN AND AXEL UHL

7.1 Introduction

Knowledge workers are regarded as autonomous individuals who enjoy occupational advancement and mobility, and resist a commanding and controlling culture (Horwitz, Heng and Quazi, 2003). They 'think for a living', where their knowledge can be seen as an asset to any organization as it enables corporations to achieve sustainable and competitive advantage in hyper-competitive environments (Alavi and Leidner, 1999). However, the advancement of digital technologies such as robotics as well as predictive and prescriptive analytics is revealing the potential for automating human cognitive work altogether, thereby questioning the need for knowledge workers in future Digital Enterprises.

This chapter presents the Effective Knowledge Worker as one of the Digital Capabilities required for Digital Enterprises. Google is used as a case study to illustrate how having a high maturity level of the Effective Knowledge Worker capability contributes to continuous digital transformation and organizational productivity in the digital economy. The Effective Knowledge Worker Maturity Model is applied to Google, where we illustrate the use of digital technologies by Google's knowledge workers in carrying out their tasks effectively, efficiently and creatively.

Objectives of this chapter:

1. To highlight the Effective Knowledge Worker as one of the key Digital Capabilities in Digital Enterprises.
2. To showcase how digital technologies can enable knowledge workers to be creative and effective in Digital Enterprises.
3. To demonstrate the applicability of the Effective Knowledge Worker Maturity Model with Google Inc. as a case study.
4. To identify key managerial practices required for a high maturity level of the Effective Knowledge Worker Digital Capability.

7.2 Status quo

Initially, the challenge that knowledge workers faced in the digital economy was dealing with the abundance of information. While the various sources of information accessible via mobile devices, such as from websites and social media, may have provided them with the ability to make informed decisions, the increasing hyper-connectedness of users in the digital space has bombarded knowledge workers with the issue of information overload (see Karr-Wisniewski and Lu, 2010). To mitigate this, software such as (big) data analytics has provided knowledge workers with the ability to analyze and visualize information systematically, and even prescribe decision-making for management personnel. As the development of digital technologies matures over time, we begin to witness the increasing automation of not just physical, but also cognitive work, such as the introduction of Machine-to-Machine technologies, which may potentially eliminate the need for knowledge workers in the future. The question that arises from this emerging trend is then, what is left for those knowledge workers in Digital Enterprises? How can they turn around the situation, and leverage digital technologies to their advantage? To address this challenge, we first have to gain an understanding of the fundamentals in managing knowledge in organizations.

7.2.1 DEFINITION AND FUNDAMENTAL CONCEPTS

Knowledge, Knowledge Management, and the Knowledge Worker

Knowledge is acquired from the individual's experience and understanding, and then applied to decisions and actions (Alavi, Kayworth and Leidner, 2006). While the terms 'information' and 'knowledge' tend to be used interchangeably, knowledge is more than just information; knowledge is a high value form of information and can be classified into various forms (see Table 7.1). Information is the outcome when data (that is, raw facts and/or figures) is organized into meaningful patterns. It is then converted into knowledge when an individual reads, comprehends, interprets and applies the information to a particular work function (Lee and Yang, 2000). That said, one person's knowledge can be another person's information; if they cannot apply the information to anything, then it simply remains as information. As such, the effective utilization of information by knowledge workers can bring about a plethora of benefits such as better decision-making, improvements in customer service, innovation, reduced costs in people and infrastructure, rapid development of new products and services, and so forth.

Table 7.1   Knowledge taxonomies and examples

Knowledge Types	Definitions	Examples
Tacit	Knowledge is rooted in actions, experience, and involvement in specific context	Best means of dealing with specific customer or user
Cognitive tacit:	Mental models	Individual's belief about cause-effect relationships
Technical tacit:	Know-how applicable to specific work	Programming skills
Explicit	Articulated, generalized knowledge	Knowledge of major customers in a region
Individual	Created by and inherent in the individual	Insights gained from completed project
Social	Created by and inherent in collective actions of a group	Norms for inter-group communication
Declarative	Know-about	What mobile or social media technology is appropriate for collaborating with peers
Procedural	Know-how	How to interpret findings of big data analysis qualitatively
Causal	Know-why	Understanding why the social media channel works
Conditional	Know-when	Understanding when to utilize big data analytics
Relational	Know-with	Understanding how findings from big data analytics interact with cloud technologies
Pragmatic	Useful knowledge for an organization	Frameworks, best practices, project experiences, market reports

Source: Extracted and adapted from Alavi and Leidner, 2001, p. 113.

As there are different types of knowledge, managing knowledge and knowledge workers becomes an important agenda for organizations. Knowledge workers are constantly exposed to, and are involved in the creation, distribution or application of knowledge (Arthur, DeFillippi and Lindsay, 2008). As such, they play a critical role in influencing the decision-making process in organizations, where the dissemination of knowledge impacts on both their productivity and their peers (Borko, 1983), and ultimately the overall organizational performance (Maruta, 2012). We describe next the different types of knowledge workers in the context of Digital Enterprises.

Characteristics and Types of Knowledge Workers

Knowledge workers are key players in the organization as they can have an impact on the success of business activities. Examples of knowledge workers who 'think for a living' include doctors, lawyers, engineers, research scientists, physicists, consultants, economists, teachers, and so forth. Identifying the different types of knowledge workers can contribute to an understanding of what is required to manage the knowledge workers by equipping them with the necessary resources, competences, and an environment that allows them to carry out their work effectively. Researchers in the field of knowledge management have identified the various types of knowledge workers that can assist in informing industry practitioners regarding the tasks and skills required from those knowledge workers. Table 7.2 showcases how different types of knowledge workers can utilize digital technologies to enable the effective application of their knowledge for the enterprise's productivity.

Table 7.2   Typology of knowledge worker roles

Role	Description	Typical Knowledge Actions (expected)	Potential Digital Technologies
Controller	Monitor organizational performance based on raw information	Analysis, dissemination, information organization, monitoring	Data analytics, in-memory computing, cloud, mobile devices
Helper	Transfer information to teach others, once they have resolved a problem	Authoring, analysis dissemination, feedback, information search, learning, networking	Cloud technologies, social media platforms, mobile devices
Learner	Utilize information and practices to improve personal skills and competence	Acquisition, analysis, expert search, information search, learning, service search	Social media platforms, in-memory computing, mobile devices
Linker	Associate and mash up information from different sources to generate new information	Analysis dissemination, information search, information organization, networking	Data analytics, cloud, mobile, social media
Networker	Create personal or project related affiliations with those involved in the same kind of work, to share information and support one another	Analysis, dissemination, expert search, monitoring, networking, service search	Mobile and social media technologies

Role	Description	Typical Knowledge Actions (expected)	Potential Digital Technologies
Organizer	Organize and plan activities for individuals or organization-wide, e.g. to-do lists and scheduling	Analysis, information organization, monitoring, networking	Cloud technologies, social media and mobile technologies
Retriever	Search for and collect information on a given topic	Acquisition, analysis, expert search, information search, information organization, monitoring	Social media, in-memory computing, data analytics, cloud technologies
Sharer	Disseminate information in a community	Authoring, co-authoring, dissemination, networking	Cloud technologies, social media and mobile technologies
Solver	Identify and/or provide a way to resolve a problem	Acquisition, analysis, dissemination, information search, learning, service search	Social media, data analytics, in-memory computing, cloud technologies
Tracker	Monitor and react on personal and organizational actions that may become problems	Analysis, information search, monitoring, networking	Data analytics, in-memory computing, mobile and social media technologies

Source: Adapted from Reinhardt, Schmidt, Sloep and Drachsler, 2011, p. 160.

It should be noted, however, that a knowledge worker might hold more than one of the roles listed above. For instance, project managers may have the role of the networker and organizer knowledge workers, as they are required to liaise with and coordinate particular activities or processes. Those processes can be identified as being Knowledge-Intensive Business Processes (KIBP) or non-KIBP, as differentiated in Table 7.3. As knowledge workers in Digital Enterprises are exposed to – if not bombarded with – massive amounts of data and information, Digital Enterprises can therefore be identified as knowledge-intensive firms. Hence, having a high maturity level in the knowledge worker as a Digital Capability is imperative to ensure effective business operations.

Having an awareness of KIBP and non-KIBPs can improve the decision-making of the knowledge workers in Digital Enterprises. In particular, they can apply Transactional Managerial Capabilities for non-KIBPs, and Transformational Managerial Capabilities for KIBPs. This is because Transactional Managerial Capabilities ensure that the business processes adhere to existing approaches that are known to have worked, albeit in the past (see Safrudin, Recker and Rosemann, 2011). However, when unsuccessful outcomes suggest that the approach may not work for a particular event or incident, knowledge workers need to invoke Transformational Managerial Capabilities to reconfigure organizational resources by employing an ad hoc or improvisational approach, for example, (re-) designing user personas and strategizing for a digital business model.

Table 7.3   Contrasting knowledge-intensive business processes

KIBP	Non-KIBP
Mostly complex	Simple or complex
Mostly hard to automate	Mostly easy to automate
Mostly repeatable	Highly repeatable
Predictable or unpredictable	Highly predictable
Need lots of creativity	Need less creativity
Structured or semi/unstructured	Structured

Source: Extracted from Isik, Mertens and Van den Bergh, 2013, p.519.

Having described the different types of knowledge, knowledge workers, KIBPs and non-KIBPs, the next section outlines how knowledge can be managed in Digital Enterprises.

7.2.2 KEY PROCESSES OF KNOWLEDGE MANAGEMENT

Generally, the process of managing knowledge involves four distinct yet interdependent processes, namely *Knowledge Creation, Knowledge Storage and Retrieval, Knowledge Transfer and Knowledge Application*. While the four processes of managing knowledge are presented as discrete, it is imperative to note that this does not necessarily imply a linear sequence (Alavi and Leidner, 2001). At any point in time, an enterprise and its workers can be involved in multiple knowledge management process chains. The key processes are outlined below, along with how Information Technology (IT) can enable each process.

Knowledge Creation

Knowledge creation involves developing new content or replacing existing content within the enterprise's body of tacit and explicit knowledge (Pentland, 1995). Knowledge can be seen as moving through individual, group and organizational levels via four modes:

1. Socialization – converting tacit knowledge to new tacit knowledge via social interactions and joint experience among knowledge workers (e.g. interacting on Enterprise Social Networking platforms).
2. Externalization – converting tacit knowledge to new explicit knowledge (e.g. jointly documenting best practices over cloud technology).
3. Internalization – creating new tacit knowledge from explicit knowledge (e.g. understanding gained from discussion on social media channels).
4. Combination – creating new explicit knowledge via merging, (re-) classifying, and synthesizing existing explicit knowledge (e.g. real-time, collaborative document analysis via cloud technologies).

In the knowledge creation process, IT designed for collaborative and communicative purposes can facilitate teamwork, which subsequently enhances the knowledge worker's interaction with other individuals and the growth of knowledge creation (Nonaka, 1994). Additionally, computer-mediated communication may increase the quality of knowledge creation by enabling a forum for developing and sharing beliefs, affirmation of consensual interpretation, and to allow expression of new ideas (Henderson and Sussman, 1997).

Knowledge Storage and Retrieval

Also referred to as 'organizational memory', knowledge storage and retrieval includes knowledge embedded in various component forms, such as documented organizational procedures and processes, structured information stored in electronic databases, as well as tacit knowledge obtained by individuals and networks of individuals (Tan et al., 1999). Organizational memory can be classified into:

1. *Semantic memory* – explicit and articulated knowledge (e.g. archived annual reports stored using cloud technologies).
2. *Episodic memory* – context-specific knowledge (e.g. particular instances of organizational decisions and outcomes, place and time via in-memory processing).

IT can serve as an important role in enhancing and expanding both semantic and episodic organizational memory, whereby advanced computer storage technology and sophisticated retrieval techniques can be effective tools in boosting organizational memory and the speed at which the organizational memory can be accessed.

Knowledge Transfer

Explicit and tacit knowledge transfer can occur at various levels: between individuals, from individuals to explicit knowledge sources, from individuals to groups, between groups, across groups and from the groups to the organization. These transfers are stored as both semantic and episodic memory. Communication processes and information flows drive knowledge transfer in enterprises, which can be disseminated via four channels:

1. *Informal channels* – Includes ad-hoc meetings via teleconferencing systems, or private messaging on social media channels.
2. *Formal channels* – Includes on-line training sessions and briefing teleconferences for wider dissemination of knowledge.
3. *Personal channels* – Includes face-to-face interaction of personnel that may be more effective for disseminating highly context-specific knowledge.
4. *Impersonal channels* – Includes knowledge repositories on cloud technologies that may be most effective for knowledge generalizable to other contexts.

As enterprises tend to have a distributed nature of organizational cognition, it is important to consider the organizational configuration for knowledge transfer to locations where it is required and can be utilized. This is not a straightforward process as businesses typically do not know what they know, and have sub-par systems to locate and retrieve their embedded knowledge (Huber, 1991). IT can play a role in increasing knowledge transfer by extending the individual's reach beyond physical and organizational boundaries. Configuring the infrastructure for knowledge transfers, such as the use of metadata (information about where knowledge resides), can help to quickly locate the required knowledge and/or other knowledge workers.

Knowledge Application

Knowledge application refers to the integration of knowledge to build the enterprise's capability. There are four primary mechanisms to do so:

1. *Directives* – specific set of rules, procedures, instructions and standards developed by converting specialists' tacit knowledge to explicit knowledge that can be communicated efficiently to non-specialists.

2. *Organizational Routines* – development of task performance and coordination patterns, process specifications and interaction protocols that enable knowledge workers to apply and integrate their specialized knowledge without needing to articulate what they know to others.

3. *Routines* – can be relatively simple (e.g. time-based activities such as assembly line) or highly complex (commercial pilot flying a passenger aircraft).

4. *Self-contained Task Teams* – establishing groups of knowledge workers with prerequisite specialties to address uncertain and complex tasks not specified in directives or organizational routines, e.g. dedicated group of engineers, designers and researchers for a particular solution development project.

IT can enhance the integration and application of knowledge by facilitating the capturing, updating and accessing of organizational directives, and can enhance the speed of knowledge integration by automating organizational routines or establishing rule-based expert systems to capture and enforce well-specified organizational procedures.

Before we demonstrate how contemporary, digital technologies can further enhance each knowledge management process, we first describe what constitutes a Digital Enterprise with a high maturity level of the Effective Knowledge Worker capability, and contrast this with that of a low maturity level.

7.3 Digital Capability Maturity Model for the Effective Knowledge Worker

The Digital Capability Maturity Model for the Effective Knowledge Worker allows for an in-depth, holistic and integrative approach to assess capability of knowledge workers in Digital Enterprises. To measure the maturity of the Effective Knowledge Worker, the corresponding Effective Knowledge Worker Maturity Model is based on the BTM² management disciplines. Table 7.4 highlights the key characteristics of the maturity model by comparing the lowest and highest levels of the Effective Knowledge Worker.

Table 7.4   Outline of the Effective Knowledge Worker Maturity Model (contrast between a low vs. high maturity level)

Discipline	Level 1 – Initial	Level 5 – Excellence
Meta Management	• Little or no consideration of establishing a working culture • Limited communication and team cooperation • Knowledge management and sharing is deemed to be unimportant	• Knowledge of all employees along the value chain is a core competence • Leaders are thought leaders in their subject areas, and are visionary and pragmatic thinkers • Employees are intrinsically motivated, coached, and work according to defined goals and values, including sharing knowledge within the environment
Strategy Management	• Lack of vision and goals, as well as execution of strategies • Business models are built on high automation and tailored business processes	• Vision includes the Effective Knowledge Worker across the entire value chain • Strategic goals across the ecosystem • Utilization of internal and external resources and partners in contributing to the business model, with joint collaboration platform and initiatives
Value Management	• Unaware of the value of the Effective Knowledge Worker • No planning of value realization • Do not know the value of transforming employees to Effective Knowledge Workers	• Understand how the knowledge worker contribute to the value realization • Develop and implement an established value realization plan • Continuous evaluation of the outcomes of their Effective Knowledge Workers across the entire ecosystem
Risk Management	• Little to no consideration of risks associated to the Effective Knowledge Worker • No planning of risk management activities	• Strategic risk management, including a risk register, planning and mitigation approaches across entire value chain • Risk mitigation results in significantly less negatively impacted Effective Knowledge Worker
Business Process Management	• Little to no process governance • Neglect tools, approaches and execution to manage knowledge	• Effective governance mechanisms are in place to ensure knowledge is accessible within the entire ecosystem via established tools and methods • Definition of relevant KPIs like patents, public presentations and/or publications

Discipline	Level I – Initial	Level 5 – Excellence
Transformational IT Management	• Little consideration in deploying technologies for their knowledge workers • Lack of knowledge management systems, enterprise data warehouses, collaborative platforms, etc.	• Invest in value-added technologies to provide their workers and advantage among their competitors • Analyze data from various sources including internal and external social media platforms • Workers bring their own devices and contribute to the information sharing in established knowledge management systems
Organizational Change Management	• No identification of key stakeholders to manage organizational change for knowledge workers • No conduct of auditing communication needs, or have any change management activities	• Concrete plan to enhance the Effective Knowledge Workers • Provide training for knowledge workers to improve their skills • Established communication structures across the entire ecosystem, and an ongoing evaluation of the effectiveness of change management activities
Competence and Training Management	• No consideration of training needs for knowledge workers • Sparsely distributed training within some units and departments, i.e. not standardized throughout the enterprise • Little to no training or curricula are in place for knowledge workers to be effective	• Understand the need for and the importance of training for their Effective Knowledge Workers • Training needs are constantly being evaluated and updated by involving key partners within the ecosystem • Execution of the training program and curriculum is extended across the entire value chain to ensure the knowledge workers are equipped with the required skills and capabilities
Program and Project Management	• Lack of established frameworks or standards as a reference kit for knowledge workers to manage initiatives as a program or project • Little to no communication and knowledge exchange between initiatives	• Established program and project management methods and tools, which are shared across the entire ecosystem • Program and project management skills are an integral part of personnel development programs for HR managers

The Effective Knowledge Worker Maturity Model assumes that the maturity level increases if the following aspects are realized in Digital Enterprises:

• Knowledge is accessible and shared from anywhere at any time;
• Leaders are visionary and pragmatic thinkers;

- Continuous improvement of knowledge workers' skills and competences;
- Integration of knowledge-related activities across the entire ecosystem.

Digital Enterprises with the highest level of maturity (Level 5 Excellence) consider the knowledge and their knowledge workers as exceedingly valuable. Such enterprises have reached the maximum level of process and system standardization, and a holistic and global view on the Effective Knowledge Worker. They also leverage new technologies to support the Digital Capability and follow a systematic approach to acquire and retain the best possible employees. The maturity model presented in this chapter provides an important guideline for companies as it defines achievable goals for all important methodological disciplines, as illustrated with our case study in Section 7.4. But first, we present some digital use cases that can be achieved by those Digital Enterprises with a high level of Effective Knowledge Worker capability.

7.4 Digital Use Cases for the Effective Knowledge Worker Capability

Globalization and the constant innovation of (digital) technologies are contributing to the evolution of the business environment. For Digital Enterprises to stay competitive, it is essential for them to transform their practices strategically. Table 7.5 provides some examples of how digital technologies can enable the knowledge workers of a Digital Enterprise to perform their tasks effectively.

Table 7.5   **Potential Digital Use Cases for Effective Knowledge Workers in Digital Enterprises**

Knowledge Management Processes	Mobile	Big Data	Social Media	Cloud
Knowledge Creation				
Socialization	Exchange of tacit knowledge via video conferencing from mobile or tablet devices, e.g. Skype	Interpreting findings from various data sources, e.g. social media sentiments	Forum discussion beyond 'normal' business hours, e.g. LinkedIn	Real-time interaction in a virtual environment (PaaS), e.g. Google Hangout

Knowledge Management Processes	Mobile	Big Data	Social Media	Cloud
Externalization	Documenting tacit knowledge via voice-recognition and photo/image capture, e.g. via wearable technologies such as Google Glass	Documenting tacit knowledge based on interpretation of big data analytics, e.g. predictive analytics	Sharing tacit knowledge via social media channels, e.g. Twitter and linking to personal/ organization website or blogs	Storage of explicit knowledge that is accessible by peers anytime and anywhere (IaaS, HaaS)
Internalization	Accessing meeting minutes or progress reports on the go, e.g. via emails	Interpreting findings from big data analytics to create and apply tacit knowledge	Receiving updates on recent via internal enterprise social network, e.g. Yammer	Real-time, collaborative documentation (SaaS), e.g. Google Docs
Combination	Annotating documents using mobile apps, e.g. Pages	Results from data analytics and intuition contribute to business intelligence, e.g. in-memory computing	Using hashtags to organize explicit knowledge	Provision of Information as a Service (using SaaS, PaaS, HaaS)

Knowledge Storage/Retrieval

	Mobile	Big Data	Social Media	Cloud
Semantic	Accessing and storing explicit knowledge via wearable technologies, e.g. Smartwatches that allows voice-to-text commands	Efficient in-memory processing to retrieve archived information, e.g. SAP HANA	Sharing of articulated knowledge in weblogs that has social-networking affordances, e.g. Google+	Storage of archival records of reports accessible anytime and anywhere, e.g. DropBox
Episodic	Searching and storing context-specific knowledge on mobile phones	Real-time analysis of results from various sources, e.g. responses from announcing news on websites vs. social media channels	Recorded images and descriptions specific to particular incidents, e.g. Instagram's geo-tag and timestamp features	Real-time updates of events, e.g. Google Calendar

Table 7.5   Potential Digital Use Cases for Effective Knowledge Workers
in Digital Enterprises – Continued

Knowledge Management Processes	Mobile	Big Data	Social Media	Cloud
Knowledge Transfer				
Informal	Sharing knowledge via mobile phones or applications, e.g. WhatsApp, SMS, MMS	Websites bearing presentation materials, e.g. Slideshare	Sharing knowledge via enterprise networking software, e.g. Salesforce	Note-taking shared with selected peers, e.g. Evernote
Formal	Virtual training and facility tours on mobile or tablet devices, e.g. augmented reality incorporating Google Maps	Amalgamation of materials gathered from internet and websites	Sharing curriculum development materials e.g. via official company/ department account on Yammer	Dissemination of information pertaining to the organization and practices, e.g. via Sharepoint
Personal	Mirroring space setup via real-time collaboration network technologies, e.g. Cisco Room Endpoints with mobile device, tablets, wearable technology (Google Glass)	Real-time streaming that supports and integrates various sources of data, e.g. SAS Event Stream Processing Engine with data-driven audio, motion controller or sensors, virtual reality headsets	Tagging via dedicated social media account for content-specific knowledge, e.g. daily updates on work environment via 15-second video on Instagram	Pointing to training and educational materials accessible anytime and anywhere (PaaS), e.g. Dropbox
Impersonal	Video tutorials or training guide accessible via mobile and tablets, e.g. YouTube	Repository of public data sets, e.g. Amazon Web Services	Distributing knowledge content on social media channels, e.g. on Facebook	Dissemination of templates, e.g. via Google Docs

Knowledge Management Processes	Mobile	Big Data	Social Media	Cloud
Knowledge Application				
Directives	Communicating or disseminating relevant formal documented, procedures off-site, e.g. maintenance instructions on tablet devices	Insight-to-action, e.g. propose actions based on analysis of user access patterns (big data analytics)	Real-time application of knowledge, e.g. rapid response to enquiry via enterprise social media platforms	Uploading, updating or consolidating documented procedures (PaaS), e.g. after merger or acquisition
Organizational Routines	Recommending next steps based on performance, e.g. real-time monitoring of KPI via mobile apps	Automating decisions via use of signals or thresholds, e.g. SAP HANA	Coordinating tasks among peers and broadcasting performance, e.g. earning badges via gamification	Scaling experimentation of new product developments, e.g. via on-demand cloud resources (IaaS)
Routines	Approving co-workers' request remotely, e.g. via mobile apps Applying augmented reality using mobile technology affordances, e.g. via built-in camera and voice recognition on tablet devices or wearable technologies to diagnose situation at hand	Automation of simple routines, e.g. assembly lines Automation of complex routines, e.g. predictive or prescriptive analysis and simulation for cockpit crew flying large passenger airline	Real-time and direct interaction with customer, e.g. attending to customer enquiries via Twitter	Immediate adoption of business processes based on customer input, e.g. real-time engagement with clients distributed globally via Google Hangout
Self-Contained Task Teams	Collaborating with other knowledge workers dispersed all over the world, e.g. using mobile or tablet devices and Cisco Room Endpoints functionalities	Analyzing data gathered from internet, e.g. web, social media etc. to simulate user experience or outcome	Documenting experiences and interacting with other knowledge workers and end-users or customers, e.g. via Instagram using hashtags and geo-tag location affordances	Accessing documents with real-time collaboration, e.g. Google Docs Rapid and scalable prototyping, e.g. Amazon Web Services or Elastic Computing

7.5 Case Study Research

Google Inc. (commonly known as Google) is a renowned Digital Enterprise whose main business is to search and provide information to end-users. Google is also recognized for providing useful information in clever and innovative ways, enabled by the use of advanced, digital technologies. Not only does this suggest that the knowledge workers at Google are effective in carrying out their tasks, the company is also known to provide a dynamic work environment that is conducive to harnessing the creativity and talent of their workers, all for the benefit of its end-users. As such, we deem Google as a perfect case to examine how they manage their knowledge workers, and to demonstrate the application of the Effective Knowledge Worker Maturity Model. Our investigation is based on the following research questions:

RQ1. How do the knowledge workers at Google utilize digital technologies in order to meet their mission?
RQ2. How does Google rank the Effective Knowledge Worker Maturity Model?

Before addressing these questions, we outline some background information about Google, its establishment and the teams of knowledge workers that contribute to the development of innovative solutions at the Digital Enterprise.

7.5.1 ABOUT GOOGLE

Snapshot of the Establishment

Google was founded in 1998 and has since grown to serve millions of users and customers around the world. Founders Larry Page and Sergey Brin met at Stanford University in 1995. The duo started up the company with the Google Search engine, with the mission to organize the world's information and make it universally accessible and useful (Google, 2014). Since its inception, the company has developed a reputation that coincides with its vision to be a leading developer of great products, which contributes to the incremental growth in revenue of up to USD37,422 million in 2013. With more than 49,829 workers distributed worldwide (as of Q1, 2014), it is no secret that the knowledge workers at Google represent the primary driving force for the company's success. Google is also known to provide a working environment that is conducive to innovation. For three years in a row, Google has earned its number one rank in 'Fortune 100 Best Companies to Work For' in 2014 (Fortune, 2014).

Information as Core Offering

With searching as the core business of Google, the Digital Enterprise has leveraged its reputation and technological capabilities by innovating agile, digital business models. Information has been made available to users in various formats through the web including contextual information (Google Search, Google Translate), analytical information (Google Trends, Google Analytics), information sharing via applications (Google Docs) and also via social networks (Google+, Google Hangout). Recognizing the incremental uptake of mobile devices, Google has also made other forms of information accessible through mobile phones and tablet devices such as images and geo-spatial information (Google Maps and Google Earth), and videos (YouTube).

A Track Record of Innovative Digital Solutions

2005: Launched Google Maps and Google Earth to feature live traffic information, transit directions and street-level imagery, previously inaccessible to the public, such as having a close up view of the ocean and the moon which formerly were only accessible via military-standard technologies.

2007: Announced joint venture with Android in developing an open platform for mobile devices and the Open Handset Alliance.

2011: Introduced Google+ project, which aims to bring the nuance and richness of real-life sharing on the web. The objective of Google+ is to develop a platform that enables social engagement, where people have the ability (and reachability) to share their personal thoughts and interests via the Internet.

2013: Developed a wearable technology with an optical head-mounted display, known as Google Glass. Developed by Google Project Glass based in New York's 9th Avenue Google Glass Basecamp. Their mission is to be a mass-market producer for ubiquitous technologies.

Digital and Physical Presence

What is also admirable about Google is how the company has established its presence not just in the digital world, but in the physical world as well. Once a purely service-oriented enterprise, Google has since expanded its value proposition; the company is now also a product-oriented business that endeavors to provide information via mobile devices, for example, Nexus smartphones and tablets, and more recently with wearable technology, Google Glass. The transformation from intangible to tangible products proves that Google is a highly capable, boundary-spanning enterprise.

This innovation extends to its physical, working environment. Throughout our investigation, we observed from the images taken at Google's office branches[1] how the company provides a dynamic atmosphere across various workplaces, such as:

- Having Google bicycles at its Googleplex headquarter in Mountain View California;
- Adding novelties at the Google New York office, such as having scooters to commute around the building, a food truck on the 8th floor, a Lego room, etc.;
- Celebrating the birthday of Google's Creative Lab inception;
- Constantly renewing inspirational quotes, such as those at Googleplex California and in Google New York's office lobby;
- Inviting live entertainment (e.g. a jazz band) and influential figures (e.g. Sir Richard Branson) to ensure its knowledge workers have a 'Googley' work experience.

While such initiatives are meant to encourage and inspire the knowledge workers at Google, this of course does not necessarily imply that all Digital Enterprises should adopt the exact same practices. Such enhancements need to be considered and tailored to the specific culture of the business. The underlying concept of cultural revitalization however is key – cultural revitalization can alleviate collective anxiety, which may result from the pressure to constantly deliver innovative solutions (Phelan, 2005). Cultural revitalization facilitates the transfer of subordinates' dependency on their leaders, to self-driven motivation. With Google providing its employees all the necessary resources, guidance and inspiration, the knowledge workers are subsequently able to further develop their way of thinking, conducive to creativity and innovation, which are at the very core of Google's values.

7.5.2 MEET THE GOOGLERS

For any organization to be successful, it is essential to value their knowledge workers (Bogdanowicz and Bailey, 2002). Google believes that the company is successful because of its people, where the company truly values their knowledge workers. CEO Eric Schmidt said (Finkle, 2011, p.880):

> *I looked at Google as an extension of graduate school; similar kinds of people; similar kinds of crazy behavior, but people who were incredibly smart and who were highly motivated and had a sense of change, a sense of optimism. It was a culture of people who felt that they could build*

---

1   Accessed via Geo-Tag location feature on Instagram, e.g. 'Googleplex', 'Google Glass Basecamp'.

things; they could actually accomplish what they wanted and ultimately people stay in companies because they can achieve something.

A recent study on Google's knowledge workers also shows that the Googlers carry out tasks well beyond what is required, reflecting a healthy 'Organizational Citizenship Behavior' and facilitating creativity and innovation (Dekas, Bauer, Welle, Kurkoski and Sullivan, 2013).

Big Data for Bigger Creativity

One of the main sources of Google's revenue is from advertising (for example, AdWords). The concept of 'Programmatic Buying' is where digital technologies and insights from the audience can be used to automatically buy and run a campaign that reaches the right user in real time, and with the right message. The challenge with digital advertisements however, is that big data is pressuring digital marketers to ensure that every impression reaches the right people at the right price, in real-time and in the right format (for various devices). Consequently, marketers are more conversion-oriented than customer-oriented, which results in a lack of focus on the attention-grabbing design elements of a digital advertisement. Peter Crofut, who is Google's Head of Creative Platforms Strategy, states that marketers can utilize data signals from Programmatic Buying to inform their creative message (Crofut, 2014). He labels the infusion of creative design in digital advertisements with big data analytics as 'Programmatic Creative', which is achieved in two ways by the digital marketers at Google:

1.   Utilize information about the audience on how they are viewing the ads, including location and demographic information, as well as user behavior on websites obtained from first-and third-party data. For example, fashion designer Tony Burch successfully found her audience and captured viewers across the web by broadcasting her New York Fashion Week show live on multiple, high-traffic fashion sites and blogs such as Style.com and Glamour.com.
2.   Integrate data regarding the context and environment in which the digital advertisement is being viewed. For example, one of the UK's largest Telco, TalkTalk, noticed how its Flash ads were not viewed as intended on mobile devices (where Flash is not supported) and as a result presented a static backup image. TalkTalk's creative agency then utilized Google Web Designer to incorporate HTML5 which allows for consistent quality across various devices, thereby preserving the company's creative message and even gained new insights from the ad viewers.

Think With Google, a collective group of digital marketers at Google, lists Google Analytics as one of their product offerings. As the knowledge workers themselves work at Google, one can reasonably assume[2] that they have access to Google's digital solutions, such as Google+ and Google Analytics to serve their clients (see Think With Google, 2014a). Google also works closely with its clients, involving knowledge workers external to the company. The case of ELEKS[3] was a collaborative initiative among knowledge workers that are internal and external to Google. Their intent was to inspire their audience to immerse themselves in a new digital reality and imagine sports from a new perspective. Data was captured via Google Glass, analyzed with Google Analytics, and transmitted as information to the audience who subscribed to the (Google Glass) user's posts on social media channels such as Google+, YouTube, LinkedIn, Facebook and Twitter. The knowledge workers of Google Glass consists of Art and Video Directors, Producers, Enterprise Mobility Business Developer, R&D Android Stream Lead, and Business Development Program Manager for Digital Production and Mobility. These knowledge workers understand that the users need to be able to convey their experience hands-free, and from the lens of a mountain-biker, for instance. Clever application of big data analytics enables reachability and connectedness among like-minded users, where the knowledge workers strive to provide information for professional and aspirational mountain-bikers, thereby tapping into the emotive factor of end-users for a profound impact. ELEKS managed to successfully increase brand awareness of up to 40,000 unique visits per month.

In short, creativity can be achieved using big data analytics and digital solutions, by collaborating with knowledge workers that have the pertinent types of knowledge, and also complementary interests and competences that span across the technical and socio-behavioral factors.

Crossing Boundaries with Wearable Technology – A Fashion Statement

Google is infamous for its boundary spanning initiatives. The knowledge workers of the Google Glass project reflect the characteristics of a Digital Enterprise bearing Effective Knowledge Worker Digital Capability by establishing synergy with two other types of knowledge workers, namely, their end-users and also those from cross-industry. By involving the end-users or potential

---

2   Based on Google's Creative Sandbox and Think With Google case studies (sourced http:// thinkwithgoogle.com) and content analysis of posts on Google+ (https://plus.google. com/+ThinkwithGoogle/posts).

3   See for instance, http://www.thinkwithgoogle.com/campaigns/eleks-google-glass.

customers of Google Glass in the prototyping phase, the project team is able to gauge the potential customers' response via social media sentiments analysis. Based on the sentiments obtained from Instagram (via #GoogleExplorers or #throughglass hashtag search functionality), product and software engineers can iteratively improve their artefact development prior to the launch. This is also an instance of subliminal marketing by Google Glass' social networkers (as knowledge workers), whereby they understand the affordances of social media technologies, and utilize this knowledge to create the hype around Google Glass. The marketable content embedded in those hashtags is amplified by the end-users, where the photos or 15-second videos posted on Instagram using Google Glass ensure that the content classified under #throughglass comprises mainly of positive sentiments. The positive impressions can subsequently boost the demand for the product once it is made available to the general public.

The other key group of users is the ambassadors of the fashion industry. The fact that Google Glass is a piece of wearable technology means that Google will have to compete in two highly dynamic industries, namely: a) the fashion world, and b) the digital world. The knowledge workers at Google utilize this perspective to their advantage, where they have engaged with various users from the fashion industry such as Nina Garcia, who is Creative Director of *Marie Claire* magazine. The fashion icon has been seen alongside supermodel Heidi Klum wearing Google Glass before the general public can purchase one. This was during the annual New York Fashion Week 2013 where social media platforms such as Instagram could show viewers from all over the world what was happening in real-time from the use of hashtag #NYFW2013. The knowledge workers at Google saw this as an opportunity to promote Google Glass as a *fashionable, wearable technology*, and thus received endorsements from fashion bloggers who are widely known in the digital world (for example, social media, blogs) and who also have the ability to broadcast wearing Google Glass as a fashion statement to over 1 million followers the moment they post a picture of themselves wearing the product on their social media accounts. As a result, the Googlers are able to bring forward the concept of a fashionable, wearable technology for Google Glass through cross-industry collaboration of knowledge workers.

For Google, Everyone is Involved

The capitalist philanthropic way of doing business at Google has also included serial entrepreneur, Sir Richard Branson who is the founder and CEO of Virgin Group, within its knowledge ecosystem. Sir Richard Branson can be seen via his own personal account on Google+ (https://plus.google.com/+RichardBranson). The celebrity was also observed to have interacted with Google's knowledge workers on Google Hangout. Due to the accessibility of such digital technologies, other Internet users are able to access the information provided by Branson. Google's decision to share its knowledge reflects an organizational culture with consistent behavior norms, which is not just a powerful motivator for the efficient and effective productivity of knowledge workers, but is also a vital element of organizational mental health (Phelan, 2005). The affordances of digital technologies allows for purposeful and accessible information for Googlers, as well as to connect like-minded users to engage in a dialog within a trusted connected community, subsequently contributing to Google's knowledge bank.

Amalgamation of Knowledge Worker Actions with Digital Technologies

Google reflects the classical characteristic of an ambidextrous organization (see O'Reilly III and Tushman, 2004) where the knowledge workers understand how to explore and exploit the different types of knowledge to their advantage, enabled by digital technologies. Table 7.6 summarizes our key findings on how the different types of knowledge workers (introduced in Table 7.2) at Google go about their work with a mission to improve the world (Finkle, 2011).

Table 7.6   **Applying the typology of knowledge workers on the Google case study with future implications**

Type of Knowledge Worker	Example of Knowledge Workers at Google[4]	Implication of Insights for Knowledge Workers
The Solver	Social Scientists at Google Research, Digital Marketers at ThinkWith Google, Engineers for Google Driverless Car initiative are several instances where the Googlers play the different type(s) of knowledge worker role	• Data Scientists working closely with Creative Directors utilizing insights (qualitative, interpretive) from big data analytics and to supplement and/or validate findings from prescriptive and predictive analysis, i.e. balancing act of evidence-driven vs. intuition-driven[5] • Intrapreneurs within large corporations working alongside entrepreneurs from small-medium Digital Enterprises, thereby requiring integrated cloud technology platforms and services
The Retriever		
The Learner		
The Helper		
The Sharer		

---

4   Based on qualitative, interpretive data analysis on job positions/roles and responsibilities at Google (listed in each team per http://www.google.com.au/about/careers/teams) as well as content posted by Googlers on Google+ (e.g. Google Research, Google Code Jam, Google Driverless Car), YouTube and Instagram.

5   Refer Chapter 3 on Innovation Digital Capability (specific managerial capabilities).

Type of Knowledge Worker	Example of Knowledge Workers at Google	Implication of Insights for Knowledge Workers
The Linker	The 'Social' Networker[6] for Google Glass (i.e. from Google Glass Basecamp, Google+ and Google-affiliated accounts on Instagram demonstrating coordination of socio-behavioral and technical systems of operation across both digital and physical environment	• Physical setting cannot be substituted for product launch and provision, e.g. Commercial Bank with Travel Agent, can be via M&A and/or strategic alliance • Interpretive, qualitative analysis skills required as part of Data Scientist role to analyze insights from big data analytics (user/customer sentiments from social media channels, research articles, etc.) • Prescriptive analysis via big data analytics
The Networker		• Automated cognitive analysis using big data analytics, cloud technologies, and transmitted to user via mobile devices and social media channels with image, video, audio, and textual affordances (e.g. via Instagram, Twitter, YouTube, Google Hangout)
The Tracker		
The Organizer	The Googlers in charge of organizing Google Glass product launch event, including monitoring sentiment of #googleglass on Instagram, and comments on Google+ and YouTube	• Automation of transactional requirements such as alert from 'digital' personal assistant via mobile devices and applications, company's social network platforms using big data analytics; or via geo-location check-in features[7] from social media affordances and mobile devices in digital space; or sensors for machine-to-human communication, etc.
The Controller		

The different types of knowledge workers in Digital Enterprises, and the future implications of their roles in Table 7.6 shows several instances where knowledge workers can utilize digital technologies to perform their work effectively. Several emerging, contemporary IT solutions that can enable knowledge workers to work effectively in Digital Enterprises include wearable technology, data analytics, integrated social networking platforms and Machine-to-Human communication (for example, sensors, geo-tag information, mobility, etc.). The implications from the current and future digital uses cases are twofold. First, knowledge workers in Digital Enterprises should be well-versed in balancing the use of particular capabilities, for example, one of each management discipline per the BTM² framework. Secondly, knowledge workers who understand the various types of knowledge (see Table 7.1) may be able to operate effectively and efficiently. They do so by applying and amalgamating

---

6   When a computer network connects people or organizations, it is a social network (Garton et al., 1999: 75).

7   Refer Chapter 3 Innovation Capability on potential digital use cases for mobile technologies.

the different types of knowledge in deciding whether to reuse, or reconfigure, organizational resources. Existing studies (see Safrudin and Recker, 2013) suggest that reusing existing approaches and methods requires Transactional Managerial Capabilities that enforce known organizational routines such as rigorous application of Program and Project Management methodologies (for example, PRINCE2, PMBOK, MSP), or adherence to those benefits defined and agreed upon in Value Management. On the flip side, Transformational Managerial Capabilities does not make use of existing approaches (because 'best practice' is past practice). Carrying out those past practices would result in obtaining the very same outcome that they are trying to change. Instead, knowledge workers perform ad hoc reconfiguration of organizational routines and methods (for example, design thinking competences, design digital business model).

7.5.3 MATURITY MODEL – GOOGLE'S EFFECTIVE KNOWLEDGE WORKER

In order to identify how well Google's knowledge workers carry out their tasks, we assessed the maturity level of their Effective Knowledge Worker Digital Capability. We apply the Effective Knowledge Worker Maturity Model based on conducting qualitative, interpretive analysis on the work practices and job requirements of Google's knowledge workers via various social media platforms, and also synthesize other existing research works and case studies conducted on the corporation. We specifically examined how certain individuals, and groups of individuals, such as the teams of engineers,

EFFECTIVE KNOWLEDGE WORKER AT GOOGLE INC.								
EFFECTIVE KNOWLEDGE WORKER	DIRECTION			ENABLEMENT				
META	STRATEGY	VALUE	RISK	PROCESSES	IT	CHANGE	TRAINING	PROGRAM
Culture	Vision and Goals	Value Identification	Risk Identification	Governance	Information & Analytics	Change Impact Analysis	Training Need Analysis	Framework
Leadership	Business Model	Value Realization Planning	Risk Management Planning	Methods & Tools	Business Applications	Change Management Planning	Curriculum Development	Organization
Values	Execution	Value Realization	Risk Mitigation	Process Optimization	Communication Technology	Change Management Execution	Training Execution	Execution

Information missing   Scale   Initial   Reactive   Defined   Managed   Excellence

Figure 7.1   Heat map of the Digital Capability Maturity Assessment of Google's Effective Knowledge Worker

designers, researchers, marketers and product developers utilize their knowledge and creativity with aid from the digital technologies. The result from the assessment is illustrated in Figure 7.1, and shows that Google has a high maturity level of the Effective Knowledge Worker Digital Capability.

Keeping it Googley with the 20 percent Project

Knowledge workers in Google share common values with the organization, which is why Google has been investing in creating collaborative workspaces conducive to innovative and lucrative works, that is, the Googley way. Employees at Google are also self-determined, and work according to defined goals and values. This shows that Google strives for a healthy working culture, with an emphasis on confidence in the individual through their hiring process and team-oriented working environment. In a recent interview, the Vice President of Google highlighted the importance of consistency in its leadership (Bryant, 2013):

> We found that, for leaders, it's important that people know you are consistent and fair in how you think about making decisions and that there's an element of predictability. If a leader is consistent, people on their teams experience tremendous freedom, because then they know that within certain parameters, they can do whatever they want. If your manager is all over the place, you're never going to know what you can do, and you're going to experience it as very restrictive.

In addition to having a distinctive culture and clear values, employees at Google spent 80 percent of their working time on regular tasks and the other 20 percent on non-core initiatives (Gargiulo, 2011), which is also known as organizational slack (Finkle, 2011). According to Marisa Mayer, who is Vice President of Search Product and User Experience (and the first female engineer hired at Google), the slack time gave engineers the opportunity to be creative and pursue whatever they were passionate about. The outcome can be exceptionally rewarding – Google Mail (GMail) is but one example of a successful outcome of the 20 percent project. Providing such autonomy to knowledge workers is in line with Larry Page's mission to revolutionize the Google experience by emphasizing the novel factor in its solutions, which the co-founder believes can be achieved by encouraging 'new and weird ways' of working at Google (Verge, 2013). Those novel solutions are enabled by the digital technologies at Google, since the Digital Enterprise also has the Digital Capability to innovate and transform with its digital technologies.

Repurposing Affordances of Digital Technologies

Knowledge workers at Google have demonstrated awareness of the affordances of digital technologies. Software and hardware engineers, together with product designers, have demonstrated their ability to apply and integrate their knowledge to reuse or reconfigure organizational resources, including configuration of digital business models enabled by digital technologies. The Google Glass initiative for instance, re-uses existing technologies such as prompting information via voice recognition (similar to the 'Siri' feature of the Apple iOS mobile devices) where users are able to access information by prompting Google Glass with the command, 'OK Glass', followed by a request for specific information, for example, 'Google what is the name of this song?'. Google Glass will then return results of the song currently playing to the user, however, the medium of delivery is novel in that the provision of such service is via wearable technology, which is unique not only to Google's existing range of products, but also in the global market. Table 7.7 opposite summarizes the implications for the Effective Knowledge Worker, by drawing upon affordances of contemporary digital technologies, such as that of Google Glass. These affordances can

Table 7.7   Description of personas for Google Glass

Digital Technology	Digital and Physical Affordances	Implications for Effective Knowledge Worker
Google Glass as a wearable, fashionable, digital technology	• *Voice recognition*: iPhone's 'Siri' inquiry, e.g. 'Ok Glass, show the quickest route to the office' • *Real-time information*: retrieval of information, e.g. Google Maps • *Audio transmission*: dissemination of information, e.g. headpiece • *Image capture*: High resolution from camera with ability to manipulate data, e.g. mobile photo editing applications, camera filters, etc. • *Social media*: Real-time integration of information with hash-tag use and geo-tag location functionalities • *Big data*: In-memory processing to enable real-time communication, e.g. predictive or prescriptive analysis • *Cloud computing*: Scalable access and storage • *Mobility*: Can be used anytime and anywhere, e.g. wearable technologies, micro-sensors, robotics, etc.	• *Orchestration of those digital capabilities* by re-using or re-configuring the digital affordances for a Digital Enterprise transformation • Identifying ways to *leverage the use of those affordances*, e.g. Data Scientists to collaborate with Social Scientists in interpreting both quantitative and qualitative data, enabled by big data analytics softwares such as Google Analytics, SAP HANA • *Real-time mitigation strategies* in response to short- and long-term goals via user/customer sentiments, e.g. sentiment and prescriptive analysis based on critical incidents such as customer complaints or praises, number of 'likes' on social media platforms, interpretive analysis on adjectives used on product, etc.

be applied even to knowledge workers of other organizations in order to leverage those affordances for organizational productivity towards a digital transformation.

Figure 7.2 shows what type of Managerial Capabilities to invoke, that is, Transactional or Transformational, for the different contexts experienced by knowledge workers in carrying out their tasks.

The contexts specified in Figure 7.2 are derived from the Cynefin Framework (Snowden and Boone, 2007). Simple and complicated, as well as chaotic contexts may benefit from invoking Transactional Managerial Capabilities by applying established approaches in order to reinforce and restore order to the situation respectively. Yet at the same time, complicated and chaotic contexts require Transformational Managerial Capabilities to reconfigure existing organizational routines and resources, in the same way that complex contexts require design-led innovation and creativity from knowledge workers to identify a new way of working. As we can observe from the digital use cases presented, digital technologies can assist in exploiting or exploring the knowledge workers of a Digital Enterprise.

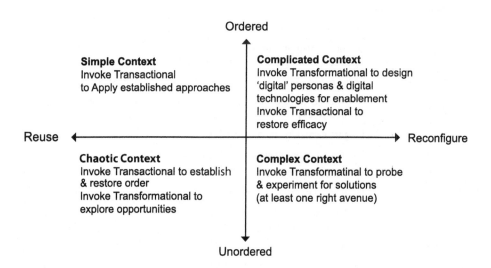

Figure 7.2   **Decision-making matrix to reuse or reconfigure resources based on context of situation**

Source: Adapted from Cynefin Framework.

7.5.4 IMPLICATIONS AND FUTURE OUTLOOK

Digital Assets – Challenges and Opportunities for the Effective Knowledge Worker

One of the key challenges of a Digital Enterprise addressed by Google is the management of digital assets. This includes the dissemination of information and knowledge among the different types of knowledge workers, enabled by digital technologies. As knowledge is an intellectual corporate asset, it may be purposeful for Digital Enterprises to be aware on the different types of knowledge embedded within their organization and also an awareness of the different types of knowledge workers required as this will inform the necessary means to reuse and/or reconfigure the resources for the Effective Knowledge Worker to achieve a high maturity level in its Effective Knowledge Worker Digital Capability. Table 7.8 below provides several examples on instantiating the different knowledge types based on the Google case study that other Digital Enterprise may be able to apply with respect to their business domains.

Table 7.8   Application of knowledge taxonomies and examples from Google

Knowledge Types	Examples from Google Case Study
Tacit	Best means of dealing with customers of Google Glass
Cognitive tacit	Understanding of cause-effect relationships such as involving celebrities to endorse Google Glass as a fashionable technology
Technical tacit	Social media skills, software or product development skills
Explicit	Knowledge of major customers in New York City (e.g. New York Fashion week)
Individual	Insights gained from completed projects such as product launch events
Social	Norms for inter-group communication, e.g. Google+
Declarative	Which social media platform is appropriate for mass reachability
Procedural	How to administer and boost the effectiveness of a social media platform
Causal	Understanding why the social media platform, e.g. Instagram, is successful in marketing Google Glass with power users in the fashion industry
Conditional	Understanding when to post updates on social media
Relational	Understanding how the affiliation of renowned fashion icon impacts the sentiment and perceptual value of Google Glass
Pragmatic	Utilization of available products such as Google Hangout to disseminate knowledge, e.g. Sir Richard Branson's experience with users within and beyond Google's ecosystem

A study of digital ethnographies states that 'everyday life' for much of the world is becoming increasingly technologically mediated (Murthy, 2008). As such, Digital Enterprises require special consideration of the roles and responsibilities of senior level knowledge workers such as the emerging role of a Chief Digital Officer or CDO (Fitzgerald, 2013; Weiss, 2013), and also to foster alliance between Chief Information Officer or CIO and Chief Marketing Officer or CMO. Additionally, the role of the Chief Cultural Officer (CCO) is important to ensure a culture that is conducive for effective knowledge workers to demonstrate creativity as an intermediate outcome, which subsequently leads to organizational performance.

Digital Natives – Preparing the Next Generation of Knowledge Workers

In Google, some of the key challenges faced include losing their knowledge workers for reasons unrelated to Google, for example, career progression factors where the workers opt to leave Google to pursue their own startup companies. Such factors, which are beyond the control of Google, can be identified as strategic risks for knowledge workers across the ecosystem. Another identified strategic risk that Larry Page has been trying to address since taking over as CEO from Eric Schmidt is having Google itself as its biggest threat (Miller, 2011). Mr Schmidt commented that, '*The problems at a company at Google's scale are always internal at some level*', where one of the key statements made was how companies slow down decision making as they get bigger. As such, preparing for the next generation of knowledge workers in the near future becomes important for enterprises seeking digital transformation. Having resources that are equipped with the fundamental capabilities per the BTM² to manage business transformations holistically allows the enterprise to undertake the initial transformation. Then, digital technologies can enable the journey towards becoming a Digital Enterprise. For this, it is necessary for knowledge workers to be well-versed in at least those Digital Capabilities specified by the Digital Capability Framework (see Chapter 2). Once these 'technical' skills are honed, they can then be complemented with a design thinking approach to derive the 'persona' of the end-user.

Digital Personas – Empathizing the End-User

Digital Enterprises with a high Effective Knowledge Worker maturity level can contribute to the development of novel and value-added offerings. The knowledge workers at Google understand that leveraging their knowledge regarding Google's digital solutions can satisfy certain 'digital' personas, such as those individuals who wish to be transported safely from one destination to another, which resulted in the development of Google's driver-less car, or those athletes from the ELEKS project who utilize the affordances of the wearable technology Google Glass, mobile and social media and web 2.0 technologies, such as YouTube, iTunes Podcasts, Spotify, SoundCloud, Instagram, Twitter, and so forth. Knowledge workers recognize the value of those digital technology, and convert it to their advantage.

Based on the practices of Google's knowledge workers, plus the clever utilization of digital technologies and their affordances, Google is assessed as having a high maturity level in according to the Maturity Model of their Effective Knowledge Worker Digital Capability. They have acquired and applied their knowledge to satisfy the needs of their end-users, well beyond the sheer provision of information that is universally accessible and useful (hygiene factor); they have also managed to tap into the psychological or emotional needs of their users, to create a seamless user experience that were not possible prior to the advancements in digital technologies.

7.6 Conclusions

In a nutshell, knowledge workers are autonomous individuals who are key players in organizations. They have the capacity to influence the success of business activities, and are not bound by restrictions or controls to effectively apply their knowledge and creativity. In Digital Enterprises, the Effective Knowledge Worker is one of the key Digital Capabilities where employees are the main resource for companies to be competitive, by leveraging digital technologies to their advantage. One of the ways to assess and develop the maturity level of the Effective Knowledge Worker Digital Capability is by utilizing the Effective Knowledge Worker Maturity Model. The case of Google demonstrates how the corporation's distinctive culture and thirst for novel, technology-driven ideas can bring about innovative solutions for its end users, and ultimately, for the benefit of Google as a whole. The knowledge workers have repurposed the existing affordances of digital technologies, whilst maintaining the integrity of the distinctive 'Googley' culture. They do so by blending not just the digital and physical environment, but also through collaboration with other knowledge workers cross-industry and repurposing the affordances of contemporary, digital technologies. Google's knowledge workers show that the automation of human cognitive work with digital technologies is not a threat to their role; rather, such advancements can serve as an ally so they can focus on the psychological needs of their end user for an extraordinary and seamless experience across both digital and physical worlds.

References

Alavi, M., Kayworth, T.R. and Leidner, D.E. (2006) An empirical examination of the influence of organizational culture on knowledge management practices. *Journal of Management Information Systems, 22*(3), 191–224.

Alavi, M. and Leidner, D.E. (1999) Knowledge management systems: issues, challenges, and benefits. *Communications of the Association Information System, 1*(2es), 1.

Alavi, M. and Leidner, D.E. (2001) Review: Knowledge Management and Knowledge Management Systems: Conceptual Foundations and Research Issues. *MIS Quarterly, 25*(1), 107–136.

Arthur, M.B., DeFillippi, R.J. and Lindsay, V.J. (2008) On being a knowledge worker. *Organizational Dynamics, 37*(4), 365–377.

Bogdanowicz, M.S. and Bailey, E.K. (2002) The value of knowledge and the values of the new knowledge worker: generation X in the new economy. *Journal of European Industrial Training, 26*(2/3/4), 125 – 129.

Borko, H. (1983) Information and knowledge worker productivity. *Information processing and management, 19*(4), 203–212.

Bryant, A. (2013) *In Head-Hunting, Big Data May Not Be Such a Big Deal.* http://www.nytimes.com/2013/06/20/business/in-head-hunting-big-data-may-not-be-such-a-big-deal.html?_r=0, last accessed 15 November 2013.

Dekas, K.H., Bauer, T.N., Welle, B., Kurkoski, J. and Sullivan, S. (2013) Organizational Citizenship Behavior, Version 2.0: A review and Qualitative Investigation of OCBs for Knowledge Workers at Google and beyond. *The Academy of Management Perspectives, 27*(3), 219–237.

Fitzgerald, M. (2013) CDOs Are Reaching New Heights – and Quickly. *MIT Sloan Management Review.*

Gargiulo, S. (2011) *How employee freedom delivers better business.* Retrieved 2 June 2013 from http://edition.cnn.com/2011/09/19/business/gargiulo-google-workplace-empowerment/index.html.

Hacini, S., Boufaida, Z. and Cheribi, H. (2007) Mobile Agent Protection in E-Business Application A Dynamic Adaptability Based Approach. In *On the Move to Meaningful Internet Systems 2007: CoopIS, DOA, ODBASE, GADA, and IS*, edited by R. Meersman and Z. Tari (Vol. 4804, pp. 1821–1834). Berlin, Heidelberg: Springer.

Horwitz, F.M., Heng, C.T. and Quazi, H.A. (2003) Finders, keepers? Attracting, motivating and retaining knowledge workers. *Human Resource Management Journal, 13*(4), 23-44.

Karr-Wisniewski, P. and Lu, Y. (2010) When more is too much: Operationalizing technology overload and exploring its impact on knowledge worker productivity. *Computers in Human Behavior, 26*(5), 1061–1072.

Lee, C.C. and Yang, J. (2000) Knowledge value chain. *The Journal of Management Development, 19*(9/10), 783–793.

Maruta, R. (2012) Transforming Knowledge Workers into Innovation Workers to Improve Corporate Productivity. *Knowledge-Based Systems, 30*, 35–47.

Miller, C.C. (2011) Google's Biggest Threat Is Google. *The New York Times – Technology,* http://bits.blogs.nytimes.com/2011/09/27/googles-biggest-threat-is-google/, last accessed 7 July 2014.

O'Reilly III, C.A. and Tushman, M.L. (2004) The Ambidextrous Organization. *Harvard Business Review, 82*(4), 74–81.

Phelan, M.W. (2005) Cultural Revitalization Movements in Organization Change Management. *Journal of Change Management,* 5(1), 47–56.

Picard, R. (2011) Strategic Uses of Social Media for Businesses. In *Nordic Contributions in IS Research,* edited by H. Salmela and A. Sell (Vol. 86, pp. 1–1). Berlin Heidelberg: Springer.

Reinhardt, W., Schmidt, B., Sloep, P. and Drachsler, H. (2011) Knowledge Worker Roles and Actions – Results of Two Empirical Studies. *Knowledge and Process Management, 18*(3), 150–174.

Verge, T. (2013) Redesigning Google: how Larry Page engineered a beautiful revolution. http://www.theverge.com/2013/1/24/3904134/google-redesign-how-larry-page-engineered-beautiful-revolution, last accessed 7 July 2014.

Weiss, T.R. (2013) Chief Digital Officer: Hot new tech title or flash in the pan? http://www.computerworld.com/s/article/print/9241033/Chief_Digital_Officer_Hot_new_tech_title_or_flash_in_the_pan_, last accesed 29 July 2013.

Chapter 8

Operational Excellence

THERESA SCHMIEDEL, JAN VOM BROCKE AND AXEL UHL

8.1 Introduction

Operations are at the core of every organization. They are what organizations do. Operations refer to business processes in and across all functions of an organization. Against this background, Operational Excellence is a key precondition for organizational success. As one of the six major Digital Capabilities, Operational Excellence means outperforming competitors by leveraging the potential of new technologies. Mobile and real-time business, social media, and big data analytics are examples of a new generation of technologies that has fundamentally changed the degree of Operational Excellence that can be realized in modern organizations. These technologies are disruptive, and in the long run, the adoption of such technologies will determine which organizations are competitive in the market and which are not.

While it is tempting for organizations to adopt new technologies immediately, they often struggle in doing so, as organizations do not always meet the fundamental preconditions for Operational Excellence – such as overcoming corporate silos by integrating systems, processes, and data – that are required in order to leverage the potential of new technologies. This integration requires enormous effort, particularly for global organizations, which for historical reasons often have highly diverse systems and processes in place. Building a solid foundation of integrated processes is an important precondition for Operational Excellence and thus for digital transformations. At the same time, organizations need to remain sufficiently flexible and agile to experiment with new technologies in their operations to extend and embrace business opportunities.

This chapter describes the foundations of Operational Excellence and points out the kinds of opportunities the digital age offers so that organizations can realize new levels of Operational Excellence. The chapter also reflects the management dimensions that firms should consider when they move toward Operational Excellence. We demonstrate our findings using a number of practical examples, particularly the Hilti case, in order to exemplify ways in which firms can realize Operational Excellence today and in the future. Hilti developed a strategy called 'solid core and flexible boundary' to balance its needs for both stability and agility in pursuing Operational Excellence in the digital world.

Objectives of this chapter:

1. Explain the fundamental preconditions for Operational Excellence.
2. Show the potential of new technologies for Operational Excellence.
3. Present the Hilti case to exemplify ways in which firms can move toward Operational Excellence.

8.2 Foundations of Operational Excellence

8.2.1 DEFINITION AND CLASSIFICATION

Many organizations provide similar or identical products. As competition increases, it is important for such organizations to excel in both operations and transformations in order to remain competitive and be successful. There are many ways a firm can excel, but since operations are what organizations basically do, Operational Excellence is a central capability for any organization that wants to compete, particularly in a digital world. Operational Excellence requires managing all business processes of an organization, whether they are core processes or support processes, so that their performance is outstanding. Such process management includes both continuous improvement and the innovation of processes.

Operational performance has two dimensions. First, business processes must be effective such that the organization carries out the operations required to realize its business goals. For example, an operation that sends out paper-based feedback forms to teenage customers is probably less effective than an operation making use of digital opportunities, such as using social media for the purpose of surveying young generations. Second, business processes must be efficient such that organizations carry out their operations with the fewest costs and errors. For example, the integration of organizational data and systems enables real-time, evidence-based business decisions that would not be possible with silo solutions.

8.2.2 CHALLENGES AND BENEFITS

A major difficulty for many organizations, particularly global organizations, is the almost countless operations that go on daily, which often differ from location to location in terms of the systems, processes, and data used. In addition, managing the digital transformation of these operations is often narrowly focused on methods and IT, neglecting aspects such as the overall strategic alignment of goals and cultural change management. Thus, Operational Excellence still presents a huge challenge for many organizations in terms of devising fully integrated processes and data as a foundation for the Digital Enterprise.

Nevertheless, Operational Excellence has huge potential for overall performance. While realizing Operational Excellence requires considerable effort in terms of time and money, the benefits of constantly improving and innovating operational processes pay off. Companies that consciously manage Operational Excellence outperform those that do not, in terms of financial well-being, reputation, market share, and other factors (for example, Kaynak, 2003).

8.2.3 ORIGIN AND RECENT DEVELOPMENTS

Operational excellence has its origins in the approaches of scientific management, or Taylorism, at the beginning of the 20th century, when production processes were closely analyzed to eliminate waste that occurred through, for example, inefficient movement by the workers. Considering the past few decades, process management has two main ancestors (Hammer, 2010): approaches like total quality management (TQM), which focuses on incremental improvements in business processes, and business process re-engineering (BPR), a more radical approach that undertakes larger changes in business operations.

Today, Operational Excellence is considered a holistic approach to process change that includes aspects of management like strategy, value, change, and competence management (Rosemann and vom Brocke, 2010). From a business transformation perspective, Operational Excellence bears significant potential for firm performance (vom Brocke et al., 2012). Thus, Operational Excellence is a key goal for digital transformation and as such one of the key capabilities of the Digital Capability Framework.

8.3 New Technologies and Use Cases for the Future of Operational Excellence

Today's new technologies give firms access to new ways of achieving Operational Excellence. We introduce several of these technologies as examples to show the impact they can have on organizations' Operational Excellence. In particular, we look into the potential for increasing the Operational Excellence of typical core operations through new technologies and illustrate some specific use cases of these technologies.

8.3.1 THE INTERNET OF THINGS AND BIG DATA ANALYTICS

In-memory technologies allow large amounts of data to be analyzed instantly (vom Brocke et al., 2014), thus enabling big data analytics. The advantage of big data analytics is that firms can base decisions on massive amounts of evidence from the past and on predictions of the future. An important field of application of big data analytics is the Internet of Things since machine-to-machine communication produces enormous amounts of valuable data for businesses. For example, sensors in products can automatically initiate maintenance activities and predict maintenance requirements, which enable efficient scheduling of customer support.

8.3.2 MOBILE AND REAL-TIME TECHNOLOGIES

The ubiquity of devices that allow real-time access to data sources completely transforms the way in which business processes can be executed. For example, real-time technologies significantly accelerate sales processes since current information on the availability of goods and services can support purchase decisions instantly. Another example is the completely new dimension of real-time technologies that comes with the development of 3D-printers. In the future, these printers may even allow real-time printing of required products, on demand, anywhere, anytime.

8.3.3 SOCIAL MEDIA

Social media tools like Twitter and Facebook, which millions of people use daily, provide many new opportunities for organizations to improve their Operational Excellence. An obvious possibility is to improve customer-facing operations which also relate to the capability of Customer Centricity (for example, increasing customer loyalty by having people follow the organization on social media). Other possibilities include analyzing social media discussions on specific products to feed the warranty process (Richter et al., 2011). The direct contact with customers and the assessment of their sentiments about the organization enables new dimensions of Operational Excellence in sales and marketing operations, as well as in complaints-handling and product improvement.

8.3.4 USE CASES OF NEW TECHNOLOGIES IN INDUSTRY 4.0

New technologies, particularly the Internet of Things, are expected to result in a fourth industrial revolution called industry 4.0 that will yield completely new dimensions of Operational Excellence. Using typical core operations in a goods-producing company, we now examine the potential that new technologies offer in terms of transforming Operational Excellence. Table 8.1 provides an overview of use cases of new technologies, illustrating how such technologies may support a typical core process. In this process, we distinguish *purchasing, warehousing, production, distribution,* and *support.*

Table 8.1   **Use cases of new technologies in typical core operations**

Core Processes Operations	Internet of Things and big data analytics	Mobile and real-time technologies	Social media
Purchasing	• Purchasing based on storage sensors • Purchasing based on customer data analytics	• Real-time integration with suppliers • Real-time notifications of sales via mobile technologies	• Supplier relationship management
Warehousing	• Smart stock consumption • Automated material check-out	• Smart inventory • Monitoring of storage conditions	• Prediction of demand based on social media analytics
Production	• Machine control via product parts • Parts compatibility detection	• Augmented reality in assembling through special glasses • Monitoring of production conditions	• Identification of production improvements
Distribution	• Transportation incompatibility detection • Automated product check-out	• Car routing based on product RFID tags • Real-time automated payment at the moment of delivery	• Distribution channel for products and services
Support	• Product maintenance indications • Sensor-based maintenance orders	• Real-time notification of sales persons on maintenance issues • Provision of mobile services apps for customers	• Distribution of information on product functionalities

Purchasing (or procurement) can be supported through opportunities provided by the Internet of Things and big data analytics. For example, sensors in the storage system can recognize when resources should be refilled and automatically trigger purchase orders. Additionally purchase orders can be triggered through analyzing historical customer data. Further, mobile and real-time technologies can support the purchasing process, for example, through cloud services that enable an integrated process with supplier companies or through real-time notifications on sales that require specific production materials to be purchased. Beyond, social media can support purchasing as it enables organizations to maintain relationships with their suppliers for example, keeping them informed about the latest activities.

As part of the organizational core process, *warehousing* can also be supported through the introduction of new technologies. The Internet of Things for example, allows: parts in stock to automatically indicate which part to use next in the production process, to prevent parts in stock from becoming out-dated, and it also allows for parts to be automatically checked out from the warehouse as they are taken off the shelf. Real-time technologies further simplify inventory when all materials in stock contain RFID (radio frequency identification) tags and they also support a quality process that monitors the storage conditions (for example, temperature, air quality) to protect material quality. Warehousing can additionally be supported through analyzing interests in certain products expressed on social media platforms, thus predicting sales – that is, demand for specific products, and thus, also, the raw materials that need to be available in the warehouse.

Production can also be supported by the various possibilities of new technologies, for example, through controlling machines via product parts that are being processed (for example, automated shut down of machines when parts have passed) or through automated detection of whether parts are compatible for the assembly of a specific product. Further, the production process can be enhanced through the use of special glasses that augment reality and show how to assemble the parts of a product. Production can also be supported by sensors that monitor the production conditions for factory workers (for example, temperature, air quality) to ensure that health and safety requirements are met. Finally, involvement with customers via social media may help to identify ideas for production improvements that increase the quality of the product.

Distribution can also take advantage of the broad range of capabilities of new technologies. For example, the distribution process can be improved when incompatibilities in transportation (for example, flammable next to explosive materials) are detected automatically for quality and safety reasons, or when products that are taken off a car or truck are automatically checked out. Further possibilities to improve the distribution process include that the products that are loaded into a car or truck automatically determine the route for delivery based on the destination information that is available via RFID scanning. Also, real-time automated payments which are triggered through RFID scanning at the moment of delivery could be a way to enhance the distribution process. Finally, depending on the product or service, social media can be used as a distribution channel.

Finally, *Support* as a core operation can be facilitated through new technologies. For example, sensors in products can indicate maintenance requirements or even automatically initiate maintenance orders at the manufacturing or service company. It is further possible to notify salespersons on a real-time basis when product maintenance is required at customer sites. In addition, customer support can also be facilitated through mobile service apps that help customers manage or monitor products and related maintenance services. Finally, social media can further support customers, for example, when information on product functionalities is provided and distributed through community channels.

In the next section we take a look at the Operational Excellence Maturity Model as part of the Digital Capability Framework and examine management areas to be considered when working toward high maturity levels of Operational Excellence. We then examine the case of the Hilti Corporation as an example of how to realize Operational Excellence.

8.4 Operational Excellence Maturity Model

From the perspective of Digital Enterprises, Operational Excellence is far more than merely process improvements in operations. Such an approach could lead to disregarding considerable potential for expanding a company's business to other fields, which is essential for survival in the digital world. Reaching higher maturity levels of Operational Excellence is a journey towards building efficient and sustainable businesses based on opportunities that result from innovative technologies. This journey does not have a beginning and a definite end, but represents a continuous approach that needs to be incorporated into the organization's culture (Schmiedel et al., 2013, 2014). Being able to innovate and transform with regard to Operational Excellence is essential for rapid adaptability to new market conditions and hence for the long-term success of companies. Therefore, it is becoming increasingly crucial that management pays attention to Operational Excellence as one of the critical business capabilities.

The pursuit of Operational Excellence requires comprehensive efforts. Alongside efficient business processes, leadership, strategic direction, organizational structure, people, and systems must also be aligned. Hence, Operational Excellence as a key capability of a Digital Enterprise needs to be considered as a holistic endeavor. For assessing the specific maturity level of Operational Excellence an overarching Operational Excellence Maturity Model can be used. This maturity model builds on the BTM² approach (see Chapter 2) which integrates major management disciplines, such as Strategy Management, Risk Management or Change Management. Increasing the maturity in each of these management areas fosters the digital organization's overall maturity with regard to Operational Excellence. In the following, we look into each management area, comparing low and high levels of maturity of Organizational Excellence as one of the Digital Capabilities (see Table 8.2).

Table 8.2   Outline of the Operational Excellence Maturity Model (contrast between a low vs. high maturity level)

Discipline	Level 1 – Initial	Level 5 – Excellence
Meta Management	• Short-term operational goals • Risk-averse approaches • Top-down process management	• Long-term transformation initiatives • Vision of a Digital Enterprise • Employee participation
Strategy Management	• No strategy for OE in place • Lack of managerial commitment • Poor strategy communication	• Corporate strategy focused on OE • Strong executive management support • Integrated strategy communication
Value Management	• Focus on turnover as indicator of OE • Lack of value measurement	• Systematic business benefit planning • Monitoring of business objectives
Risk Management	• Lack of consideration of strategic risks in risk mitigation strategies • Focus only on operational and tactical risks	• Active risk identification and risk mitigation planning • Strategic risk management anchored at top managerial level
Business Process Management	• Operational silos between global units • Varying quality standards	• Globally integrated processes across all units • Consistent quality levels

Discipline	Level 1 – Initial	Level 5 – Excellence
Transformational IT Management	• Large number of separate IT solutions • Lack of standardized interfaces • Disregarding the potential of new technologies for business purposes	• Strategic selection of user-friendly systems • Integration into an overall system landscape • Adoption of suitable new technologies
Organizational Change Management	• Lack of stakeholder involvement in change initiatives • Improvement projects perceived as disturbance of daily operations	• End-to-end involvement of employees, top management, and customers • Culture shift towards perceiving OE as an ongoing endeavor
Competence and Training Management	• Minimum amount of training for employees • Lack of competence management	• Strong focus on developing required transformation skills • Peer-to-peer exchange of competences
Program and Project Management	• Lack of integration of few OE projects • Lack of resources available for OE initiatives	• Integration of projects into an overall strategic roadmap towards OE • OE initiatives become part of the budgetary process

This overview of the Operational Excellence Maturity Levels provides a starting point for Digital Enterprises that want to realize state-of-the-art Operational Excellence. In the next section, we provide insights into the Hilti Corporation's global transformation using the nine management areas to outline how the company managed the large-scale change.

8.5 Case Study

Based on findings from previous studies, company documentations, and in-depth interviews with key representatives from the IT function of the Hilti Corporation, we report on the Hilti case to showcase their journey towards Operational Excellence as a basis for developing into a Digital Enterprise.

8.5.1 THE HILTI CORPORATION

Hilti is a global leader in the construction and building maintenance industry that provides products, services, and software for professional customers. With more than 20,000 employees in more than 120 countries, Hilti achieved sales of around 4.2 billion Swiss francs in 2012, resulting from more than 200,000 customer contacts every day. To ensure that their operations are efficient and effective, Hilti pays special attention to the continuous improvement and innovation of its business processes.

In 1999, Operational Excellence was already part of the Hilti strategy, however, the top management at the time was dissatisfied with the company's performance in this strategic dimension. The company did not face financial difficulties or other severe external pressure, but was simply convinced that Hilti would not succeed in the long run if it did not make progress in the area of Operational Excellence. At this point a transformation initiative called 'Global Processes and Data' (GPD) was born that would require enormous efforts over the next decade (vom Brocke et al., 2010).

Today, after completion of this transformation, Hilti's business processes are globally executed in a fast and consistent manner (vom Brocke et al., 2011). The worldwide standardization of data, processes, and systems facilitated Operational Excellence. Beyond standardization, the GPD project also facilitated the company's ability to realize local initiatives at a global level. While the Hilti market organizations once lacked resources to realize their improvement ideas, today globally shared processes mean that the Hilti headquarters can offer the infrastructure and other resources that the market organizations need. Hilti created a basis on which to synchronize activities and ideas and to provide the transparency that allows Hilti to benchmark its Operational Excellence globally.

8.5.2 KEY ELEMENTS IN HILTI'S JOURNEY TO OPERATIONAL EXCELLENCE

When Hilti's management decided to transform the company's operations through the GPD initiative, Hilti had many locally optimized business solutions in place. The goal of the GPD project was to integrate the processes and data from these individual solutions into a single SAP solution. To realize this global objective, Hilti made huge technical and social investments. This investment in the GPD program became the overall foundation for harvesting new business potential and leveraging new technologies on the way towards a Digital Enterprise. Figure 8.1 illustrates the three major phases of Hilti's journey to Operational Excellence.

Based on Hilti's IT strategy, which envisions a balance between reliability and agility in IT service delivery, the company's CIO derived the concept of a 'solid core and flexible boundary'. While Hilti developed this concept recently, it ties in well with the GPD approach: the investment phase enabled Hilti to develop a central foundation for Operational Excellence – that is, a solid core – that today facilitates harvesting by means of a flexible boundary. Next, we explain this concept in more detail.

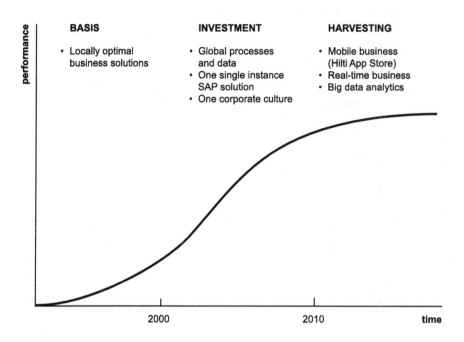

Figure 8.1   Hilti's phases to Operational Excellence

Solid Core and Flexible Boundary

While Hilti's management knew that a solid core of integrated processes, systems, and data is a key prerequisite for Operational Excellence and consistent performance, they also knew that this solid core could not be too rigid. Therefore, a one-size-fits-all approach, in which every part of the business globally had to perform exactly the same processes in exactly the same way and get exactly the same result, was not considered adequate. Instead, there had to be a flexible boundary that allowed for a differentiation between information demands and ways to do business (see Figure 8.2).

The first step of the GPD initiative was to eliminate silos and integrate the business into a solid core of global processes and data. Hilti implemented GPD in 50 sales organizations, all eight plants, and the company's headquarters. Based on this complete integration, the second step of shaping a flexible boundary was possible: specializing again and looking into the differences between the market organizations. For example, market reach initiatives do not have to use only 'the' global solution. Hilti established Regional Market Reach Summits that address regional needs.

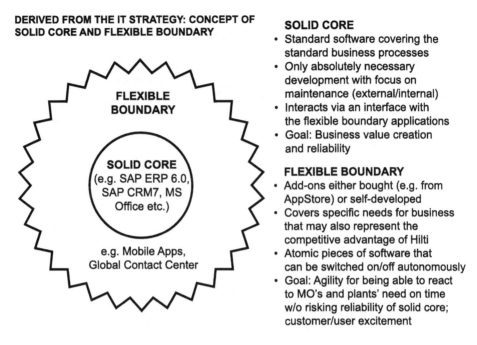

DERIVED FROM THE IT STRATEGY: CONCEPT OF SOLID CORE AND FLEXIBLE BOUNDARY

FLEXIBLE BOUNDARY

SOLID CORE
(e.g. SAP ERP 6.0,
SAP CRM7, MS
Office etc.)

e.g. Mobile Apps,
Global Contact Center

SOLID CORE
- Standard software covering the standard business processes
- Only absolutely necessary development with focus on maintenance (external/internal)
- Interacts via an interface with the flexible boundary applications
- Goal: Business value creation and reliability

FLEXIBLE BOUNDARY
- Add-ons either bought (e.g. from AppStore) or self-developed
- Covers specific needs for business that may also represent the competitive advantage of Hilti
- Atomic pieces of software that can be switched on/off autonomously
- Goal: Agility for being able to react to MO's and plants' need on time w/o risking reliability of solid core; customer/user excitement

Figure 8.2   The solid core and flexible boundary concept
Source: Petry et al., 2013.

Today Hilti is focusing on business modularity to create a flexible boundary around the fully integrated solid core. The development of this modularization is considered important because some of Hilti's business areas require more standardization than others. Therefore, Hilti differentiates between areas in which there is no value in deviating from standards, such as accounting, and areas where deviation is beneficial. For example, sales representatives in Dubai and Appenzell have fundamentally different jobs, as the one in Appenzell works primarily with smaller construction companies where loyalty is highly valued, while the one in Dubai might work on one large construction project for several years with only one customer. Because of these differences, their demands for information and solutions also differ. While they have many things in common (solid core), they also have some business needs that require a flexible boundary.

Another example of the modularity is the hub structure that Hilti introduced to improve the quality of process management in the regions. The idea was to support small local units with a shared service structure because they do not have the capacity to run the full business model. The regional hubs serve as a knowledge pool to support small units with training and also provide operations like repair, logistics, finance, product marketing, and HR. Overall, the concept of a solid core and flexible boundary is a key element that supports Hilti's way towards Operational Excellence and its ability to leverage the potential of new technologies.

8.5.3 ANALYZING HILTI'S JOURNEY TO OPERATIONAL EXCELLENCE USING THE OPERATIONAL EXCELLENCE MATURITY MODEL

To deeper understand how Hilti realized new levels of Operational Excellence, we used the Operational Excellence Maturity Model to examine the case regarding its maturity in the individual management disciplines. We first conducted a qualitative assessment through face-to-face interviews with representatives of the IT function, and then send out a survey for a quantitative assessment of Hilti's maturity in the management areas. This assessment is also based on the perspective of the Hilti IT function.

Meta Management

Regarding culture and values, Hilti pays close attention to creating a shared understanding of the company. Hilti's values of integrity, courage, teamwork, and commitment are perceived as the foundation for business goals like Operational Excellence. Therefore, the company makes considerable effort to shape and affirm the Hilti culture and its values through a well-documented and shared culture training program called 'Our Culture Journey'. As part of this program, all employees participate regularly in team camps to gain additional insights on how best to work together.

The company's values strongly support Operational Excellence. For example, courage is required when change decisions are made that affect the company on a global scale, and commitment is necessary if these decisions are to be realized and their desired results achieved. The GPD project also brought the Hilti culture to a new level in the area of teamwork, as employees worked together with other employees outside their departments and countries. When the GPD project started, it was the first time that many of the people involved had sat in the same room as people from other departments or organizations.

Generally, the Hilti culture means that employees on all levels share awareness of the need for Operational Excellence on all levels, but this is particularly the case on the leadership level. Operational Excellence has been a well-known strategic goal in the management teams for many years. As new employees learn about the Hilti culture and the importance of Operational

Excellence from their supervisors, Hilti ensures that employees consider the bigger picture in each action.

Strategy Management

Regarding vision and goals, Operational Excellence has been part of the Hilti strategy since its creation in 1996. In fact, the GPD project was initiated because the company's top management assessed the corporate strategy in 1999 and found no significant progress with regard to Operational Excellence. A key argument for launching the program was that good ideas on process improvements were not transferred effectively from one market organization to the next.

While the execution of the Hilti strategy with regard to the capability of Operational Excellence was tightly linked to realizing the GPD initiative, Operational Excellence is also anchored in the Hilti business model as a continuous effort beyond the GPD program. In fact, Operational Excellence is represented in two key parts of the business model: as part of the corporate strategy (where Operational Excellence is called a 'strategic imperative') and as part of a continuous review cycle of the company's core business processes.

The Hilti business model is distributed to, and shared among, all employees as part of the Culture Journey. For this reason, Operational Excellence is more than an abstract strategic goal that resides only at the managerial level; instead, it is communicated to all levels of employees, and there is considerable awareness of its importance in overall firm performance. The business model also helps employees think about processes and their improvement in an integrated way.

Value Management

Regarding Value Management of corporate initiatives in general and Operational Excellence initiatives in particular, it is Hilti's policy to identify the business value of a project as a first step, so the initiative's business case and its added value are defined up front. After the value identification, the costs and benefits of the project are evaluated over suitable short- and long-term periods. The planning for realizing the value in the initiative begins after the decision to pursue the initiative has been made.

While the business value identification is a prerequisite for launching a project, the value realization is also monitored closely during the project's implementation, as the creation of business value is double-checked throughout the project phases. At the end of the project, the business value must be visible.

Therefore, the GPD initiative was not launched for the purpose of Operational Excellence but for the business benefits (value) that could be achieved through Operational Excellence. Thus, the Operational Excellence initiative is not seen at Hilti as *l'art pour l'art* but as a means to improve customer satisfaction and to realize business value for the company. The value of the GPD project was constantly evaluated for its business impact.

Risk Management

The risks related to each project at Hilti must be assessed at the outset. Apart from risk identification, these risk analyses include evaluating the probability of the risks and developing a contingency plan, a 'plan B' that contains ways to mitigate realized risks. The risk analysis is usually reviewed monthly and shared with the project's sponsor.

Especially with a global program like GPD, the risks associated with its realization can change over time since some risks disappear over time, such as people's buy-in, and other risks appear, such as the extension of the program's timeframe for completion. In fact, the risk analysis at the beginning of the GPD project was very different from the risk analysis at the end. Therefore, Hilti's management considers tracking the risks continuously and adapting risk mitigation plans accordingly to be critical to success.

Business Process Management

Regarding the governance of Business Process Management, Hilti defined global process owners (GPOs) and global process managers at the beginning of the GPD program, and these employees worked full-time on the projects for the first five to six years to build global processes. Since then GPOs have been reintegrated into the lines of business, so today, for example, the GPO for logistics is the head of logistics, responsible not only for processes and Operational Excellence but also for operational results, down to the daily fulfilment rate.

This approach improves the inputs for process optimization, as they come straight from the line of business, where there is direct feedback on what is working and is useful, and what is not. Today, the process organization is integrated into the line of business to the degree Hilti finds necessary and useful.

This integration is seen as an important element of success because it ensures that the responsibilities for value creation are well established and supported by a web of people who are working on Operational Excellence, including GPOs, Hilti IT, regional and local process experts, and the line of business.

A key characteristic of Hilti's Operational Excellence initiative is a methodological approach to process management, which focuses on the review cycle of the business model. The review cycle requires the company to reflect constantly on whether the current activities lead to the goals set, and if not, to have the courage to look at the bare facts and to take pragmatic action accordingly.

Transformational IT Management

Generally, Hilti implements and uses only those IT artifacts that support Operational Excellence, as they otherwise have no business value. Therefore, all systems at Hilti, whether they support analytics, communication, or business, are required to foster the Operational Excellence that generates business value.

Hilti has minimal process management systems in the sense that it does not deploy many available tools, such as ARIS, to model processes in detail because the contribution of these tools to process excellence and the value they add to the company is considered insufficient. The guiding idea in Hilti's Transformational IT Management is to provide systems that support the users – the consumers of the information.

Hilti's global process management system includes process documentation, compliance documentation, guidelines, and policies on how to do things. It serves several key objectives, including maintaining a clear description of Hilti's key processes and their implementation in IT systems, storing all binding and compliance documents, capturing and sharing knowledge, supporting end-user training and communication, improving global and local communications, gaining clarity about which documents are relevant to policy, and ensuring ISO compliance. Overall, Hilti's global process management system supports Operational Excellence. The system has been revised to include missing processes and procedures but also to exclude for example, documents that are outdated in order to make it more practical and useful.

Organizational Change Management

Regarding organizational change, Hilti focuses on stakeholder management, particularly at the executive management level. For initiatives the size of the

GPD project, members of the executive board are typically involved in order to facilitate organizational change by 'beating the drum'. Their support in communicating the vision and benefits of such programs helps to deliver results at an operational level, however, once the top managers have announced such a change program, it is up to the change management execution team to ensure that the change materializes.

In addition to involving those at the executive management level, it is important to involve a first mover as an example of the benefits of the change. In the case of the GPD project, Hilti communicated and celebrated the success of the first market implementations in such a way that the desire of other market organizations to be next in the rollout grew rapidly. GPD was ultimately perceived as an integral part of Hilti, rather than an IT project dictated from headquarters.

As part of Hilti's stakeholder management, it was important to involve the operational level and provide transparency regarding the initiative's benefits. The support of the employees closest to the market, such as those on the regional level, proved to be a key success factor in cascading information about the benefits of the organizational change.

Competence and Training Management

It is generally part of Hilti's strategic manpower-development process to ensure that its employees have the competences and skills they need to perform well in their jobs. This means that each employee and the employee's team leader assess and discuss the employee's current status and also objectives and identify the training required based on the person's potential, rather than on a pre-established list of skills.

In implementing the GPD initiative, Hilti used a detailed process for training and competence management that included a to-be profile for each position. Comparing the as-is-profile with the to-be-profile revealed deltas in two directions. If employees exceeded the to-be-profile, a move to a new position was discussed, and if employees were lagging behind the to-be-profile, coaching activities were started. This approach was particularly helpful in facilitating the change in the early stages of the program. For Hilti IT, for example, GPD required a change from Oracle Applications skills to SAP skills and from a Rhine Valley team to a global team. Since positions changed completely over the course of the GPD program, Hilti had to ensure that its employees had the opportunity to grow into their positions.

Hilti applied a wave approach to managing training in the market organizations during the GPD rollout. The market organizations with the most recent rollouts coached the market organizations next in line to be rolled out. This transfer of skills and competences at an operational level had two effects: it increased the pride of the market organizations that performed the coaching and provided hands-on support from top trainers for the learning organizations. Overall, this training approach was more successful than having an outside trainer come from the headquarters.

Program and Project Management

Hilti uses a standardized methodology for Program and Project Management that focuses on results and a clear, lean structure. Two tactics were crucial success factors in the organization and execution of the GPD rollout: site preparation meetings and stress tests.

As to site preparations meetings, Hilti first had a 'site opportunity meeting' with each market organization to provide employees with a rough understanding of the actual change required at the site and the opportunities the change would bring. This meeting was followed by two on-site operational review meetings: one to assess in detail what needed to be prepared in terms of data quality, process changes, and skills development, and one to follow up and assess the progress made to then decide on the rollout. This second meeting was central to creating a sense of discipline needed for the rollout.

As to the stress tests, Hilti did two stress tests at each site. Both repeated full business days that were copied out of the old system and replayed in the new environment. The first stress test was used to reveal gaps in the trainings, and the second one was used to give people confidence that they were ready because they had done their homework. While stress tests are an important tool in project management, they are not commonly used in the industry because it costs a considerable amount of money to spend two days stress-testing hundreds of people, however, this investment prevents later struggles and the waste of many person years in recovery procedures. Announcing the stress tests early and monitoring progress in the market organizations also had a psychological element, as no one wanted to lag behind, and the key users wanted to give a good performance.

OPERATIONAL EXCELLENCE AT HILTI AG								
OPERATIONAL EXCELLENCE	DIRECTION			ENABLEMENT				
META	STRATEGY	VALUE	RISK	PROCESSES	IT	CHANGE	TRAINING	PROGRAM
Culture	Vision and Goals	Value Identification	Risk Identification	Governance	Information & Analytics	Change Impact Analysis	Training Need Analysis	Framework
Leadership	Business Model	Value Realization Planning	Risk Management Planning	Methods & Tools	Business Applications	Change Management Planning	Curriculum Development	Organization
Values	Execution	Value Realization	Risk Mitigation	Prozess Optimization	Communication Technology	Change Management Execution	Training Execution	Execution

Scale — Initial — Reactive — Defined — Managed — Excellence

Figure 8.3 **Results of the maturity assessment for Operational Excellence at Hilti AG**

Status of Operational Excellence

Figure 8.3 shows an overall assessment of Hilti's Operational Excellence, as seen from the perspective of Hilti IT. Each management dimension was assessed on a maturity scale from 1 (the lowest rating) to 5 (the highest). The heat map in Figure 8.3 illustrates the perceived maturity levels through colors. It shows that, generally, Hilti has realized high performance levels in Operational Excellence, with an average maturity level of 4. While this level is already very mature, the company still has some room for even further improvement of Operational Excellence.

The maturity that Hilti has achieved in terms of Operational Excellence builds on the achievement of integrated systems, processes, and data. This foundation allows Hilti to see the potential of new technologies to realize overall Operational Excellence and to further develop into a Digital Enterprise. Hilti has already started a number of initiatives to add business value through new technologies. The next section outlines some of these ideas and provides additional thoughts on performance increases of business processes.

8.5.4 USE CASES OF NEW TECHNOLOGIES

Based on the solid core of global processes and data, Hilti is today able to further develop its digital capabilities and to support its business processes through new technologies. Harvesting the benefits of this foundation, Hilti can now consider several technologies – mobile and real-time technologies, big data analytics, the Internet of Things, or social media – and integrate them into the flexible boundary of Hilti's IT landscape, supporting specific business needs.

Mobile and Real-Time Technologies

Considering that a large share of Hilti's business is conducted by territory salespersons, mobility has always been a key element in Hilti's operations, and it has gained significant momentum with the availability of smart phones, which connect the sales representatives to necessary data when they are on the job site.

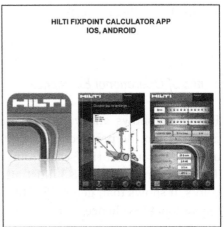
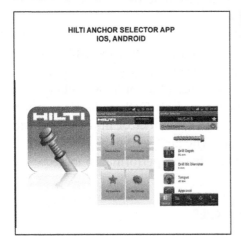

Figure 8.4   Examples for customer-facing Hilti apps

Source: Petry et al., 2013.

This new dimension of mobility has significant implications for the development of mobile applications at Hilti. For example, the company developed sales area applications that support the sales process: territory sales representatives are provided with real-time information on construction sites in their regions, including a contact sync app that loads all the contacts in a territory onto a phone, a customer data app that allows the representative to change customer attributes and is fully synced with the CRM (Customer Relationship Management) system, and a pricing app that provides detailed product pricing information. In addition to these examples that satisfy sales representatives' immediate on-site business needs, Hilti has also developed innovative apps for customer support processes, such as one that assists in selecting the right product (see Figure 8.4). Hilti has also been working on apps that provide customer purchase suggestions based on the analysis of purchases made on similar construction sites. Such apps significantly improve the performance of sales and support processes at Hilti and help to enhance the Operational Excellence of the company.

Big Data Analytics and the Internet of Things

Technologies that enable high-speed in-memory analyses of large amounts of data (for example, SAP HANA (high-performance analytic appliance)) mean that reporting processes at Hilti are now up to 1,000 times faster than previously. At the intersection of mobile technologies and big data analytics, Hilti has been working on a shopping proposal app that uses data mining techniques to analyze product baskets and determine shopping patterns. The analysis of customers' buying behavior can then support cross-selling and up-selling proposals. These technological opportunities can strongly support the customer support process and also trigger higher revenues. Big data analytics also make what was once unthinkable possible. For example, internal customer care notes can be analyzed automatically for patterns of product and service perceptions that may provide valuable information for process improvements. Considering that Hilti has 200,000 customer contacts per day, automated high-speed analyses are highly beneficial as they bear huge potential for increased Operational Excellence. Big data analytics also gain importance in the context of the Internet of Things. With increased connectivity, the analysis of machine-to-machine communication offers new possibilities for Operational Excellence. For example, processes like product development and product maintenance can benefit from an analysis of the conditions under which construction tools are used and related patterns of required maintenance services. Sensors in the tools can automatically trigger information processing from the tool to a central database. The Internet of Things is an exciting innovation that provides entirely new possibilities also for customer support processes. For example, it enables features for customers, such·as apps that determine the exact position of tools on a construction site and alarm signals to prevent the use of construction tools on certain materials. Thus, the Internet of Things has a strong influence on the service operations that Hilti can offer its customers.

Social Media

Linking big data analytics with social media, Hilti also makes use of the possibilities of analyzing public data from social platforms like Twitter and Facebook. These analyses yield insights into customers' perceptions of marketing campaigns and Hilti tools as well as general customer satisfaction, all of which can be useful for deciding on process improvements and hence for increasing Operational Excellence. For example, the identification of perception patterns from social media through sentiment analyses is particularly valuable to Hilti, as the perceptions of a large number of customers can be examined at once. Social media has become increasingly important for business-to-customer operations as well as for business-to-business processes. Analyzing customers' perceptions of competitors is also an important source of information that can feed Operational Excellence at Hilti. Because of the enormous power of social media, Hilti is further actively seeking ways to leverage the potential of this new technology for Operational Excellence.

8.6 Conclusions

This chapter provides an overview of Operational Excellence as a central capability for Digital Enterprises. It explains the foundations of Operational Excellence and presents use cases to illustrate the potential that new technologies bear for companies that seek higher maturity levels in Operational Excellence.

Key learning of the chapter:

1. Operational Excellence is a digital capability that can be realized in a two-step approach: (a) global processes, data, and systems need to be integrated before (b) the potential of new technologies can be leveraged.
2. New technologies that bear huge potential for transformation towards a Digital Enterprise include (a) the Internet of Things and big data analytics, (b) mobile and real-time technologies, and (c) social media.
3. Use cases of new technologies to enhance Operational Excellence in organizations include the improvement of (a) warehousing processes based on RFID tagged product parts, (b) product development and product maintenance processes based on real-time information of product usage, and (c) support processes based on interaction possibilities via social media.

The case of Hilti's GPD initiative shows that Operational Excellence can be seen as a two-step approach. First, organizations need to establish a standardized common platform – that is, integrated global processes, data, and systems – that help to pool resources and to transfer solutions from one part of the Hilti group to the next. Then this foundation allows new opportunities to be exploited.

Establishing integrated systems, processes, and data at Hilti relates to a high maturity level of 4 in the digital capabilities framework for Operational Excellence. However, to reach an even higher degree of maturity, the company must continue to leverage the potential of new technologies. This step can be seen as the icing on the cake in transforming into a Digital Enterprise.

Acknowledgement: The authors would like to thank the Hilti Corporation, particularly Dr Martin Petry and Isabelle Rapin, for sharing valuable company insights and also for providing vital comments that helped to improve the quality of the chapter.

References

Hammer, M. (2010) What is business process management? In *Handbook on business process management: Introduction, methods and information systems,* edited by J. vom Brocke and M. Rosemann (Vol. 1), 3–16, Berlin: Springer.

Kaynak, H. (2003) The relationship between total quality management practices and their effects on firm performance. *Journal of Operations Management,* 21(4), 405–435.

Petry, M., Nemetz, M., Wagner, A., Maschler, M. and Goeth, C. (2013) IT megatrends at Hilti: Mobility, cloud computing and in-memory technology (SAP HANA). Presentation at the *5th IT Academy,* 28 May 2013, Locarno, Switzerland.

Richter, D., Riemer, K. and vom Brocke, J. (2011) Internet social networking: Research state-of-the-art and implications for Enterprise 2.0. *Business and Information Systems Engineering (BISE),* 3(2), 89–101.

Rosemann, M. and vom Brocke, J. (2010) The six core elements of business process management. In *Handbook on business process management: Introduction, methods and information systems,* edited by J. vom Brocke and M. Rosemann (Vol. 1), 107–122, Berlin: Springer.

Schmiedel, T., vom Brocke, J. and Recker, J. (2014) Development and validation of an instrument to measure organizational cultures' support of business process management. *Information and Management*, 51, 43–56.

Schmiedel, T., vom Brocke, J. and Recker, J. (2013) Which cultural values matter to business process management? Results from a global Delphi study. *Business Process Management Journal (BPMJ), 19*(2), 292–317.

vom Brocke, J., Debortoli, S., Müller, O. and Reuter, N. (2014) How in-memory technology can create business value: Insights from the Hilti case. *Communications of the Association for Information Systems* (CAIS), forthcoming.

vom Brocke, J., Petry, M. and Gonsert, T. (2012) Business process management. In *The Handbook of Business Transformation Management*, edited by A. Uhl and L.A. Gollenia, 109–139, Farnham: Gower.

vom Brocke, J., Petry, M. and Schmiedel, T. (2011) How Hilti masters transformation. *360° – The Business Transformation Journal*, 1(Jul 2011), 38–47.

vom Brocke, J., Petry, M., Sinnl, T., Kristensen, B. and Sonnenberg, C. (2010) Global processes and data: The culture journey at Hilti Corporation. In *Handbook on business process management: Strategic alignment, governance, people and culture*, edited by J. vom Brocke and M. Rosemann, (Vol. 2), 539–558, Berlin: Springer.

Chapter 9

Digital Supply Chain Management

CHRISTOPH MEIER

9.1 Introduction

The chapter presents examples towards a Digital Transformation Roadmap based on Digital Use Cases for Supply Chain Management (SCM). SCM involves several business areas such as operations management, production, logistics, procurement, or IT, and is therefore a practical showcase to present the ongoing developments and future possibilities of digital technology. Talking about the future of SCM, managers and researchers predict the movement into the digital age and claim a digital SCM for the coming decades.

The Digital Transformation Roadmap and the Digital Use Cases are two building blocks of the Digital Capability Framework (see Chapter 2). Basically, the roadmap provides an overview of the realization timeframe for the individual Digital Use Cases and is the basis for strategic decisions on which activities need to be executed in order to strengthen digital maturity. Each use case requires a detailed understanding of benefits, and business impact, as well as implementation efforts. In the area of SCM, we identified an initial set of 18 digital use cases, which are relevant for a number of different industries. In addition, we introduce a possible method to assess the priority and impact of the individual use cases, which is the basis for the concrete development of a Digital Transformation Roadmap. Certainly, these use cases can also be mapped to other management areas as well.

Investigating the vision of a digital SCM and its potential use cases makes a differentiated view onto the big picture of SCM necessary. Therefore, we first introduce the foundation of SCM and explain the principles of the Supply Chain Operations Reference model (SCOR). The SCOR model is the basis for the assessment of the individual use cases regarding customer oriented parameters (reliability, responsiveness, agility) and internally-oriented parameters (costs, assets). Next, we describe each digital SCM use case in detail and highlight its major benefits, as well as the assessment results. We conclude the chapter by positioning the digital SCM use cases into a strategic effort-benefits portfolio.

Objectives of this chapter:

1. Explain the key characteristics of SCM and the SCOR model.
2. Introduce 18 digital use cases related to SCM.
3. Assess the digital use cases based on the SCOR model.
4. Position the digital use cases into a strategic effort-benefits-portfolio.

9.2 Introduction to Supply Chain Management

9.2.1 WHAT IS SUPPLY CHAIN MANAGEMENT?

A supply chain consists of all parties involved, directly or indirectly, in fulfilling a customer request. The supply chain includes not only the manufacturer and suppliers, but also transporters, warehouses, retailers, and even customer themselves (Chopra and Meindl, 2013).

SCM involves various approaches utilized to effectively integrate suppliers, manufacturers, and distributors in performing the functions of procurement of materials, transformation of these materials into intermediate and finished products, and distribution of these products to customers in the right quantities, to the right locations, and at the right time in order to meet the required service level with minimal cost. SCM also involves managing a connected series of activities that are concerned with planning, coordinating, and controlling movement of materials, parts, and finished goods from the supplier to the customer. For this to occur, material, financial, and information flows are managed as decisions are made at strategic, tactical, and operational levels throughout the supply chain (Chandra and Grabis, 2007).

9.2.2 KEY CHARACTERISTICS OF SUPPLY CHAIN MANAGEMENT

Both in theory and practice one will find the integration of value-adding networks as the key task of SCM. The term 'Supply Chain Management' goes back to the 1980s and was developed and shaped by the two consultants Keith R. Oliver and Michael D. Webber. They were convinced that a holistic consideration of a supply chain would lead to planning and logistics tasks being required to move up to the corporate level.

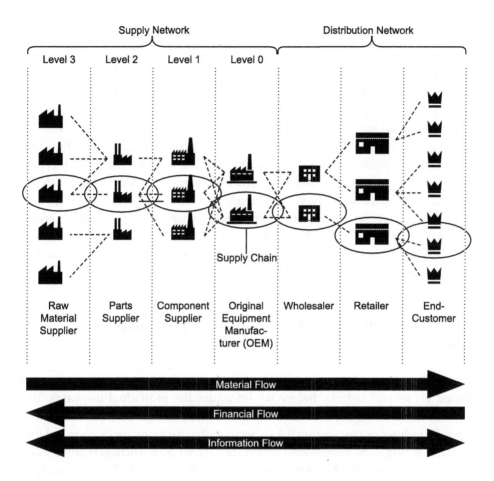

Figure 9.1   Key characteristics of supply chain management

Scanning literature one will not find a consistent and comprehensive definition of SCM. Nevertheless, most of the authors refer to recurring key characteristics, which in total provide an extensive picture of the scope of SCM (see Figure 9.1).

SCM operates initially between companies and therefore considers both upstream and downstream business partners. SCM covers value-adding chains, networks or logistics networks and defines the value-add as supplying, transforming and distributing different types of (raw) material and (semi) finished goods. SCM claims a strict end-customer orientation and focuses on customers' needs (at the right time, in the right quality, to the right place). SCM takes an end-to-end perspective, from the end-customer back to the raw material suppliers and promotes an integration of all participants under optimization of holistic time, cost and quality objectives (adequate service level, minimal costs (inventory costs etc.)). Also the synchronization of demand and supply is key in SCM, as production produces just what the end-customer demands and these demands have to be synchronized with the upstream supply chain. That means that all types of flows (material, information and financial flows) must also be integrated and synchronized. To enable such an integration and synchronization, management activities such as configuring, coordinating, planning, executing and monitoring must be performed as part of SCM. In that context, decisions with different time horizons (strategic, tactical, and operational) have to be made, and finally SCM is also a generic term for management methods and approaches such as 'Just-In-Time', 'Vendor Managed Inventory' and others (Kuhn and Hellingrath, 2002; Simchi-Levi et al., 2004; Christopher, 2005; Chandra and Grabis, 2007; Weber, 2008; APICS, 2010; Stadtler, 2010; Wilke, 2012).

9.3 Assessment of the Digital Supply Chain Management Use Cases

The digital use cases presented in this chapter have been analyzed and assessed based on several criteria. Before we introduce the individual use cases, this section explains the basis of the assessment. First, each use case is assigned to specific industries (see section 9.3.1). Second, the use cases are categorized into corresponding SCM dimensions, which are derived from Michael Porter's Value Chain (see section 9.3.2). Third, we identified the relevant digital technology for each use case (see section 9.3.3). Finally, each use case is assessed in terms of value add (benefit) and implementation effort and horizon. The assessment of the specific benefits is consistently done based on the attributes and metrics of the SCOR Model (see section 9.3.4). Overall, this enables us to position the use cases within a strategic portfolio, which will be discussed in the last section of this chapter.

9.3.1 SEVEN STRATEGIC INDUSTRIES CONSIDERED FOR A DIGITAL SUPPLY CHAIN MANAGEMENT

The digital use cases presented in this chapter are defined for seven strategic industries: Automotive, Machinery, High Tech, Consumer Products, Chemical, Pharma, and Retail.

Table 9.1   Supply chain management dimensions

Suppliers	Integration, collaboration and development of suppliers
Production Systems	Value adding processes that transform products and services
Logistics and Inventory	In-/outbound, transportation, warehousing and inventory management and control
HR and Talent	Attraction, selection, training, assessment, and rewarding of employees in SCM context
IT and Technology	Study, design, development, application, implementation, support or management of computer-based information systems and further SCM related technology
Performance Measurement Systems	Collecting, analyzing, and reporting information regarding the performance of an individual, group, organization, system or component in SCM context
Customers	Connection, integration and collaboration with customers

9.3.2 SEVEN DIMENSIONS OF SUPPLY CHAIN MANAGEMENT

Derived from Michael Porter's Value Chain Model we arranged the digital SCM use cases for seven dimensions within SCM, as shown in Table 9.1, with the intention to demonstrate the extensive intersection of SCM related tasks within and between companies.

Table 9.2   Digital technology trends in supply chain management

Mobility	Mobile applications for performing business processes at any time and any place
Big and Smarter Data	(Near) live analysis of large volumes of structured and non-structured data to get deeper insights and enable reliable decision making
Cloud Computing	Internet-based IT infrastructure to enable collaborative processes and scalable Total Cost of Ownership (TCO)
Social Media	Private and business oriented networks for communication and collaboration purposes to be leveraged as additional data sources and sinks
Predictive and Prescriptive Analytics	Analysis of structured and non-structured data and recognition of specific patterns (through usage of advanced algorithms) to enable more precise predications of future behaviors
Internet of Things	Seamless integration of physical objects (e.g. machines with sensors, labor etc.) into the information network to make use of high amount of additional data
3D Printing and Scanning	Mass customization of different types of products to most individual customer needs
Robotics	Machines with appropriate intelligence to perform specific processes faster, cheaper, safer and with better quality results

9.3.3 RELEVANT DIGITAL TECHNOLOGY TRENDS

The presented digital use cases leverage eight emerging technologies related to SCM, which were derived from Gartner's Hype Cycle on Emerging Technologies. Some of the technological areas were introduced in detail in Chapter 1. For the sake of completeness and convenience the trends are briefly presented once again in Table 9.2.

9.3.4 SCOR MODEL

Introduction to the SCOR Model

The Supply Chain Operations Reference model (SCOR) is a product of the Supply Chain Council, Inc. (SCC), a global non-profit consortium whose diagnostic, methodology, and benchmarking tools help organizations make dramatic and rapid improvements in supply chain processes. SCC established the SCOR process reference model for evaluating and comparing supply chain activities and performance. The SCOR model comprises SCC's consensus view of supply chain management. The unique framework links business processes, metrics, best practices and technology into a unified structure. This helps to support communication among supply chain partners and to improve the effectiveness of supply chain management and related supply chain improvement activities (Supply Chain Council, 2012).

The purpose of the SCOR model is to describe the business activities associated with all phases of satisfying a customer's demand. The model is structured into several sections and is organized based on the six primary management processes of Plan, Source, Make, Deliver, Return and Enable. Based on these building blocks the model can describe very simple or very complex supply chains using a common set of definitions. One outcome is that disparate industries can be linked to describe the depth and breadth of virtually any supply chain. The model is successfully used to describe and provide a basis for supply chain improvement for global projects as well as site-specific projects (Supply Chain Council, 2012).

The essence of reference models is to describe the process architecture in a way that makes sense to key business partners. With process architecture we mean the way processes interact, how they perform, how they are configured and the requirements (skills) on staff operating the process. The SCOR reference model therefore consists of four major sections (Supply Chain Council, 2012):

- Performance: Standard metrics to describe process performance and define strategic goals;
- Processes: Standard descriptions of management processes and process relationships;
- Practices: Management practices that produce significant better process performance;
- People: Standard definitions for skills required to perform supply chain processes.

For the sake of the assessment of digital SCM use cases the performance section of the SCOR model was chosen and will be described in more detail in the following part.

Table 9.3   Relevant SCOR performance attributes for the assessment of the Digital Use Cases

	Attribute	Attribute definition	Attribute measured by
Customer oriented	Reliability	The attribute addresses the ability to perform tasks as expected. Typical metrics include on-time, the right quantity and the right quality	RL.1.1 Perfect Order Fulfillment
	Responsiveness	The attribute describes the speed at which tasks are performed. Examples include cycle-time metrics	RS.1.1 Order Fulfillment Cycle Time
	Agility	The attribute addresses the ability to respond to external influences, such as non-forecasted changes in demand or natural disasters, and the ability to change	AG.1.1 Upside Supply Chain Flexibility AG.1.2 Supply Chain Upside Adaptability AG.1.3 Supply Chain Downside Adaptability AG.1.4 Overall Value at Risk (VaR)

Table 9.3   Relevant SCOR performance attributes for the assessment of the Digital Use Cases – Continued

	Attribute	Attribute definition	Attribute measured by
Internal oriented	Costs	The attribute describes the cost of operating a process and includes labor costs, material costs, and transportation costs	CO.1.1 Supply Chain Management Cost CO.1.2 Cost of Goods Sold
	Assets	The attribute addresses the ability to efficiently utilize assets. Typical metrics include inventory days of supply and capacity utilization	AM.1.1 Cash-to-Cash Cycle Time AM.1.2 Return on Supply Chain Fixed Assets AM.1.3 Return on Working Capital

Source: Based on Supply Chain Council, 2012.

SCOR Performance Attributes and Metrics

The performance section of SCOR consists of two types of elements: Performance Attributes and Metrics (Supply Chain Council, 2012). A performance attribute is a grouping of metrics used to express a strategy. An attribute itself cannot be measured; it is used to set strategic direction. Metrics, in contrast, measure the ability of a supply chain to achieve these strategic attributes. The five SCOR attributes together with their desired level-1 metrics are summarized in Table 9.3.

Reliability, Responsiveness and Agility are considered to be customer-focused. Cost and Asset Management Efficiency are considered to be internally-focused. All SCOR metrics are grouped within one of the performance attributes. Each Performance Attribute has one or more level-1/strategic metrics. These level-1 metrics are the calculations by which an organization can measure how successful it is in achieving its desired positioning within the competitive market space. The detailed definition of the SCOR level-1 metrics can be found in Table 9.4.

Table 9.4   Detailed definition of the SCOR level-1 metrics

Level-1 metric	Level-1 metric definition
RL.1.1 Perfect Order Fulfillment	The percentage of orders delivered on-time, in full
RS.1.1 Order Fulfillment Cycle Time	The average actual cycle time consistently achieved to fulfill customer orders
AG.1.1 Upside Supply Chain Flexibility	The number of days required to achieve an unplanned sustainable 20% increase in quantities delivered
AG.1.2 Supply Chain Upside Adaptability	The sustainable reduction and increase or decrease in product quantities that can be achieved in 30 days (without back-orders, cost penalties or excess inventory)
AG.1.3 Supply Chain Downside Adaptability	The sustainable reduction and increase or decrease in product quantities that can be achieved in 30 days (without back-orders, cost penalties or excess inventory)
AG.1.4 Overall Value at Risk (VaR)	The sum of the probability of risk events times the monetary impact of the events which can impact any core supply chain functions or key dependencies
CO.1.1 Supply Chain Management Cost	All direct and indirect expenses associated with the operation of supply chain business processes across the supply chain
CO.1.2 Cost of Goods Sold	The cost associated with buying raw materials and producing finished goods. This cost includes direct costs (labor, materials) and overhead
AM.1.1 Cash-to-Cash Cycle Time	The time it takes for cash invested in materials to flow back into the company after finished goods have been delivered to customers [calendar days]
AM.1.2 Return on Supply Chain Fixed Assets	The return an organization receives on its invested capital in supply chain fixed assets
AM.1.3 Return on Working Capital	Return on working capital assesses the magnitude of investment relative to a company's working capital position verses the revenue generated from a supply chain. Components include accounts receivable, accounts payable, inventory, revenue, cost of goods sold and total supply chain management costs

Source: Based on Supply Chain Council, 2012.

9.4 Digital Supply Chain Management Use Cases

In this section, we describe 18 use cases of a digital SCM, in terms of current challenges and proposed solutions – how the specific business area (for example, demand and supply matching) leverages certain technology trends. Additionally the benefits and efforts are shown to the right of each description, illustrating the assessment based on SCOR metrics (benefits) and further important effort values (necessary one-time investment, resulting annual variable costs and estimated maturity time horizon for implementation readiness). At the end of each section the reader will find the assignment of the use case to the desired industry, SCM dimension, and the leveraged emerging technologies.

9.4.1 DEMAND SENSING AND SIGNAL MANAGEMENT

The amount of consumer data is steadily increasing particularly because of today's multi-channel commerce however, this data can often be stored and analyzed only on an aggregated level (for example, per product group, per storage location, per week etc.) with limited functions on a granular level in real-time. In order to sense and respond to a future customer-driven supply chain in real-time, in-memory computing provides a single repository of all shipment, point-of-sales, social media and syndicated data, as well as other influential demand data points, applying the concept of big data (storing of high volumes of granular data at the lowest level). Combined and enriched with unique modeling capabilities and algorithms from predictive and prescriptive analytics, in-memory platforms can rapidly analyze, plan

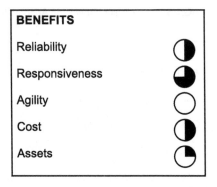

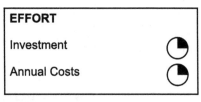

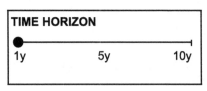

and manage huge amounts of demand data in real-time. The in-memory process innovation can thus greatly improve responsiveness to customer and end consumer demand with low latency.

The concrete benefits of demand sensing and signal management are the reduction of out-of-stock situations in stores. Customers always receive the required products, which results in increasing sales figures. In addition, forecast accuracy improves as the input for the demand forecast calculation becomes more granular and realistic. This enables a better granular planning, lower inventory levels and therefore reduces costs for the supplying company. Overall, the consumer orientation improves and the customer relationship is much better understood along the entire upstream supply chain.

Industries: Consumer Products, Retail
SCM Dimension: Customers
Technology: Big Data, Social Media, Predictive and Prescriptive Analytics

---

9.4.2 ADVANCED SELLING PATTERN AND CUSTOMER BEHAVIOR ANALYSIS

A detailed understanding of selling patterns and customers buying behavior is necessary to effectively deliver promotions. This is relevant for all industries, which sell additional services to customers besides the primary products. Selling patterns and customer behavior can be analyzed by geography, product, time horizon and line of business and provide answers to questions like: 'Where are products sold?', 'Who purchases the products?', or 'When are the products demanded (every week, always at the end of the month)?' The results are combined and dynamics can be built, meaning that it is possible to analyze how customers behave over time. Big data concepts and in-memory technology enable such analyses and support accurate promotion planning.

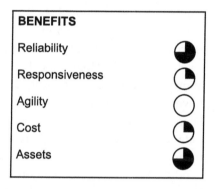

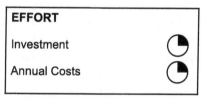

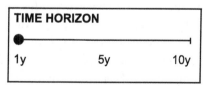

The concrete benefits are an increasing visibility of all sales- and trade-related processes in order to facilitate collaboration and improve forecasting and promotion planning to ultimately increase revenue. Furthermore, the analysis of the company's own selling patterns enables detection of improvement potential (for example, selling peaks within a week, a month or a year, which leads to undesired peaks in other lines of business like transportation capacity) and therefore reduces internal costs.

Industries: Automotive, Machinery, High Tech, Consumer Products, Chemical, Pharma, Retail
SCM Dimension: Customers
Technology: Big Data, Social Media, Predictive and Prescriptive Analytics

---

9.4.3 REAL-TIME GLOBAL SERVICE PARTS DEMAND AND SUPPLY MATCHING

The quick and precise matching of demand and supply for service parts on different levels of granularity within a complex network of companies and/or plants is a major business challenge for many companies. The current inventory is not visible on a global or on a regional level. New technology, like big data, allows the capture of inventories at the lowest level of granularity (per stock keeping unit and per location). This data can be aggregated in real-time to any level of interest (for example, product family XY for region Z for the next two weeks). In this scenario, in-memory databases are an enabler as they support fast decision making, using highly sophisticated simulation models which leverage the captured (big) data in real-time. In addition, an in-memory database provides insight into current service parts demands

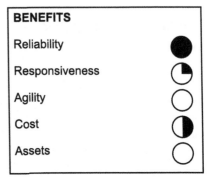

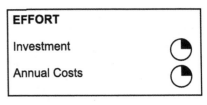

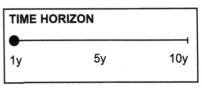

and matches these with inventory levels in real-time and with early alerting. In-memory databases also serve as a central data platform for prediction and simulation, thus enabling global planning and simulation of service parts demand and supply by different company areas. Furthermore, required service parts coming from predictive maintenance activities using automatic defect detection might be considered useful as an input on the demand side.

Concrete benefits of real-time demand and supply matching for service parts are a significant increase in customer satisfaction, as the desired service parts are stored at the right location. Also, planning costs and inventory holding costs are reduced. Overall, the company gets much more as well as deeper insights and is able to plan and execute faster and more precisely.

Industries: Automotive, Machinery
SCM Dimension: Production Systems, Logistics and Inventory
Technology: Big Data, Predictive and Prescriptive Analytics

9.4.4 ADVANCED PICKING AND COMMISSIONING USING AUGMENTED REALITY

Augmented reality, enabled by computer wearable devices like Google Glass, can improve the performance of employees and companies. These devices provide employees with real-time information, no matter when they work, where they work (for example, in front of a shelf), or on what task they work (pick article XY). For example, in the area of picking and commissioning activities, where workers are constantly on the move, it is very useful for them to have their needed information continuously updated in front of their eyes. Also it is helpful and sometimes necessary to have both hands permanently free and/or clean (for example, when working in a food storage location). Warehouse pickers might use Google Glass to be guided through the entire process from package pick-up, through to scanning

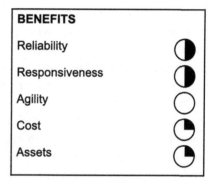

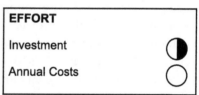

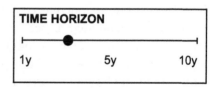

and drop-off for shipment, and to receive details about the exact location, weight, size and type of each package while retaining full situational awareness about safety in the warehouse.

The concrete benefits of such computer wearable devices providing augmented reality are that they can improve the performance of employees/

workers who are constantly on the move and need updated information, whose efficiency and safety depends on keeping their hands free, or who can benefit from visual alerts (for example, if the wrong product was picked) and reminders, or increased environment-awareness.

Industries: Automotive, Machinery, High Tech, Consumer Products, Chemical, Pharma, Retail
SCM Dimension: Logistics and Inventory
Technology: Mobile, Internet of Things

9.4.5 CONSUMER 360°

Stationary retailers are threatened by the increasing competition of online stores and require new ways to improve sales growth. Some retailers are experimenting with applying online-techniques to in-store processes, for example, by tracking in-store customer behavior. This transformation from simple brick and mortar shops to digitally-integrated showrooms might create significant consumer value along with a unified customer experience. The foundation for providing specific information to customers is capturing and analyzing relevant data upfront. It is essential to know who your customers are and what they want (or maybe not want but also should buy). Concrete customer profiles are generated based on so called 'Consumer 360° programs'. Customers are invited to share their

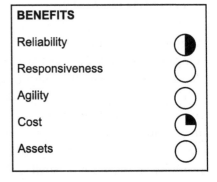

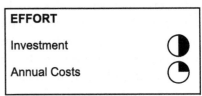

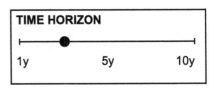

preferences and buying history (for example, in online stores or using loyalty cards). This data allows the provision of better customer experience. For example, customers can be greeted by name and receive personalized product suggestions. In another scenario, Radio-Frequency IDentification (RFID) tags attached to clothing items might communicate with mobile devices of customers and provide additional information on specific products. In-memory computing is one prerequisite for achieving this kind of intuitive customer experience. It can analyze big data fast enough for sales staff to react to customers' preferences. In combination with big data and social media for data capturing, cloud computing for data storing, analytics for any kind of predictions and mobile for data presentation, allows putting the customer into focus.

The immense benefit of such a 360° program is that it creates an extraordinary in-store experience for customers. It also provides sales assistants (who might wear Google Glasses) with information about their customers. Moreover, better customer insights allow retailers to optimize product placements, enhance promotions, make better staffing decisions and increase cross-selling.

Industries: Retail
SCM Dimension: Customers
Technology: Big Data, Cloud Computing, Mobile, Social Media, Predictive and Prescriptive Analytics, Internet of Things

---

9.4.6 INTELLIGENT STORAGE LOCATIONS

Storage locations across the entire ecosystem, for example vending machines on customer's side or in-store shelves, can be equipped with sensors and Internet connectivity. This provides a real-time awareness of sales data across the entire network. The stock level can be monitored anytime and anywhere, and sales actions can be taken. For example, this allows making ad-hoc customized offers (such as seasonal stock discounts). Storage locations, like vending machines, can also be equipped with video cameras, facial recognition software, wireless connectivity and touch screens. The collected information helps to map social networks and buying patterns or even allows sending personalized offers to people passing by, using mobile phones.

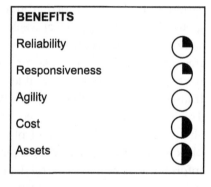

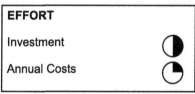

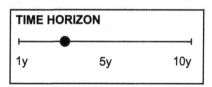

This new technology enables the company to gain real-time insight into who is buying what, from which machine, or taking which product from the shelf. In addition, customers' response rates to special offers and data on which vending machines should be prioritized for stocking can be detected. Intelligent storage locations design their own customer-dependent marketing campaigns and automatically order the desired products from upstream supply chain locations. Next-generation vending machines also accept mobile payments.

The concrete benefits of intelligent storage locations are an improved and easier stock management, as well as tailored offers for consumers and therefore more precise sales combined with a unified customer experience.

Industries: Automotive, Machinery, High Tech, Consumer Products, Chemical, Pharma, Retail
SCM Dimension: Logistics and Inventory, Customers
Technology: Big Data, Cloud Computing, Mobile, Social Media, Predictive and Prescriptive Analytics, Internet of Things

9.4.7 REAL-TIME GEOLOCATED SHIPPING

Products are often shipped around the globe with delivery times of weeks and sometimes months. In order to keep track of the delivery process, products have to be somehow visible and transparent within the supply chain. This can be achieved using geolocated shipping. The geolocations of physical objects are permanently tracked and the information is sent to a central data hub using latest connectivity technology (for example, RFID chips with GPS integration). Another approach is to use the GPS device of mobile phones during the shipping process. For example, staff use their mobile phones on the ship, the train or the truck to send their location in short time frames. In any case, huge amounts of data are captured, stored (in the cloud) and analyzed to enable predictions and also simulations in terms of arrival times. The information

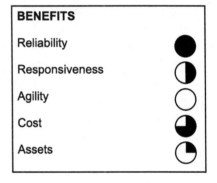

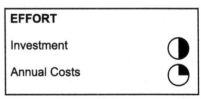

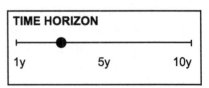

can further be enhanced with data like weather or traffic forecasts or the telematics of the transportation vehicles. Logistics service providers can offer such real-time data publicly to their customers as additional services.

The benefits of such scenarios are an obvious increase of visibility within the supply chain allowing preparation or even reaction upfront if disruptions are notified. Therefore penalties will be reduced if on-time deliveries increase.

Industries: Automotive, Machinery, High Tech, Consumer Products, Chemical, Pharma, Retail
SCM Dimension: Suppliers, Logistics and Inventory, IT and Technology, Customers
Technology: Big Data, Cloud Computing, Mobile, Predictive and Prescriptive Analytics, Internet of Things

---

9.4.8 DIGITAL PRODUCT HISTORY

The digital product history can be considered as one of the first steps towards the Internet of Things. Every product (or component, module, packaging unit, etc.) gets its own identity and stores its own history which can be retrieved through RFID, barcodes or integrated SIM-cards. Every detail of a product's life cycle can be recorded, ranging from product characteristics, to manufacturing history, to operational or machine data, ingredients and batch numbers and also repair and maintenance data. All information is centrally available for customers, suppliers, distributors, service providers, production and development departments. With the help of a digital product history, products can, for example, steer production, because a product can send its production parameters directly

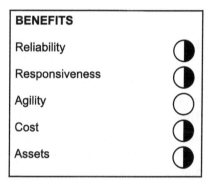

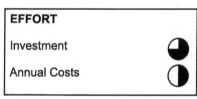

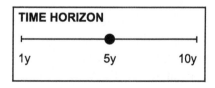

to the machines that produce it. Improvements in product quality are also possible as data from the production process and machines in use can be interrelated. The implementation of self-service portals for customers is another innovation that can include detailed information on each individual machine.

Overall any product becomes individual and serves as decentralized data storage, permanently (or on-demand) connected to its environment.

Concrete benefits of implementing a digital product history are an increased transparency across the installed base which helps to safeguard a company's competitive position in the market as well as an increase in service revenue through new value added services. In addition there is only one single point of truth in terms of product data available and many other scenarios will be enabled by such a digital product history: adaptive logistics, self-steering factories and so forth.

Industries: Automotive, Machinery, High Tech, Consumer Products, Chemical, Pharma, Retail
SCM Dimension: Suppliers, Production Systems, Logistics and Inventory, IT and Technology, Performance Measurement Systems, Customers
Technology: Big Data, Cloud Computing, Mobile, Internet of Things

9.4.9 CONSUMER MASS CUSTOMIZATION USING 3D SCANNERS

3D technologies pave the way towards profitable mass customization. Those companies recognizing this opportunity could benefit from higher loyalty, increasing revenues, and a competitive advantage. Mass customization becomes profitable if companies manage to provide real value for customers on the one hand, while managing an appropriate cost structure within the complex manufacturing process on the other hand.

Social media and online configuration wizards can be used to gather customers' preferences and analyze the value for customers attached to existing or proposed product components. In addition, 3D scanners can be used (for example, in-store) to analyze the shape of real-world objects such as exact body

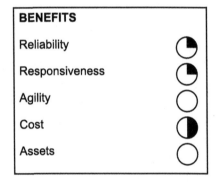

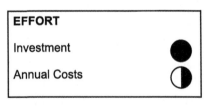

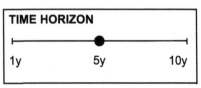

measurements and utilize the collected data to construct 3D digital models (for example, for individualized products tailored to fit). Such a concept might be also interesting for companies manufacturing products like cars (to tailor seats or maybe touchpad positions), machines (for example, production or infrastructure equipment) or even high tech products like tablets.

The concrete benefits of mass customization are: increasing revenue and competitive advantages, improving customer loyalty and cash flow, and reducing waste through on-demand production. It can also generate valuable data that can be used in the development of standard products and in marketing campaigns. Furthermore, the number of returns will be reduced dramatically as the products fit customers' needs more precisely.

Industries: Automotive, Machinery, High Tech, Retail
SCM Dimension: Customers
Technology: 3D Printing and Scanning

9.4.10 TRENDMINING

Predicting trends and future behaviors of customers has proven to be very difficult in the past, however, new technologies such as big data and predictive and prescriptive analytics can considerably facilitate the detection of new trends and help companies to react quickly to new developments. To make forecasts as accurate as possible, large amounts of data are needed, covering topics such as 'what did customers buy', 'when', 'where', or 'which marketing strategy was successful'. Most of the data that is collected is unstructured which is why trendmining algorithms are needed to perform the analyses. Trendmining programs can filter huge amounts of data, recognize patterns and thus deduce future scenarios. Until now, primarily retailers have made use of such analytics to detect upcoming trends. For instance, they analyze

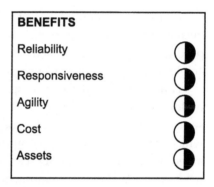

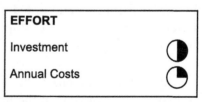

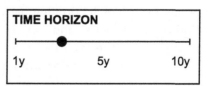

customer behavior, sales trends and weather data to determine the number of customers coming into a shop – which proves highly valuable when it comes to staff planning. Industries with no direct contact to the end consumer (for example, chemical and pharmaceutical industries) need to rely on other data sources to discover trends in their markets. In this case, trendmining can be utilized to identify recent tendencies in patent applications which can be an indication of new research and development trends.

Primary benefits of trendmining are an increase in forecast accuracy, and therefore a better foundation for planning. Companies can prepare much better for the future, for example when it comes to capacity (staff) planning, allocation, and especially utilization.

Industries: Automotive, Machinery, High Tech, Consumer Products, Chemical, Pharma, Retail
SCM Dimension: Customers
Technology: Big Data, Predictive and Prescriptive Analytics

9.4.11 ACCELERATED PRODUCT LAUNCHES USING 3D PRINTING

Customers demand a steadily decreasing time-to-market, while product launches in contrast have to be accelerated significantly. 3D printing is a technology that allows the speedy building of new prototypes and pre-series parts. Based on 3D models, which are derived from computer-aided design software or 3D scanners, new products can be manufactured in local departments and tested much faster, avoiding expensive shipment from a distant manufacturer.

3D printing is considered to be technology for everyone in the future. So far, the use of 3D printing has been limited to experts and specialized manufactures. The recent developments in 3D printing, and the resulting price drops, allow a much wider user group to participate in this technology.

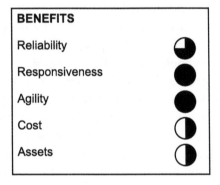

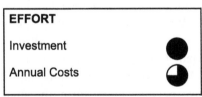

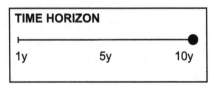

There are a lot of concrete benefits using 3D printing in a wide range of businesses. 3D printing will fundamentally change the production footprint and thus the time to market. New products can be introduced much faster and with a higher frequency – anywhere in the world. This allows a much more precise response to customer changes and is therefore a huge enabler of an agile supply chain. Also, supply chains will change their style as certain suppliers may be replaced by 3D printers. This again gives companies a flexibility to adjust products, production quantities and so forth (for example, when it comes to disruptions within certain supply chains).

Industries: Automotive, Machinery, High Tech, Consumer Products, Chemical, Pharma
SCM Dimension: Production Systems, Customers
Technology: 3D Printing and Scanning

9.4.12 3D FOOD PRINTING

Printing customized chocolates, pasta, or food at the International Space Station (ISS) is about to become reality and could revolutionize the supply chain of the food industry. In the near future, uniquely designed and customized chocolate or candies might be manufactured and delivered. Enabled by additive manufacturing using 3D printers, the concept of mass customization will be introduced within the food industry. These 3D printers could be used in every imaginable point of the food manufacturing process, for example restaurants or supermarkets. This again would provide customers with the opportunity to fully customize their desired food product to be a certain shape, size, or even color. Additionally, food production will not be limited to a certain production location anymore, and thus will bring food closer to the end consumer (especially as the world's population will constantly increase in the future).

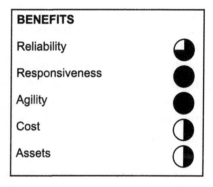

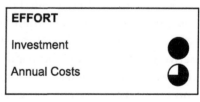

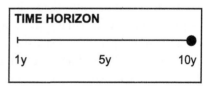

The major benefits when using 3D food printers are that the food manufacturing process becomes much more flexible and independent of the actual location. Customers can create their own variations depending on the personal tastes and preferences. Furthermore, new food products can be created and tested much faster.

Industries: Consumer Products
SCM Dimension: Production Systems
Technology: 3D Printing and Scanning

9.4.13 ADVANCED BUSINESS NETWORKS

Supply chain complexity has increased as supply chains have extended overseas in order to reduce costs. Challenges of a far-flung supply chain can be found in the increased number of trading partners, the difficulty of tracking products, a lack of transportation infrastructure and logistics data overseas, and the increased length of time that it takes for products to be delivered to end users.

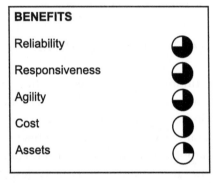

Advanced business networks based on social media can help to combat these challenges. The idea is to develop a cloud-based business network that allows companies to connect with suppliers, customers, and all kinds of partners or services. Each individual involved in the supply chain would have the ability

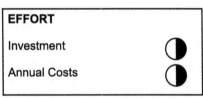

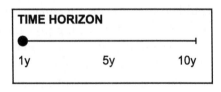

to 'friend' each other and connect to core information and updates in the process. As a cloud-based solution, the information is available to everyone involved at the same time, independent of their current location. Additionally, the network will work as single point of interaction when it comes to data interchange (sales orders, purchase orders, process data, geolocation data, etc.) and enable a real-time business within a complex network of interlinked supply chains.

Concrete benefits of advanced business networks on cloud-based platforms are end-to-end visibility within the supply chain making it easier to determine problems and disruptions, increased agility and speed when it comes to resolving problems, and continuous improvement within supply chains.

Industries: Automotive, Machinery, High Tech, Consumer Products, Chemical, Pharma, Retail
SCM Dimension: Suppliers, IT and Technology, Customers
Technology: Cloud Computing, Social Media

9.4.14 ADVANCED INVENTORY MONITORING

Companies use technologies such as barcodes or RFID chips to monitor their inventories at a certain level of detail. The Internet of Things significantly improves this monitoring. Not only are location and amount captured as inventory data, but also 3D positions, conditions, inside temperature, biological values and many more, and this data is updated every second by the item itself. As a consequence, more and more data is streamed into the monitoring systems and products moving through the supply chain. Inventory data is no longer appended to the storage location. Instead, inventory data is available anywhere and anytime. Cloud technologies come into play to store such big data, and mobile technologies like Global System for Mobile Communications (GSM) help in submitting this data if

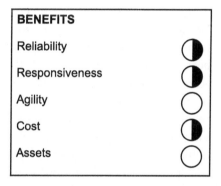

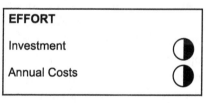

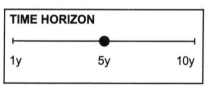

products are on their way to the customer (for example while crossing oceans). In-memory computing is the key to leveraging the big data.

Concrete benefits of an advanced inventory monitoring are that it can considerably improve supply chain efficiencies if more process (and logistics) variables are monitored. As a result, relationships like an imminent expiry data and a therefore decreasing product value can be visualized and used for further decisions. Advanced inventory monitoring also reduces scrapping costs as expiring products call attention to themselves.

Industries: Automotive, Machinery, High Tech, Consumer Products, Chemical, Pharma, Retail
SCM Dimension: Logistics and Inventory, IT and Technology, Performance Measurement Systems
Technology: Big Data, Cloud Computing, Mobile, Internet of Things

9.4.15 SAME-DAY FULFILMENT USING DRONES

Disruptive innovation is difficult to predict and the reality of 'the future of shopping' is probably far more dramatic than anyone can imagine. Yet, many innovations are based on technology that everybody quickly becomes accustomed to, and then scarcely thinks about. Delivery time is, today, the key for a successful retailer offering its products online via e-commerce. Accelerating today's deliveries needs more than just pure transportation optimization – new ways or modes of transportation are necessary. Therefore, the next big step for performing logistics operations in the retail business might be same-day fulfilment using drones, which has already started to become reality in some markets. Drone helicopters shipping to our homes could be expected soon as

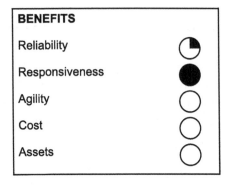

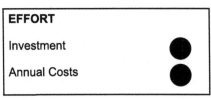

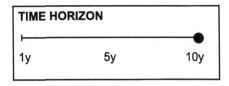

specific online retailers are already in the pilot phase of such an engagement. Drones are robots which can be connected via mobile technologies with their home base and store huge amounts of data somewhere in the cloud.

The same-day fulfilment scenario increases the speed of consumption at the customer side, as well as dramatically improves the customer experience. Real-time online shopping (and delivery) will become reality, however, such drone technology means high investment, and applications for such a delivery mode will have to be analyzed and the business case calculated.

Also the impact on the environment ('How will the drones be powered?', 'What about noise in the air?' etc.) has to be researched in detail.

Industries: Retails
SCM Dimension: Logistics and Inventory
Technology: Big Data, Cloud Computing, Mobile, Internet of Things, Robotics

9.4.16 LOCAL MINI FACTORIES

Today, many European and North American consumer products and retail companies are purchasing their products from Asian suppliers who manufacture in large factories. Due to certain demographical and economic reasons (for example, emerging markets become wealthier because of increasing wages) it may not be as profitable to source from such countries in the future. Furthermore, customers do not accept such long delivery times anymore and demand highly individualized products. These developments lead to the need to shift the location of the final product construction (or individualization to customer needs) much closer to the end customer. For that reason, companies especially from the apparel industry are planning to shift their production from big factories in Asia to smaller local factories that are closer to the consumer.

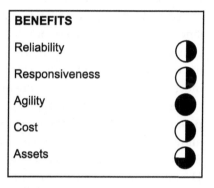

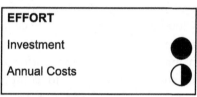

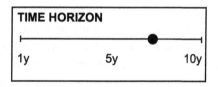

These companies want to be able to execute the production in so called 'local mini factories' and at the same time become very flexible, local, and resilient to labor cost changes. Technologies like the Internet of Things or 3D printing leverage the idea of local mini factories, and cloud technology is the foundation for steering such a decentralized factory landscape.

Concrete benefits of local mini factories are a much more flexible production process that can be responsive to customers' individual preferences and manufacture customized products, as well as independence from labor costs and trade restrictions.

Industries: Consumer Products, Retail
SCM Dimension: Production Systems, IT and Technology
Technology: Cloud Computing, 3D Printing and Scanning, Internet of Things, Robotics

9.4.17 ADVANCED AND FLEXIBLE ON-DEMAND BUSINESS IT

Although information technology is not the core business of manufacturing and retail companies, most of them suffer from huge installations and landscapes and therefore high complexity and costs. Today and in the future, companies can get most of their necessary business IT as-a-Service, on-demand and pay per use. This technology shift allows companies to move their focus from building and managing IT infrastructure back to running and optimizing their supply chains. Cloud computing, as the key enabling technology, transforms SCM and has a major impact on the performance of supply chains. Cloud computing is not only considered as a driver for innovation and differentiation but is also expected to amplify and accelerate other technology megatrends. It is the enabler or foundation for most of the other use cases presented here, as data will be stored at a provider and therefore be accessible from everywhere.

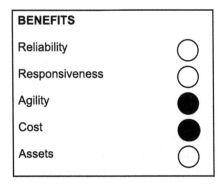

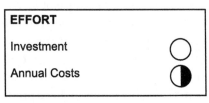

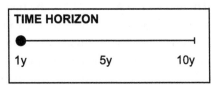

Major benefits of advanced and flexible on-demand business IT are that it supports analytics and insights from big data and allows seamless sharing of data between different devices (laptop, tablet, smartphone, wearables, etc.). Furthermore, collaboration between people is much easier as the actual work can be performed from anywhere on multiple devices. Cloud computing is boosting the speed with which new business applications can be launched, eliminating implementations lasting months and enabling the initiation of new tools and apps within minutes. Finally, significant cost savings to Total Cost of Implementation (TCI) and Total Cost of Ownership (TCO) can be observed, and large investments are no longer necessary as applications used via cloud will be subscribed to and be paid by (monthly) fee.

Industries: Automotive, Machinery, High Tech, Consumer Products, Chemical, Pharma, Retail
SCM Dimension: IT and Technology
Technology: Cloud Computing

9.4.18 ADVANCED PRODUCTION MONITORING

In today's manufacturing processes many different systems are involved at the manufacturing operations level. Each system creates masses of data records each millisecond, which have to be processed by a suitable technology platform. Factors that lead to failure are often not detected in time to take any corrective actions because of the high number of systems and the limitations on performing a holistic analysis. An advanced production monitoring system can bring the different data sources together, including the massive use of sensors associate with the idea of the Internet of Things. Having one data platform, in-memory computing is able to analyze this big data almost in real-time, and predictive (and prescriptive) analytic algorithms bring production monitoring to the next level. Cloud technology enabled production systems can be monitored from anywhere in the world and corrective decisions can be prepared and made almost in real-time. In addition, advanced production monitoring helps to avoid or minimize scrap and low quality production due to system or machine failure, by optimizing the production process through predictive and real-time analysis. Quality issues can be detected much earlier in the production chain and future issues might be predicted as well.

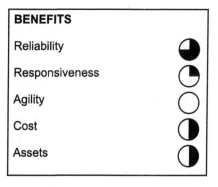

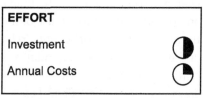

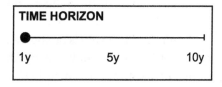

Concrete benefits are: reduced failures in production processes, lowered costs of failures and scrap, and real-time monitoring of production processes.

Industries: Automotive, Machinery, High Tech, Consumer Products, Chemical, Pharma
SCM Dimension: Production Systems
Technology: Big Data, Cloud, Predictive and Prescriptive Analytics, Internet of Things

9.5 Positioning of the Digital Supply Chain Management Use Cases into a Strategic Effort-Benefits Portfolio

The previous section outlined 18 specific use cases of a future digital Supply Chain Management. Some of the use cases are only relevant for a certain industry, such as a 'consumer 360 degree program' for retailers, but some target all strategic industries (for example 'advanced business networks'). However, what all use cases have in common is that they create a specific value to the company (benefit), but also require a certain amount of effort (cost for implementing and running of the use case). Finally, some of the use cases are more fully developed, such as 'demand sensing and signal management', meaning they are closer to implementation. Others are less developed and will take longer to appear on the corporate agenda (for example 'same-day fulfilment using drones').

Creating a portfolio helps to position and visualize the use cases in a way that enables a company to take further action, whereas an action might be also to wait and observe how the use case or the associated technology might develop. Using the assessed values of benefits (reliability, responsiveness, agility, cost and assets) and effort (investment, annual costs and time horizon) and summing them up (empty circle = 0, quarter = 1, half = 2, 3 quarter = 3, full = 4) one indicates a specific value for benefit and effort for each use case. Now every use case can be positioned in an effort-benefit portfolio as illustrated in Figure 9.2.

With the effort values on the x axis and the benefit values on the y axis a four quadrant portfolio will be spanned. The maximum values of the two axes are derived from the assessment itself as on the benefit side five criteria allow for a maximum of 20 and on the effort side three criteria lead to a maximum of 12.

Now all the use cases with their specific totalled values for effort and benefit can be positioned within the portfolio. With the first view it is obvious that most of the use cases can be found in the right lower quadrant at the border to its two closer quadrants. That means that these use cases have a healthy relation of benefits and effort, that if you invest there is a significant return on investment, and the business case is therefore positive (for example 'intelligent storage locations' or 'real-time global service parts demand and supply matching'). These kinds of use cases are worth discussing internally – of course depending on the industry focus of the use case.

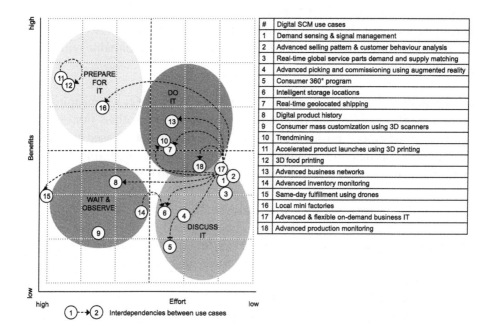

#	Digital SCM use cases
1	Demand sensing & signal management
2	Advanced selling pattern & customer behaviour analysis
3	Real-time global service parts demand and supply matching
4	Advanced picking and commissioning using augmented reality
5	Consumer 360° program
6	Intelligent storage locations
7	Real-time geolocated shipping
8	Digital product history
9	Consumer mass customization using 3D scanners
10	Trendmining
11	Accelerated product launches using 3D printing
12	3D food printing
13	Advanced business networks
14	Advanced inventory monitoring
15	Same-day fulfillment using drones
16	Local mini factories
17	Advanced & flexible on-demand business IT
18	Advanced production monitoring

Figure 9.2   Strategic effort-benefits portfolio for the Digital Use Case in supply chain management

Then there are use cases with a certain effort (somewhere between low and mid), but creating high benefit values, for example 'advanced business networks' or 'trendmining'. These use cases need to be implemented to leverage the benefits.

Use cases with a high benefit but also a high effort are more future oriented, such as the two 3D printing use cases or 'local mini factories'. Here companies should prepare for such use cases by putting them onto the radar screen and follow their increasing maturity and adoption within other industries.

Some use cases come with a high effort, but create only low to mid benefit (for the improvement of supply chain operations). These use cases can, for example, create most of their additional value within other business disciplines, like the 'digital product history' use case for the corporate Product Lifecycle Management (PLM) or the service organization, and therefore less value for SCM operations. But there are also use cases like 'same-day fulfilment using drones' that are just too far away from widespread implementation from an investment and use case maturity point of view, and also the specific benefits are not fully obvious yet. Here the corporate strategy should be to wait and observe these use cases and check from time to time whether an implementation might be attainable within the next five years.

Then, there are also dependencies between certain use cases, meaning that some use cases more-or-less rely on the implementation of others (for example leveraging 'advanced business networks' demands a cloud-based 'advanced and flexible on-demand business IT'). If one derives an implementation sequence of use cases, these interdependencies have to be considered.

Finally, new use cases are being created nearly every day as new variations of technological enablers will arise. The proposed portfolio methodology enables bringing all the potential use cases into a relationship and getting a clear overview picture to derive certain strategies for dealing with the use cases. It is therefore recommended to repeat such an exercise on a regular basis (for example, every half a year) as the maturity and also the benefits and efforts (prices for technology sometimes dramatically drop) of nearly all the use cases will change continuously.

9.6 Conclusions

In this chapter we introduced several examples of Digital Use Cases for SCM. Further, we explained how they can be mapped to a strategic efforts-benefits portfolio, which is used to derive the Digital Transformation Roadmap. Although the assessment of the Digital Use Cases is built on the SCM-specific SCOR model, the approach is rather generic and can also be mapped to other areas. The important characteristics for Digital Use Cases are: 1) description of benefits, 2) calculation of the implementation effort, and 3) calculation of the anticipated time-horizon. The identified use cases are then assessed and benchmarked against each other using any appropriate method (for example, the introduced adapted SCOR model).

In general, use cases which are easy to realize and provide a high value should be implemented right away. Those use cases, which provide little benefits and are difficult to implement should be neglected. The other use cases need to be balanced against their actual benefits and their realization effort.

Overall, the strategic effort-benefits portfolio provides an important basis for choosing the right strategic decisions for the digital future. Based on these findings a company can develop a custom-tailored Digital Transformation Roadmap.

References

APICS (2010) *Dictionary*. Alexandria, VA: APICS – The Association for Operations Management.

Chandra, C. and Grabis, J. (2007) *Supply Chain Configuration: Concepts, Solutions and Applications*. New York: Springer-Verlag.

Chopra, S. and Meindl, P. (2012) *Supply Chain Management: Strategy, Planning, and Operation*. Harlow: Pearson Education.

Christopher, M. (2004) *Logistics and Supply Chain Management: Creating Value-Adding Networks*. Harlow: Pearson Education.

Kuhn, A. and Hellingrath, B. (2002) *Supply Chain Management: Optimierte Zusammenarbeit in der Wertschöpfungskette*. Berlin: Springer-Verlag.

Simchi-Levi, D., Kaminski, P. and Simchi-Levi, E. (2004) *Managing the Supply Chain – The Definitive Guide for the Business Professional*. New York: McGraw-Hill.

Stadtler, H. (2010) Supply Chain Management – Ein Überblick. In *Supply Chain Management und Advanced Planning: Konzepte, Modelle und Software*, edited by H. Stadtler, C. Kilger and H. Meyr. Heidelberg: Springer-Verlag pp. 7–38.

Supply Chain Council (2012) Supply Chain Operations Reference Model – Revision 11.0.

Weber, J. (2008) Überlegungen zu einer theoretischen Fundierung der Logistik in der Betriebswirtschaftslehre. In *Beiträge zu einer Theorie der Logistik*, edited by P. Nyhuis. Berlin, Heidelberg: Springer-Verlag pp. 43–66.

Wilke, J. (2012) Supply Chain Koordination durch Lieferverträge mit rollierender Mengenflexibilität – eine Simulationsstudie zur exemplarischen Anwendung im Beschaffungsnetzwerk der deutschen Automobilindustrie. Dissertation Universität Paderborn. Wiesbaden: Springer Gabler.

Chapter 10

Digital Transformation at DHL Freight: The Case of a Global Logistics Provider

AMADOU DIALLO, KIM MACGILLAVRY AND AXEL UHL

10.1 Overview

In the last chapter of this book we introduce a case study of DHL Freight, the road freight division of the Deutsche Post DHL Group. DHL Freight is embarking on a journey of digital transformation to set a new standard regarding customer orientation, innovation, and efficiency. Having taken a completely new look at business models, processes, roles, and IT architecture, they collected fresh ideas that will help them prepare for the future. The Digital Capability Framework played an important role in defining the new strategic approach.

10.2 Overview

DHL Freight is a subsidiary of Deutsche Post DHL. Where the road freight business is typically managed de-centrally and decision making is dispersed, the company has systematically aligned itself to meet the growing requirements of global customers and a global economy. In cooperation with the BTA and using the Digital Capability Framework, the board of DHL Freight has developed a strategy that establishes aspirations and guidelines for transforming the company. This strategy uses new technologies to lay the foundations for new products and global processes.

The Deutsche Post DHL (DPDHL) Group was formed as a result of a number of acquisitions made by Deutsche Post. DHL Freight is the road freight division of DPDHL. It provides a full service range of Less than Truckload (LTL), Part and Full Truckload (PTL and FTL), Intermodal (for example, transportation combining Rail and Road) and Customs Services, as well as a variety of special services, such as Tradefair and Event Logistics.

Up to the year 2007, DHL Freight went through a series of internal integrations and disintegrations. The continuous process and organizational redefinitions associated with the (dis)integrations diverted management attention to internal matters and prevented decisions of a more structural nature. After 2007, when DHL Freight became a self-managed and independent unit within the DPDHL group, its focus returned to growth, profitability, and employee engagement. The business could be stabilized and has since developed strongly into being the provider, employer, and investment of choice in its industry.

DHL Freight:
With revenues of over EUR 55 billion, an EBIT of EUR 2.7 billion, and almost 450,000 employees, the Deutsche Post DHL (DPDHL) Group is one of the world's leading logistic services groups. The Group has two main brands: Deutsche Post and DHL. Deutsche Post is Europe's leading provider of standard letter mail services for private and business customers.
DHL includes the Express, Forwarding/Freight, and Supply Chain corporate divisions. It is the world's largest air freight forwarder and second largest ocean freight forwarder, one of Europe's leading road freight forwarders, one of the world's leading courier and express service providers, and the world's largest contract logistics service provider. DHL operates in more than 220 countries and has around 280,000 employees.
DHL Freight specializes in road transportation. More specifically, as a leading provider of international road transportation solutions in Europe and beyond, DHL Freight offers specific road freight expertise and sector competences that simplify its customers' most complex transportation processes.

10.3 Re-Inventing the Oldest Business in the World

The logistics business is probably one of the oldest professions in the world (see Figure 10.1). It made possible some of mankind's biggest endeavors, such as the construction of the pyramids in Egypt. It also formed the basis for some countries to develop vast military and trade operations over the centuries. For example, in the 17th century the Dutch East India Company employed 50,000 employees who sailed the world shipping more than 2.5 million tons of Asian goods to Europe.

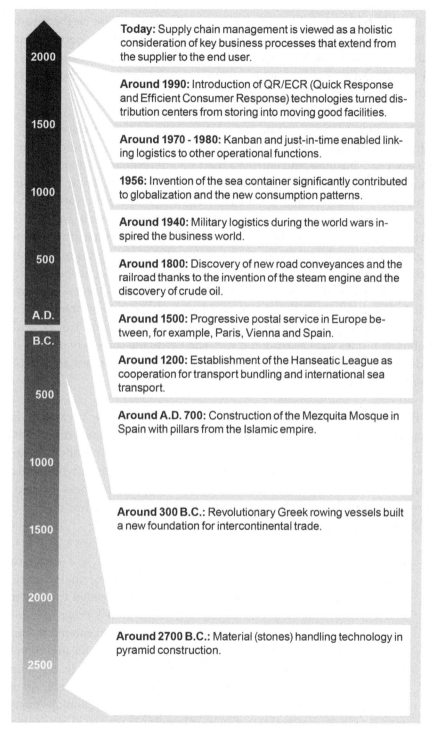

Figure 10.1   A brief history of logistics

Road freight is the oldest of all logistics disciplines. Despite the invention of the airplane and the ocean freight container, overland transport still makes up the vast majority of the logistics business around the world. At least the first and last mile of a journey must be covered on the road; most goods even stay on the ground from source to market.

The logistics freight business model is fairly straightforward. There are customers with goods and suppliers with a truck fleet. Customers focus on their own core business and entrust a road freight company with moving their goods from wherever they are to wherever they need to be. By combining the volume of many customers, a road freight provider can create a win-win situation for all parties involved; customers get their goods moved at a lower cost because they can share the carriage which is brokered efficiently by the road freight company, while the suppliers can share the business risk of filling their trucks. The difference is what constitutes the profit margin of the forwarder. Margins are typically very thin, but highly rewarding in terms of return on capital. The art of Road Freight Forwarding is doing it in an intelligent way by optimizing supply chain networks, maximizing loads on trucks, and by combining modes such as road and rail. The key to the success of this business model is the decentralized approach of ensuring that revenues and costs are closely matched and managed.

But the world has changed dramatically in the last few decades, largely through international division of labor, globalization and digitalization. Companies leverage the technological advances to improve their business, making more complicated products faster and more efficiently, while sourcing freely from around the world. Accordingly, the logistics business has become more complicated and is therefore forced to rethink its business model. Here are some of the challenges the industry is facing:

- **Productivity and efficiency**: The logistics business is a complicated task. It requires a lot of data – on the one hand for internal operational purposes and on the other hand because they are needed by customers and legislators (for example, for customs declarations). When systems do not interact seamlessly, data must be entered and often entered manually. Such internal costs do not offer immediate customer value and therefore cannot be reflected in prices. The three biggest cost blocks are: human resources, transportation and warehouse equipment, and fuel. As these resources are becoming scarcer, the industry needs to rethink its business model to make a step increase in productivity as well as in efficiency.

- **Reliability and quality expectations**: As consumer demands are changing faster, product lifecycles are getting shorter. There is increasing pressure towards reducing working capital by cutting inventory or even doing without warehouses, that is, distributing directly to end-users. As a consequence, there is greater need for speed of transportation, but – even more important – it raises expectations concerning quality and reliability. Typically, higher speed and more reliability come with higher production costs.

- **Visibility and transparency**: The fact that so much data is involved in the logistics chain makes it difficult for the right people to have access to the right information at the right time. But customers want to know where their shipments are at any time and also expect any exceptions and issues to be resolved immediately and proactively. In the data area the logistics business is not as well developed as some of their customers, who already live in the digitally enabled world.

- **Volatility**: The economic and financial crisis of 2008 and 2009 or the effects of natural disasters such as the volcanic eruption in Iceland or the tsunami in Japan shed light on how sensitive companies really are to such changes, be it banks, manufacturers, or service providers. Business-relevant events happen more often, are more erratic and bigger than ever before, a trend which is not likely to stop. Logistics companies in particular need to be able to respond immediately and effectively. Failing to do so may lead to a serious dent in your income statement. Reaction time is short, in particular for freight forwarding businesses where revenues and costs are very carefully balanced. The ability to scale your business flexibly is not only an advantage, but is becoming a necessity.

- **Customer centricity**: Across all industries there is a tendency for businesses to become commodities. The power is shifting towards the customer who has unprecedented access to relevant information and can compare and select between offerings very easily. Once your customers perceive how easily interchangeable you are, your growth and profits will inevitably falter. Only those companies which can distinguish themselves through innovation and customer service will do well. This is especially true for road freight providers. Studies have shown that in the eyes of the customers all logistics providers offer more-or-less the same services. This reduces the relationship to the simple discussion of price versus product quality. Creating loyal customers who promote your company requires not only a more customer-centric organization, but also the instruments to serve them better.

In addition, the decentralized road freight business model leads to a very fragmented company that makes it even tougher to deal with the aforementioned challenges. Its heterogeneous way of working:

- is usually rooted in local legacy organizations and system environments;
- drives a lot of complexity and costs that do not bring any immediate value to the customer;
- stands in the way of delivering consistent operational and service quality;
- demotivates people and distracts them from being truly customer-centric.

These issues are not new to any road freight company, and it is clear that substantial improvements and harmonization cannot be achieved without transforming the entire company.

10.4 Preparing DHL Freight for a Business Transformation

As a prerequisite for successful transformations a company must have a clear vision of what it wants to become and of its own particular current and future competitive advantages. The future product portfolio can be derived from this vision. Processes must be harmonized and standardized throughout the entire company to ensure consistent product and service quality and to achieve uniformly high customer satisfaction. Following this logic, DHL Freight has developed a clearly structured program to prepare the company for a possible business transformation. This includes the following steps:

1. There must be a clear vision, a common purpose and a shared value proposition.
2. The next pillar is a single, uniform product portfolio.
3. It is necessary to have harmonized, standardized processes and standards across the company to be able to deliver consistent product quality and customer experience.
4. A single, state-of-the-art IT platform is required.
5. All this has to be provided by an aligned organization with clearly distributed roles and responsibilities.

10.4.1 DEFINING THE VISION, COMMON PURPOSE, AND VALUE PROPOSITION

To implement a transformation successfully, it is critical that everyone in the organization shares the same view of the company's purpose, its value added for the customer and what the company should look like in the future. In many companies, however, this is neither well defined nor fully documented. If you ask the management what the company stands for you are likely to get as many answers as there are board members. In this case it would be pointless to move on. Even if a company has a strong brand and culture, it is a huge challenge to agree on a future vision, a common purpose, and a value proposition for the company. Therefore, to get the transformation of DHL Freight on the right track, its *Vision* of the future was developed using the Digital Capability Framework, as will be explained in the next paragraph.

The *Common Purpose* is equal to the DNA of the company. It defines 'who' the company is, and it is the glue that holds the organization together. Especially during a transformation it is very important that everyone knows what the transformation rationale consists of. It is not something that can be drawn up by one isolated department or an external agency and then force-fed to the organization. In the case of DHL Freight, the management invested a lot of time for discussing and defining the one sentence which perfectly captures the *Common Purpose* – until everyone could give their consent.

The *Value Proposition* is a set of claimed benefits a company promises to its customers. These claims constitute the most desirable experiences for its customers, and set the company apart from its competitors. The challenge when defining the *Value Proposition* is to really understand the customers' wants and requirements. In the case of DHL Freight, 700 customers were asked to describe their ideal road freight provider. Interestingly, while an acceptable price and reasonable quality are considered as the ticket of entry, what really drives customer satisfaction and loyalty is the ease of doing business with their provider.

Today, the *Vision, Common Purpose,* and *Value Proposition* together form the guiding principle for DHL Freight and set the direction for the three business transformation workstreams described in the following sections.

10.4.2 CREATING A UNIFORM PRODUCT PORTFOLIO

To materialize the benefits from transformation, a certain level of standardization of the business needs to be accepted and achieved. Especially in the services business and in companies which are managed locally, there is a risk that the products and services that are sold to the customers differ from one place to the other. Even services that share the same name label and/or are considered as being identical are often very different in practice. This drifting apart is something that simply happens over time when organizations believe that tailoring things to the local level makes the company more flexible and adapted to specific customer needs. But the resulting increased complexity usually outweighs the benefits while creating an inconsistent customer experience. For example, look at the difficulty of managing quality levels, both operationally as well as from a customer service perspective. A lack of standardization might be easy to carry for a while, but it becomes a real issue when a company needs to transform towards a common vision.

The challenges are not restricted to the customer-facing part of the product and service portfolio. Real end-to-end thinking is required, including the service elements and functional capabilities that need to be provided. At the end of the day, the products and services that the customers buy are a combination of the different capabilities of a company. A deep understanding of the relationship between the customer-facing side of products and their production is essential to translate commercial values into functional requirements for a successful transformation.

10.4.3 HARMONIZING PROCESSES AND STANDARDS ACROSS THE COMPANY

Standardized products and services are based on harmonized processes. A common pitfall is to take only a functional view and carve up the processes along the functional organization of the company. Most processes are connected in some way with several other functions. The solution is to define the key end-to-end processes that determine the business model. Some of them are obvious as they are very similar in every business – typically, the finance or HR processes, like order-to-cash and payroll processes. What makes a company unique, however, are its core business processes. In case of DHL Freight those are the operational processes.

It will be impossible to define all processes in one go and at the granular level which is usually needed to start any sort of IT development, but this is not necessary at an early stage of a business transformation. At the beginning it is usually sufficient to map some high-level process flow charts. Getting an agreement on those will be difficult enough to start with. At a later stage, the processes can be elaborated in more detail.

It is important to figure out where a company's pain points are which need to be addressed. Then the innovations to be built into the future business have to be defined. All ideas and suggestions need to be tested against the *Vision, Common Purpose,* and *Value Proposition* set out before. Transformation takes quite some time. If you do not have enough innovative and future-oriented thinking embedded in your transformation processes, you might find you have simply replaced the business you had before with something that is more or less the same, without adding any new value. In such a case elaborating a business case that will justify the investment and risk that comes with Business transformation will be difficult. Therefore, it is key to define the business benefits as clearly as possible, so that they can be quantified and compared to the costs of business transformation.

10.4.4 DESIGNING THE FUTURE IT ARCHITECTURE

This workstream concerning the IT architecture considers how the processes of delivering the future product and the service portfolio can be supported. The aim is to sort out and reduce the system landscape as much as possible to avoid duplication and redundancies. DHL Freight has, over the years, acquired several companies that use legacy systems. Local needs were given priority and have sparked the development of various customizations of core applications. When undertaking a business transformation it is as much an opportunity as a necessity to standardize the IT platforms and to rid the company of the complexities which stand in the way of delivering a harmonized product and service portfolio through standardized processes.

Again, at an early stage of business transformation it is not necessary yet to have a definitive view of the target landscape and the precise migration path. But, based on a first view of it, getting a ballpark estimate of the cost of change should be possible.

10.4.5 ALIGNING THE ORGANIZATION WITH CLEAR ROLES AND RESPONSIBILITIES

Last but not least, the organization will need to be overhauled as a consequence of the business transformation. The standardized processes require standardized roles and responsibilities. The process blueprints imply certain roles, and this workstream aims at organizing them. In most companies, each entity is organized somehow differently from another. In order to work efficiently together, many of these differences have to be ironed out, but it is risky to start this workstream too soon, as the people needed for it might be unsettled and this might impair their work.

As mentioned above, the vision for the future of DHL Freight was drafted based on the Digital Capability Framework. This process is now explained in more detail.

10.5 How DHL Freight Leveraged the Digital Capability Framework

The management of DHL Freight was aware of the importance of the digital world for its current and future business. That is why they chose the Digital Capability Framework to support the vision setting of their transformation. The Digital Capability Framework provides a holistic picture of the Digital Capabilities that a company requires for long-term success. These capabilities are: Innovation Capability, Transformation Capability, IT Excellence, Customer Centricity, Effective Knowledge Worker, and Operational Excellence.

The basic assumption of the Digital Capability Framework is that sustainable profitability will logically result from these Digital Capabilities, however, if a company focuses solely and excessively on profitability itself, this is often to the detriment of other capabilities, such as Innovation Capability, Customer Centricity, or IT Excellence.

The Digital Capability Framework was used to initiate a process – involving the management of DHL Freight – in which the actual levels of the six Digital Capabilities were assessed first. Not surprisingly, prior to the transformation the management team did not award DHL Freight top marks for any of the above mentioned dimensions, but rather identified the following levels:

As in most large companies, the perceived strength with regard to the Transformation Capability centered on value management. Corporate governance demands a strict adherence to well-defined decision processes such as presenting a business case and securing the prescribed approvals. In the case of important projects, change and training requirements are also considered, however, this stands in contrast to the disciplines of value realization, the planning and execution of change management, and the provision of training.

The greatest problem of the Innovation Capability was the lack of management commitment. As a result, the competences in the organization to develop complex, cross-functional products and services were rather inadequate. Innovation in process and IT management was even considered a disturbance. Furthermore, the topic of innovation was not addressed by any organizational entity nor training measure. Innovations were mostly implemented on a decentralized basis, and even successful innovations remained limited to individual markets.

While Customer Centricity is highly valued within the company and employees always do their very best to help their customers, there was no clear understanding of the nature of the added value that Customer Centricity represents for the company. Furthermore, the fragmented IT landscape was seen as an important impediment for Customer Centricity. In the eyes of the customers, there was a lack of transparency in the collaboration process.

The Digital Capability Effective Knowledge Worker of DHL Freight was rated high. The company is considered to have a competitive advantage in terms of employee qualification and motivation. Given the unfavorable perception of graduates, who think that the road freight industry is not the most attractive place to work, it is important to ensure that the work environment is inviting, and that employees can focus on the most fulfilling, value-adding tasks.

Operational Excellence was rated relatively high, too. However – as is typical for the road freight industry – DHL Freight discovered significant problems in the following areas: the high cost related to a large number of manual activities, the heterogeneous operational business models, processes, and related data, and a lack of access to relevant information at the right time at the right places.

It therefore comes as no surprise that IT Excellence did not score well. The often outdated legacy systems were restrictive. The poor IT landscape is typically blamed for lowering the scores of almost all of the other capabilities. IT was therefore considered to be a strategic enabler for the future competitiveness of DHL Freight.

After the assessment of the as-is levels of the Digital Capability Effective Knowledge Worker, the discussions about the DHL Freight business vision for the future and target values for the various capabilities were very intense and quite controversial at times. In simple terms, the vision for the future can be put as follows:

- Everything that can be automated is automated.
- Logistics terminals are fully integrated and they deliver consistent quality.
- Organizational entities are interconnected and aligned.
- For customers it is easy to do business with DHL Freight.
- The IT solutions in place are completely sufficient for the job required.
- The business is run by proud, happy, and ambitious people.

While for some the Digital Capability Effective Knowledge Worker agreement was reached quickly and a high level of to-be excellence was aspired to, it was more complicated with other capabilities. For example, the perceptions and opinions concerning the future Innovation Capability varied widely, but in the end, the discussions could be concluded with suitable capability target values for DHL Freight. There is clearly an ambition to close the significant gaps between actual and target levels.

The Digital Capability Maturity Models are useful for such debate as it indicates the steps that need to be taken and helps the management team to have a structured discussion as well as reach an agreement about the most fundamental aspects of the business.

Digital Use Cases are another useful part of the Digital Capability Framework. Since not all managers and employees have in-depth IT knowledge, specific use cases are helpful to illustrate and represent the future vision in concrete terms. Based on use cases, people, process, and IT requirements can be derived from the vision.

The following three sections each introduce a Digital Use Case for DHL Freight.

10.5.1 ACTIVE TRACING MOBILE APP (ACT)

In the past, DHL Freight used various tools in different countries to allow their customers to track their deliveries. To simplify the access of shipment information for customers, all track-and-trace information was made available through a single web-based tool, and DHL Freight was the first to make the data visible on any mobile device. The mobile app 'AcT' (ActiveTracing) provides DHL Freight customers with the full event-scanning history, the history of shipments for up to six months and even an automatic shipment search in further DHL transport modes (that is, link to Ocean Freight, Air Freight and Parcel/Express track and trace databases of other DPDHL business units). Registered customers benefit from additional features such as getting an overview of their most recent shipments, a reporting functionality, and direct access to proof of deliveries (PODs).

10.5.2 DHL DOOR-TO-MORE®

More and more companies are going global to meet increased customer expectations, to reach new customers and markets, and also to lower the cost of sourcing and producing their products. This increases the complexity of supply chains. With 'DHL Door to More®', DHL Freight offers its customers a seamlessly integrated direct distribution solution which helps reduce complexity and gives them a competitive advantage. Based on a streamlined end-to-end process, the exclusive web-based DTMi application allows customers to consolidate their products at the source, for example in China, so they can be shipped cost efficiently across continents, while the delivery will be deconsolidated for distribution, for example across Europe. Customers benefit from speed to market from Asia with direct delivery straight to their final consignee in Europe, with reliable end-to-end lead times and shipment visibility, with reduced inventories through bypassing local warehouses and faster cash-cycles. The DTMi application allows customers not only to organize the pick-up online, but also prepares the customs clearance and provides track-and-trace information along the entire shipment route in one single application.

10.5.3 MYWAYS PARCEL DELIVERY™

DHL Freight launched the new MyWays platform to facilitate last-mile deliveries of parcels in Stockholm, Sweden, involving the city's residents. With the pilot platform, anyone can now deliver packages directly to other end-consumers for products ordered online. An especially developed mobile app connects those who want flexible deliveries with others who offer the transport of parcels for a small fee. DHL is the first logistics company using the 'crowd' to offer a delivery that is flexible in time and location. MyWays is organized via DHL Freight's network of service points (parcel holding stations) in Stockholm where the MyWays couriers pick up and deliver the parcels.

10.6 Key Learnings from the CEO Office

The Digital Capability Framework enabled the board of DHL Freight in developing the digital strategy and the digital roadmap. The first one establishes aspirations and the latter sets the guidelines how to achieve them. The toolset provided an invaluable support throughout the digital transformation journey of the company. There is a set of key take-aways gathered by the CEO of DHL Freight who was involved into the process from the very beginning of this journey:

1. The management board needs to be a winning coalition and fully engaged. Before acting out a strategic road map, it is important to ensure that it is completely supported by the board. This can only be achieved by means of a collaborative process, with clear leadership by the CEO. If 80 percent of your team is behind you and 20 percent is not, go ahead. If it is the other way round, change your strategy.
2. Trust within your organization is a key success factor. Employee trust in the management team of the company is crucial for success. Only in a trustful atmosphere can problems and conflicts be brought to the surface and dealt with openly and properly. When there is a lack of trust among employees, problems are either not addressed at all, or they become evident to the outside world. In both cases, successful problem resolution is jeopardized.
3. Transformation is like a steeplechase. As in a steeplechase, the transformation team must know exactly when to jump and when not. Timing is essential for certain actions. This applies as much to phases of high performance as to the necessary recovery phases. No one can work at full throttle all the time.
4. Demonstrate change and innovation day in, day out. The best way to cultivate willingness for transformation in others is to regularly demonstrate changes and the benefits associated with these changes. Also, minor changes can be used to do this.

5. Leverage your best people. It is neither good nor necessary to distract everyone from their day-to-day jobs when preparing for transformation. It is important, however, to have the right people on board. Appoint someone in the management board to drive things and give everyone on the board a role in the project so they have 'skin in the game'. Let everyone put forward their most knowledgeable experts to staff the workstreams. Change must come from within.

6. The CEO has only one chance to make history. CEOs are particularly visible and subject to scrutiny. The image and messages projected externally must be consistent. Sudden changes of direction in response to external factors make a CEO appear unreliable.

7. You do not know your future competitors yet. Nowadays, you can no longer be sure about who your competitors are. The age of digital capabilities means that companies from completely different industries with a high level of expertise can suddenly enter your market!

References

Giordano, G. and Giordano, A. (2013) Outsourcing Transformative Change, *360° – The Business Transformation Journal*, No. 8, pp. 56–61.

Houlder, D., Wokurka, G. and Günther, R. (2011) Shell Human Resources Transformation, *360° – The Business Transformation Journal*, No. 2, pp. 46–53.

Kresak, M., Corvington, L., Wiegel, F., Wokurka, G., Teufel, S. and Williamson, P. (2011) Vodafone answers Call to Transformation, *360° – The Business Transformation Journal*, No. 2, pp. 54–67.

Schmiedel, T., vom Brocke, J., Uhl, A. and Zeitz, S. (2013) A Global HR Transformation, *360° – The Business Transformation Journal*, No. 7, pp. 56–65.

Uhl, A. and Gollenia, L.A. (eds.) (2012) *A Handbook of Business Transformation Management Methodology*. Farnham: Gower Publishing.

Uhl, A. and Gollenia, L.A. (eds.) (2013) *Business Transformation Essentials*. Farnham: Gower Publishing.

Ward, J., Stratil, P., Uhl, A. and Schmid, A. (2013) Smart Mobility. An Up-and-Down Ride on the Transformation Roller Coaster, *360° – The Business Transformation Journal*, No. 7, pp. 45–55.

Index